Traditional Wooden HANDPLANES

How to Restore, Modify & Use Antique Planes

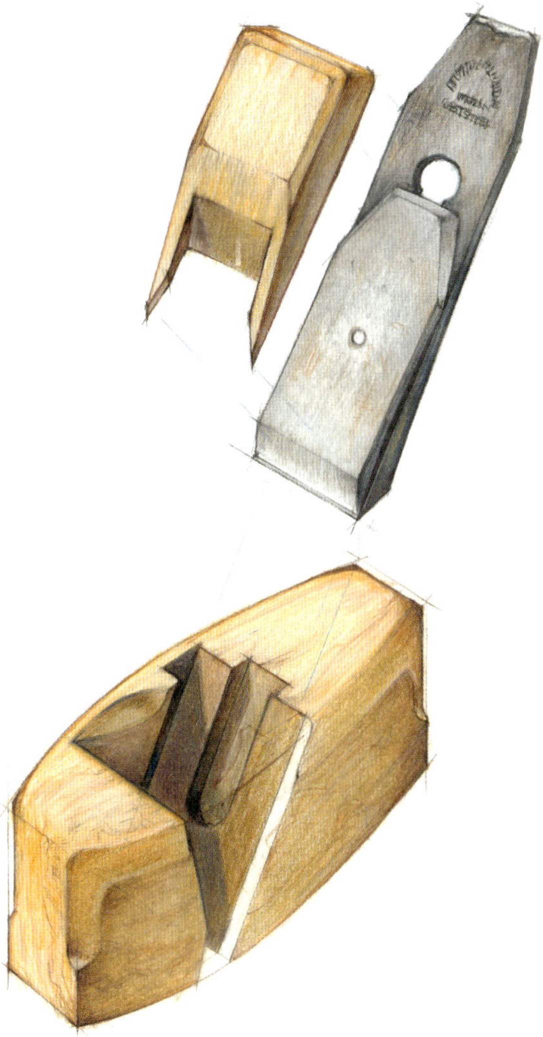

ACKNOWLEDGEMENTS

To my father, Jerry, who taught me always to watch and listen; and to my daughter, Josephine, who stands on her grandfather's shoulders watching, listening, and learning—and teaching all of us.

I would also like to acknowledge the untiring support of Kathy Tam, the helpful guidance of technical editor Rick Mastelli, and the encouragement and long hours of Jerry Konicek, whose Woodworking Academy gave me the opportunity to verify and refine my techniques.

All illustrations by Scott Wynn
All photos by Rick Mastelli and Scott Wynn

ISBN 978-1-56523-887-9

Library of Congress Cataloging-in-Publication Data

Names: Wynn, Scott, author.
Title: Traditional wooden handplanes / Scott Wynn.
Description: Mount Joy, PA : Fox Chapel Publishing, [2018] | Includes
bibliographical references and index.
Identifiers: LCCN 2017039965 | ISBN 9781565238879 (pbk.)
Subjects: LCSH: Planes (Hand tools) | Woodwork.
Classification: LCC TJ1201.P55 W95 2018 | DDC 621.9/12--dc23
LC record available at https://lccn.loc.gov/2017039965

Printed in Singapore
First printing

Traditional Wooden HANDPLANES

How to Restore, Modify & Use Antique Planes

Scott Wynn

Fox Chapel Publishing

CONTENTS

INTRODUCTION

You may ask yourself: Why bother?

I mean, when we have so many other beautiful planes to choose from that could certainly do the job well enough? Planes we are probably more familiar with, marvelously mechanical metal planes of proven reliability. And other styles of planes as well, both beautiful and functional.

Well, simply put, if you've got a lot of work to do in solid hardwood, the traditional wood plane excels at efficiently working hardwoods and is better at this than any other style of plane.

Say you have a large plank, maybe a live edge board for a tabletop, and it's too big to fit in your jointer. The traditional jack plane—maybe preceded by a scrub plane, used with the correct technique—is light, low in friction, comfortable in the hands, and will quickly take the high spots off, leveling one face of the board sufficiently to get good registration through the planer. Or maybe your planer isn't big enough either. Traditional wood handplanes, used in the traditional sequence, with the blades correctly shaped and with appropriate blade angles, will make this job doable.

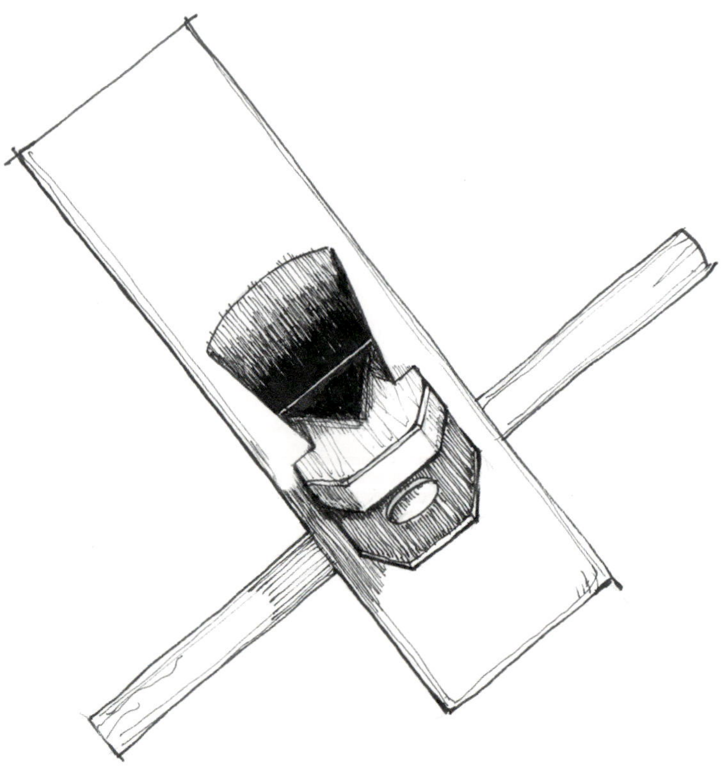

Or say you have a nice piece of figured hardwood that just wants to tear up when you go to work it. Only with a high-end two-drum sander will you get results that won't take hours of sanding to get rid of the ripples, variations at changes in hardness, and streaking that the non-industrial sanders tend to leave. Again, use of traditional wood handplanes, used in sequence with the correct blade shapes and angles—angles that you can't find on most planes—will yield crisp, smooth results at a rate competitive with sanding—and without the dust and noise and vibration and sheet after sheet of sandpaper.

After over 40 years using handplanes, many times for hours at a stretch, days at a time, with every style of plane and in every type of wood, I have developed some criteria for planes for doing serious work on hardwood (I'm talking serious work here—not the occasional edge or snipe removal). You can of course challenge these if you wish, but it will give you something to think about—and maybe you can add a few criteria to your own list.

The criteria

Weight is an important consideration: you will be lifting these planes a lot during the day, maybe several hundred times. How often can you curl an 8-pound

dumbbell (the weight of a premium #7 Bailey-type plane)? So, the planes should be comparatively light, though a balance between weight and inertia is often desirable.

The sole of the plane should be **low in friction**; like weight, the cumulative resistance adds up and it is palpably noticeable. It also interferes with feedback with how the plane is cutting.

You need **blade angles other than just 45°**. I have found that oak works tearout-free with a blade angle of 60° to 65°; walnut likes blade angles of 50° to 55° to finish. So the ideal plane should be available, or be able to be made, in a range of blade pitches; 40° to 65° is ideal, though 45° to 55° will suffice. This is for both reduced resistance when removing large amounts of stock (the low end of the scale) as well as the ability to reduce tearout for fine finishing (the high end of the scale).

Planes should be available in a **variety of widths,** with blades from 1¼" to 2¾" (3.2cm to 7cm) wide; this is because different planes do different tasks and require different width blades (much more on this in the succeeding chapters). In the same vein, you should be able to fit a variety of commonly available blades of **different steels** because different tasks and even different woods are done more effectively if the steel is matched to the work.

The **grip** of the plane must not be fatiguing, blistering, or bruising to the hands even after hours of pushing and must successfully transfer all the energy put into it to the cutting action. I have found that the larger the area of the hand the grip engages, the easier it is on the hand.

And, ideally, they should be **affordable**!

So how do the other styles of planes stack up when measured by these criteria? Let's start with the Stanley Bailey style plane. If you have a lot of work to do you'll soon realize these planes are heavier than their wooden cousins: often quite a bit. A traditional Razee-style wooden fore plane, for instance (of which plans and instructions for making are included in this book), is about 4 pounds, while the classic

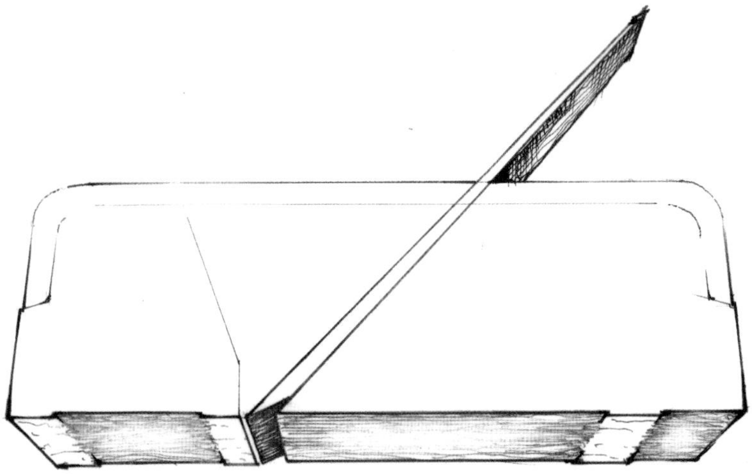

iron Stanley version is a smidgeon over 6 pounds. The premium version of the Bailey plane comes in at 7½ pounds (3.4kg)—nearly twice as heavy as its wooden counterpart! Arguments that planes of greater weight are needed to provide increased momentum to power through hardwoods (it's not needed) have a flip side; they also require greater effort to overcome the inertia of getting the plane moving. Meanwhile you're lifting twice the weight on every stroke of the plane. (Proper technique says you don't drag the plane on the return stroke; this adds wear to the blade, though you will see a lot of well-known woodworkers do it. The plane should be lifted or slightly tilted on its side or front edge to reduce wear on the blade.)

The metal sole has a noticeably higher coefficient of friction with a noticeably higher resistance to the push. You can lubricate the sole but most lubricants, such as wax, wear off in a half dozen strokes and must be repeatedly reapplied.

The blade, with the exception of a couple of expensive high-end versions, is always bedded at 45°, which works ok for a number of woods, but not so good with a lot of common hardwoods; having blade angles that match the type of work to be done, and the type of wood to be planed, can save you a lot of time, effort, and frustration. Blade-width selection, however, is good, as is the variety of blade steels now available, allowing you to customize the type of steel to the kind or work and wood you want to do.

I do have a problem with the handles, however. I find they soon blister my hands. They're too narrow, focusing the strain on narrow portions of the hand, and they're often curved and/or angled wrong. I have a vintage #8 and a vintage #6, both with beautiful rosewood handles; the handle on the #6 fatigues while the other does not. They look the same; any difference is almost imperceptible. Others may not have experienced this, but I think if you're doing significant work with these planes, eventually you will. The ball front knob is too small for doing a lot of work and concentrates the pressure on the center of the hand, which soon blisters, aided and abetted by the screw head in the center of it. The rear handle often allows the hand to slide down to its base and is angled and shaped such that the heel of the hand will start to get badly worn (and sometimes the side of the little finger). Between the weight, the friction, and the blistering handles, these planes are not made for extensive work. They can sit on the shelf for weeks at a time and be used off and on without readjustment or maintenance and they're great for most of the tasks you'll find around the wood shop, but they are just not the best choice for heavy work.

The Krenov-style plane, light, made of low friction wood, is a delightful smoother, but I don't think it's as versatile a style for all the jobs you might want to use a plane for. Because of the low position of the hand on the plane when making deep cuts to remove stock (as you might with a jack plane), the hand wants to slide forward against the blade. This takes its toll pretty quickly. Also, the selection of blades for this style of plane is limited. Those who favor Krenov-style planes might want to supplement their arsenal of planes with a traditional style jack, and maybe a jointer and scrub, depending on the type and size of work you do.

The Japanese-style plane is light, low friction, comes with some of the best blades you can get, and performs pretty well through most tasks, including stock removal—except when you have to remove a lot of stock in a hard wood. Surprisingly, despite no outward accommodation to the hand, they are not blistering, or even particularly fatiguing. But as a pull-plane, you do have to hold on to it; with a push-plane, if the grips are right, the plane is cradled in large parts of the hands so if you didn't have to lift it to bring it back very little effort would be expended holding on to it. Additionally, with a push-plane it's easier to get your body weight down and behind the push; this is more difficult when pulling a plane.

And finally, there is the issue of affordability. The traditional wood plane beats the competition here as you can often find usable vintage planes for a fraction of the cost of even a vintage Bailey—and often at one-tenth the cost of a new premium Bailey. A lot of these planes were made and a lot of them are still out there, and so far non-collectible user planes are still quite affordable. And you can get something on these planes that you can't get on a new plane: a hand-forged laminated blade—often the best choice for smoothing (more on this later). While newly manufactured versions of the traditional wood plane may be as costly as a decent Bailey plane, they maintain the advantages of lower weight, low friction, good ergonomics while often having improved adjustment mechanisms, and the advantage over a vintage wood plane of not having to invest time to repair them before you can use them.

This book is about the traditional wood planes used predominantly in Europe and North America, both vintage and contemporary, and also will touch on the planes of China and Southeast Asia and how they might be useful. It will show you how all these traditional wood planes work, how to set up a flea-market find, as well as how to tune up a new plane to get the best performance out of it. It will talk about the different types and how to use them to their best advantage; which blade angles are best, which blade steel you might want to use, and finally, how to make your own set of planes using some modern techniques that simplify construction and improve performance.

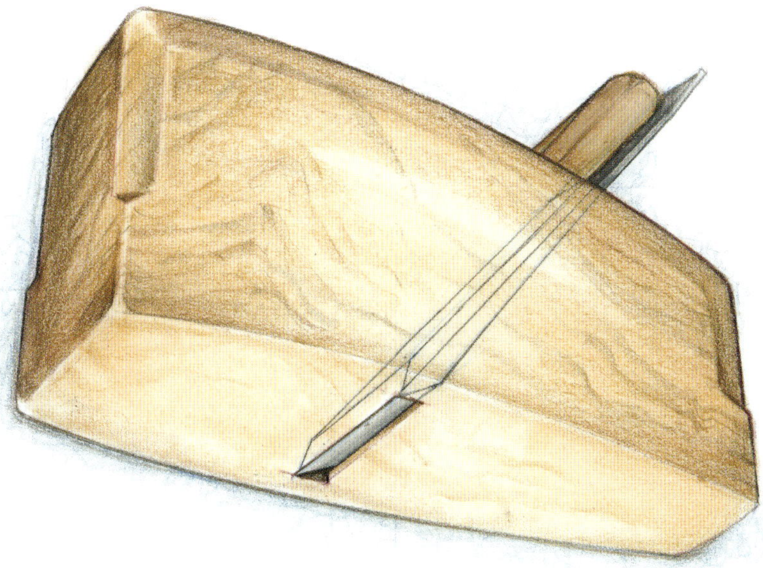

CHAPTER 1

ANATOMY OF THE TRADITIONAL HANDPLANE

A SIMPLE DESIGN

The anatomy of the traditional wooden handplane couldn't be too much simpler, really, especially when compared to the number of sophisticated parts that the Stanley/Bailey plane uses to do the same job. Up until the 18th Century it consisted of just three parts: the blade, the block, and the wedge (only the Japanese plane is simpler with only two parts: a blade and a block). Bigger planes often had a handle, or "tote." Sometime in the early 1700s the use of a chipbreaker became increasingly common, adding a fourth part.

On the left, a traditional jack plane with its wedged blade, a system in use for centuries. On the right a modern German horned jack plane, with a spring-loaded screw adjustment mechanism for adjusting the blade.

Figure 1-1. Wood Block Plane

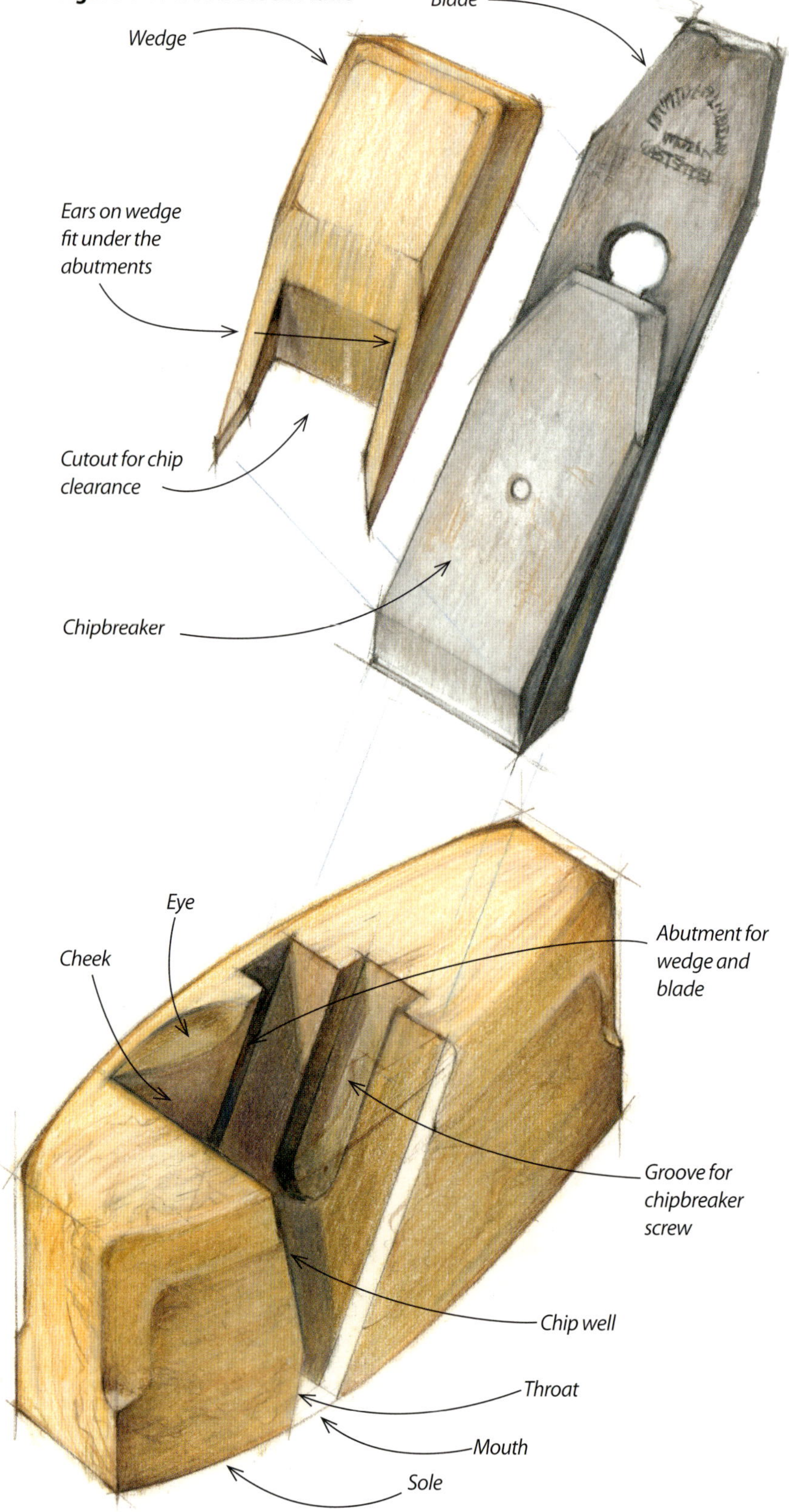

THE BLADES

Unlike today's planes, up until the early 20th century wood-body planes from Europe and North America usually had a tapered blade, thicker where the cutting edge is and thinning toward the opposite end. The main reason given for this is that the natural wedging action of a tapered blade resists being pushed back under the load of cutting wood, and also makes it easier to remove, because you can tap the blade down and it will release quite quickly (often too quickly). But it also makes it harder to adjust: if you adjust the blade down too far you may have to completely loosen the wedge and blade and start over if you want to readjust the blade back up.

I think the reasons usually given, such as this one, are the (questionable) side benefits of the method of manufacturing the blade. As we all know now—and they probably did then—parallel blades stay put just fine under the wedge. They are also easier to adjust because they do not lock in so tightly in one direction. You can move them down further than a fraction of an inch and not have to worry about them unexpectedly flying out of the mouth of the plane.

Here is my theory for the taper. When making a laminated blade by hand, you have the extra thickness of the edge steel added to the backing steel blade blank, the two of which must be forge-welded together. Then you have to hammer the assembly until the backing steel flushes with the edge steel on the top of the blade. If you do not hammer out the blade at the edge end as well—it is easier not to—then you have begun giving the blade a taper. From there, you continue the taper just making sure the back of the blade is slightly concave along its length. This guarantees the blade will bed properly at the heel despite any irregularities along its length, or irregularities in the hand-cut bed. This also means you can reduce the amount of grinding on the back. I have blades that still have the hammer marks on the back **(Figure 1-2).** A parallel blade must be accurately ground on both faces, which cannot easily be done freehand. An added benefit is you have maximized the thickness of the blade near the edge, further reducing the chances of chattering in use, especially if a substantial chipbreaker is added.

Modern versions of the traditional form have parallel blades and are only rarely laminated, though I do have a German scrub plane from the early 1980s that has a laminated blade. They were made and can be found (and laminated Japanese replacement blades for these planes are available), you just have to keep your eye out for them (for more on why you might want a laminated blade—and what it is, see the chapter on steel that starts on page 24).

Figure 1-2. If you look closely at this blade in the area of the chipbreaker screw, you can see the semicircular edges of the impressions left by the forging hammer.

CHIPBREAKER VARIATIONS

British and American chipbreakers have a slight difference (which has no effect on performance): British chipbreakers often have a "nut" of which there are a number of variations, that is proud of the top surface of the chipbreaker into which the screw is threaded; with an American chipbreaker the screw flushes out with top surface of the chipbreaker. This sometimes results in very little thread for that screw, depending of the thickness of the chipbreaker, but I haven't had one strip out yet. (More about chipbreakers in Chapter 3 on page 50.)

CHIPBREAKERS

Woodworkers throughout the world had for millennia worked with the same somewhat narrow selection of indigenous woods, often a single species, or no more than two or three, within a trade. They knew how the wood reacted, which tools and their setup worked best for those species, and they had a good selection of material and better control of their sources. New Worlds, new prosperity, greater travel and print exposure, brought a higher level of sophistication to their customers, which brought a demand for new designs and a higher degree of finish in the work. Additionally, new and imported woods often brought new challenges to providing this higher degree of finish than the indigenous woods they had worked with for centuries. The use of a chipbreaker helped solve some of these problems. It made planing these new woods more reliable, so the work went faster and with better results (see **Figure 1-1**).

The chipbreaker is almost always screwed to the blade, unlike Japanese planes and some Chinese planes. I say *almost always* because I have a French smoother (smoothing plane) by *Goldenberg* that has a chipbreaker that is not screwed to the blade, but is adjusted independent of it. This is the only time I have ever seen this in a Western plane. This setup does increase the versatility of the plane because it makes it easier to adjust the chipbreaker up and down without having to disassemble the plane to unscrew the chipbreaker from the blade.

THE WEDGE

The most common form for the wedge in antique planes is similar to that shown in the illustration (**Figure 1-1** on page 12) with the center portion of the wedge cut out for chip clearance and wedge-shaped "ears" at the edges that wedge into matching abutments cut into the block. The cutout may be done in different ways: it may have a circular shape or as frequently found in Chinese planes, it may be a simple V-shape cut. Or there may be no cutout at all, the wedge cut to thin taper at its lower edge, though this is usually found on modern planes using a cross pin (**Figure 1-3**). Besides giving added chip clearance, the use of the ears simplifies fitting the wedge to the top of the chipbreaker, which may be curved or otherwise irregular.

Figure 1-3. The top two wedges are the most common type with "ears" that fit into tapered abutments either side of the plane, the center of the wedge relieved to a thin edge to clear chips. The third wedge from the top is from a French plane (with one of its ears slightly broken) and the bottom wedge is from a Chinese plane, though occasionally you might find similar wedges on European and American planes.

The use of a wedge fitted into abutments cut into the block, besides being a nuisance to fit simultaneously to an irregular chipbreaker and the taper in the block—and it must be well fit to eliminate chatter and prevent blade shift under use—is that seasonal movement or long term change in the block can change the angle of the wedge cut, preventing the wedge from fully tightening. You must then refit the wedge by careful trimming of (usually) the top of the wedge ears to exactly fit the block. This will lower the wedge a bit, which may require trimming the ends of the ears, and in a worse case, some refitting of the wedge to the chipbreaker. This usually doesn't happen a lot in the life of the plane, especially if the block was dry when it was made and is oriented bark-side-down and quartersawn (or nearly so), but it's something to keep your eye out for.

The use of a cross pin for bearing the wedge against is a solution that avoids the labor-intensive need to exactly cut the abutments and fit the wedge to them. But you won't find this solution on any old planes. It starts showing up in early metal transition planes, but I don't think I've seen it on an old wood plane. I think the reluctance to use a cross pin was because until the late 1800s drilling technology could not be counted on (at least in woodworking) to give an accurate and reliably-sized hole—and tradition imparts a certain inertia to changing a solution that has worked for centuries anyway.

A metal cross pin can be used when it bears against metal, such as on a Japanese plane where it bears on the chipbreaker (though it only holds the position of the chipbreaker and not the blade), and on some versions of Chinese planes where the chipbreaker doubles as a metal wedge; but a metal cross pin bearing against a wood wedge will soon damage the wedge, indenting it enough that adjustment becomes difficult. A wood cross pin can be used with a wood wedge, but the difficulty with a cross pin in general is its greatly reduced cross section often doesn't provide enough resistance to keep the wedge from loosening when the plane is being used. A common response is to drive the wedge in tighter, but eventually this will damage the block, bend or break the pin, or leave an indentation on the wedge that makes adjustment difficult. German manufacturers solved these issues by using a metal cross pin with a wide flattened surface to grip the wedge, coupled with large diameter fixtures to which the cross pin is fixed to the block **(See Figure 1-4)**. These cross pin mounting fixtures greatly increase the bearing area of the pin to the block, reducing

Figure 1-4. You can see the flattened cross pin under the wedge of this horned scrub plane.

the chance that an over-driven wedge will damage the block. An additional advantage to the system is that you can push or tap the wedge sideways to loosen it, rather than beating on the plane to loosen it. From personal experience this is a very successful solution to the wedge.

James Krenov used a wooden cross pin to fix his blades, which he carved to a flat section where it engages the wedge to give it more bearing area. However, you have to glue the block up in sections in order to be able to insert it into the plane. What if you prefer—for a number of good reasons—to use a solid block? The solution is to add a wooden bearing plate to a wooden cross pin already drilled through the block **(Figure 1-5** on page 16). The wooden cross pin has a larger bearing area than a steel pin and is equal in hardness to the block, thus reducing stress and wear on the block, and the added bearing plate reduces the chance that the wedge will shift, and extends the pressure over a larger area of the wedge and blade, helping to reduce chatter. This is the system used in the planes described in the chapter "Making & Modifying Planes" (page 152).

Another wedging system in use is the screw-down lever cap (**Figure 1-6**). The lever cap is held to the plane with a screw inserted into the blade bed (rather than a cross pin), and much like the lever cap on a Stanley plane, the blade is adjusted by tapping, as with a wedge system. This can be a good system, and one that you might consider as a possible alternative for the cross pin/plate system used in Chapter 8. However, there are a couple things to look out for. First, the blade must be a parallel blade and not tapered. Second, because the blade will not move under full pressure, the lever cap cannot be tightened down fully until the blade is adjusted. However, because of the thinness of most modern blades and the curve of many chipbreakers over their length (to ensure tight contact with the blade), the chipbreaker/blade assembly is flexed to an arc when the chipbreaker is screwed to the blade.

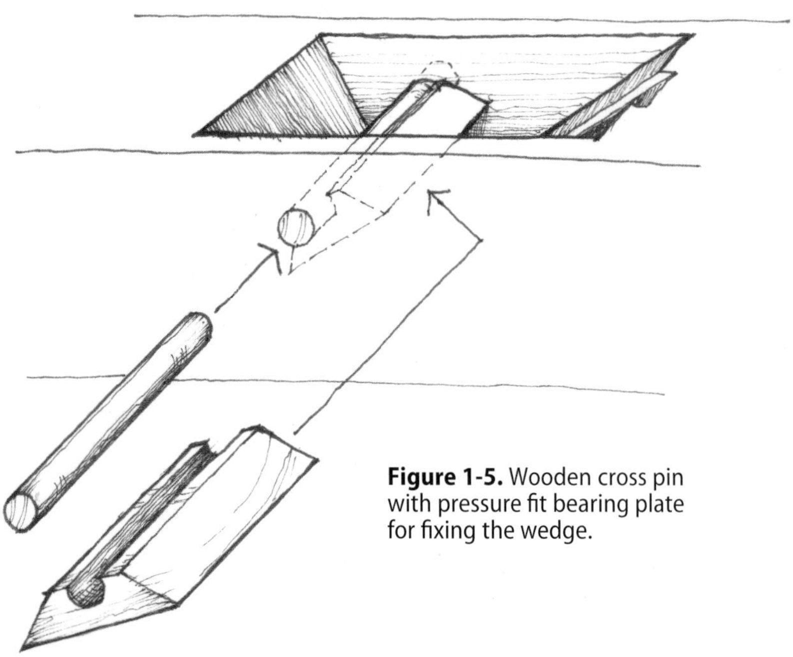

Figure 1-5. Wooden cross pin with pressure fit bearing plate for fixing the wedge.

Tapping the blade to what appears to be its final position and then tightening down the lever cap flattens out the blade/chipbreaker assembly, usually pushing the blade out of the throat slightly and changing the adjustment. You must then loosen the lever cap again, back the blade off, and second-guess how much the blade will move when the lever cap is tightened back down. This makes fine or frequent adjustments tedious. A thicker blade and/or a different chip breaker that keeps the assembly flat might remedy the situation.

Taking a quantum leap in development, a German manufacturer has replaced the wedge altogether with its Primus adjustment mechanism. The Primus blade-adjustment mechanism is one of the quickest and most precise adjustment systems. There is zero backlash on this adjuster. It can give precise adjustment on a smoothing plane, but I find it particularly useful on a jack plane, where frequent readjustment can be required to level a board; with this adjuster I can quickly and accurately readjust the blade as the board levels.

Its main drawback is its complexity. It is time-consuming to remove and replace the blade for sharpening, so frequent re-sharpening, as might be required for final finishing, is pure drudgery. To remove the blade for sharpening, first the blade-tensioning mechanism and blade adjustment must be backed off almost completely, and the blade withdrawn. Withdrawing the blade requires pushing the blade-tensioning mechanism back in and twisting and then pulling the tension rod out. Because the blade is now loose, it just flops around as you try to twist the T-bar on the end of the tension rod, because the T-bar gets wedged on the chipbreaker and must be worked off. Once the blade is out, two tight-fitting screws must be loosened to remove the chipbreaker **(Figure 1-7)**.

After sharpening the blade, the chipbreaker must be repositioned and carefully tightened down with some trial and error (the use of another type of chipbreaker is not an option as both the blade-tensioning device and the lateral-adjustment mechanism are part of the chipbreaker assembly). Then you thread the T-bar on the end of the blade-tensioning screw through the hole in the chipbreaker, rotate it, push it forward, rotate again, and pull it back to its seat on the chipbreaker. This whole process of removing and reinstalling the blade can take 5 to 10 minutes (or seem like 10 minutes). Doing it a lot gets to be quite irritating. Luckily, with its chrome-vanadium blade, if you are rough planing, you will not have to do it very often.

Over the years, other solutions to the wedge and how to adjust the blade have come about, especially with the German manufacturers, who are still one of the few manufacturers of traditional style wooden planes easily accessible to the American (and other) markets today. One type you might find is a version of the screw adjuster, with a knob similar to the Primus but working more like a Norris adjuster. It has the screw (a worm gear, actually) directly engaging threads on the chipbreaker. This version does not use a tension rod. Because the purpose of the tension rod is to eliminate backlash or play

Figure 1-6. Horned Reform Smooth Plane with Screw-Down Lever Cap
The body is pear with a lignum vitae sole. The body has had some extra rounding to accommodate the user's hand.

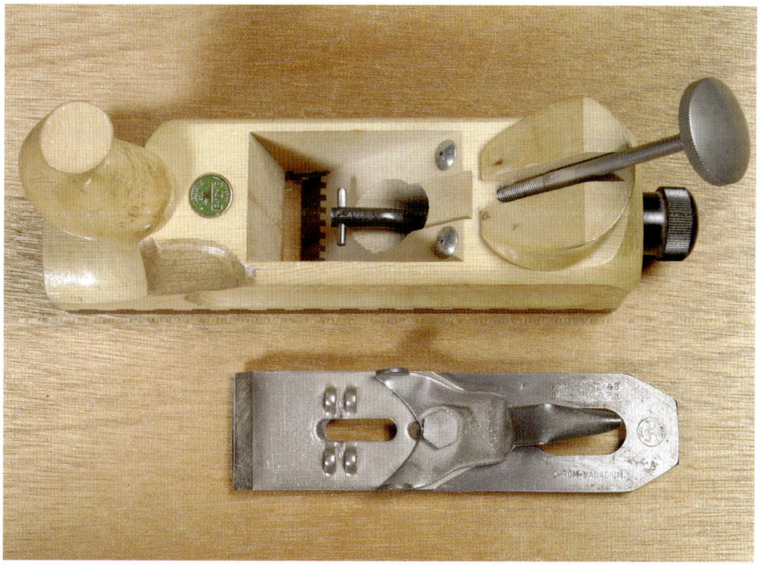

Figure 1-7. The Interior of a Primus Jack Plane
In the well of the plane you can see the two buttons that support the blade assembly at the top, and below that the T-rod that engages the chipbreaker and holds the blade assembly in the plane. The lateral adjustment is mounted to the chipbreaker. Two screws mount the chipbreaker to the blade.

Figure 1-8. This block plane by Goldenberg appears to give no accommodation to the hands.

Figure 1-9. A less common grip often used on small block planes, such as this Goldenberg plane, has the fingers of both hands bear on top of the plane in front of the blade, with the thumbs behind.

Figure 1-10. This coffin-shaped plane is typical of smoothing planes of the 1800s. This one dates probably to before the 1860s.

in the adjustment mechanism, this version does have some play, but it is not too bad and is a serviceable adjuster.

THE BLOCK

The basic block, or body of the traditional wood handplane has evolved into a few variations.

There is, of course, the basic block shape that is used for all the different types of these planes—jack, jointer, smoother—and on the larger versions, with an added handle or two. This shape may literally be a simple block with straight edges and sharp corners that appears to give no accommodation to the hands. I collected such a plane (the *Goldenberg* plane I mentioned earlier) because of its unusual blade and chipbreaker set-up, but also because its severe geometry seemed not just uncomfortable, but possibly damaging **(Figure 1-8)**. It appears well used and taken care of, but it has all its straight rectangular corners intact, giving no suggestion of how you could push this plane—in the manner we are used to, like with a Stanley plane—without bruising your hands. This befuddled me. Then, just recently I saw (again) a video of the Swiss cooper Ruedi Kohler, filmed (coincidentally by Rick Mastelli, the technical editor and photographer of my first book) in 1992. In the film I noticed Herr Kohler used a series of hollowing planes to curve the inside of the staves. These planes were a plain block, not shaped, like the Goldenberg I had. But instead of using the planes one hand in front of the blade, the other behind, he gripped the planes on both sides, thumbs behind the blade and first fingers down flat on either side ahead of the blade. Mystery explained. This is very similar to the grip used for cross-handled Chinese and Southeast Asian planes. Without the cross handles it doesn't seem to be a grip of great power like you might want in a jack plane to remove a lot of stock, but it provides sufficient power for smoothing and light shaving, especially in softer woods. The position also seems to give good control. It is most comfortable to use, however, when pushing straight ahead on short pieces; standing to one side as you might do when a piece is dogged onto the bench is more awkward with this symmetrical grip (**Figure 1-9**).

For smoothing planes that require more power, the coffin shape was developed (**Figure 1-10**). This configuration works pretty well for shorter smoothing planes, directing the energy efficiently forward and down, and giving wide distribution on the hand, even on the older planes that have not been particularly rounded off. The only real improvement I can see making here is to add a "thumbpiece" behind the blade to catch the crotch of the thumb and first finger; otherwise there is a tendency for the hand to ride up and chafe on the back of the blade.

The Razee (from the French *vaiseau rasé*, a wooden warship with the upper deck cut away) style of plane has the top of the body cut away behind the blade, lowering the handle and reducing the weight (**Figure 1-11**). These were often used to train students and apprentices because it was felt the full block versions were not only heavy (you have to remember these kids were 13 to 15 years old and mostly pretty small), but also easier to control than the full-block

Figure 1-11. Razee fore plane, 15" (38.1cm) long
The term Razee derives from the French *vaisseau rasé*, a wooden warship with the upper deck cut away. Razee planes have the top of the body cut away behind the blade, lowering the handle and reducing the weight.

versions. This is because the high position of the handle on the jointer plane, while initially awkward, once mastered, gives greater feedback as to the angle of the plane to the work when shooting an edge. This is basic geometry: the further away you are from the face of the work the more exaggerated the tilt must become in order to maintain the same angle. Thus it makes it easier to tell when you're going out of square.

I find the reduced weight of the Razee style useful for preparatory planes such as the jack and fore plane. I also find it useful for my panel plane (more on this to come), because not only is it lighter, the low position of the handle gives good feedback when smoothing.

HANDLES

Larger planes are fitted with handles or "totes." These can be either open or closed, though functionally it makes little difference to the hand. The closed tote is perhaps a bit stronger, though if you're pushing hard enough to break one of these handles, you're working too hard! It may make it easier to pick up a larger plane for the return stroke as the larger planes almost always have a closed tote. The older planes are usually meant to be used with a three-finger grip, so they may be a little small for the modern hand or someone who prefers a full grip. Modern versions usually are larger and meant for a four-finger grip.

The larger planes also no longer have a front handle. Moxon depicts a bent-over curlicue of a handle that I could never figure out and have never seen an example of, even in a museum, but such a handle has not been used for at least 300 years, so it must not have been very effective. Occasionally, longer Scandinavian planes would be fitted with a horn or variation of the horn handle up front, similar to those they used on their shorter planes, but this is also uncommon now.

Figure 1-12. Horned Plane with a Lignum Vitae or Hornbeam Sole

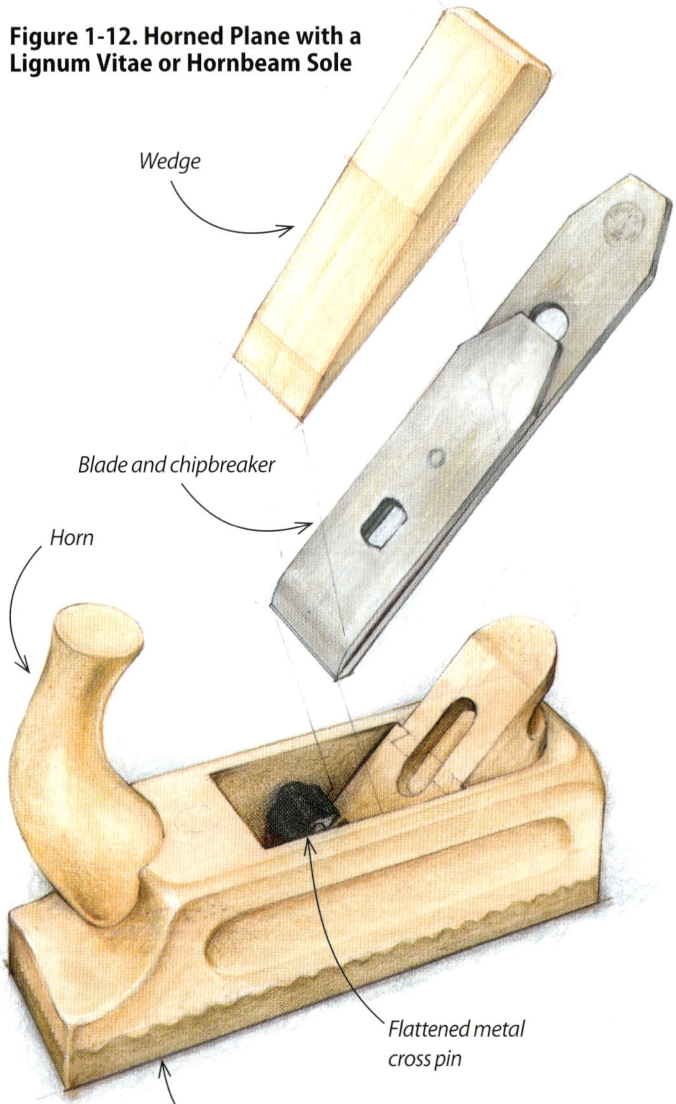

The bigger planes are intended to be used with the forward hand gripping the block cross-handed with the thumb toward the user, though they can also be used with the hand on top, the thumb on the far side of the plane. You can see long planes in the Tool Museum (*Maison de l'Outil*) in Troyes, France, where the block is worn to the shape of the forward hand and its thumb, and while perhaps some of these may have been shaped, it is believed that this is a result of wear. One of the planes is nearly worn through where the thumb would be (you can see light coming through!). That's a lot of time spent holding on to that plane.

Northern and Eastern Europeans developed the "horn" for the forward handle on their shorter planes, the back of the block nicely rounded to fit the whole of the hand with a thumbpiece to keep your hand from riding up and chafing on the blade. I like this plane a lot for heavy work. I think the horn is a successful design **(Figure 1-12)**.

While the cross handle today is most widely used on planes from Asia, antique examples from Europe can be found, particularly on two-man planes and larger one-man planes. It's a pretty effective grip that can apply a lot of downward pressure, necessary for very hard woods, though this power dissipates pretty quickly the

ANATOMY OF THE HORNED PLANE

Horned planes commonly come with 45° or 50° blade angles. I believe they were also made with 43° and 47.5° blade angles. Prep planes such as scrub planes sometimes have a 40° pitch; some finish planes have a pitch above 50°. A toothing plane is made with a 70° pitch. Check with the distributor if you are looking at new planes, or take a protractor to the flea market.

On premium models, the mouth opening adjusts with a movable mouthpiece (the reform plane). Chipbreakers are substantial and well-made, though some may require some refinement to function with a finely set mouth.

Primus planes use a traditional approach to bedding the blade by having it contact the bed at just its bottom and top. To do it, they have installed two metal buttons at the top of the blade bed to suspend the blade so it contacts the bed only at these points and at the bottom. This guarantees the blade is supported at the heel of the blade bevel, the most critical area for eliminating chatter. Though the blade and chipbreaker assembly bridges this distance, this assembly, further dampened by the tension rod which holds this assembly and is part of the adjustment system, is thick enough that the blade does not chatter.

The blade placement is a little more central than Bailey-style planes and most traditional wood planes, the blade edge being back from the leading edge of the plane about 40% of the length of the sole. This slightly more central position makes it a little easier to begin and complete a planing stroke.

The horn is available in both right- and left-handed versions.

further you lean out as the stroke progress. Again, it is better to have the work in front of you than to one side, but it'll work in that position too.

AND A WORD ABOUT CHINESE-STYLE PLANES...

I think the Chinese-style planes can be useful to the Western woodworker. But since they are functionally exactly like western planes, the real advantage is being able to find planes with 60° and 65° blade angles already made. I wouldn't bother buying one that has less than a 60° blade angle as there is (currently) a greater variety of quality planes and parts in the Western style in the lower angles. If you can source Chinese-style planes that have the high blade pitch, these planes can be really handy, if not indispensable, when working tropical hardwoods, many Australian hardwoods, and the harder Northern hardwoods. Conversely, if you never, or only rarely, use these woods, you

Figure 1-13. Traditional Smoothing Plane of China and Southeast Asia

will probably be able to get by without them (though my 60° Chinese jack works great on oak). The planes, with the correct pitch, work exceptionally well, and the ergonomics are easy for the Westerner to adapt to. But, if you are not comfortable with the Chinese-style form, you can always fabricate planes to your needs that have similar tactical specifications.

The planes used by Chinese cabinetmakers and furniture makers are functionally very similar to early European wood block planes (**Figure 1-13** on page 21). However, there are differences, and both these and the similarities are interesting to note. The blade-wedging techniques for the two is exactly the same: a wooden wedge holds the blade, itself held in place in a wedge-shaped slot cut in either side of the blade opening in the body. The same methods control tearout: the setup of the chipbreaker, and mouth opening; and the primary means, the blade angle. I think this is largely a result of having to plane the hard tropical woods traditionally used—a high-angle scraping cut seems to be more reliable.

Figure 1-14. The Sole of a Chinese-Style Plane
You can see the brass mouthpiece dovetailed into the sole that is used to form a tight mouth and reduce wear.

The smoothing plane has a blade angle of 65°+, no chipbreaker (which would seem unnecessary at this angle anyway), and a mouth opening of only several thousandths of an inch—barely enough to see light through when the blade is set. Often a brass piece is dovetailed into the throat to control wear (**Figure 1-14**).

The plane is pushed using a slightly oval-shaped handle that is inserted through a hole in the plane body behind the blade (though there are some variations of this from region to region, a fixed, oxbow-shaped handle being the most common). The palms of the hands straddle the plane and the handle. The fingers are on top of the plane in front of the blade and the thumbs are behind the blade. This is a comfortable position, allowing good body mechanics when planning. I am not used to it, however, and often use the plane without the cross handle. The handle itself is friction-fit and removes for storage or transport, or to accommodate the recalcitrant Westerner like myself who prefers not to use it.

The traditional blade is often laminated and parallel rather than tapered, but I would hesitate to say that this is always the case, as modern manufactured versions often use high-speed steel. The smoothing plane I bought, rather than having a laminated blade, had a piece of steel about an inch long braised onto the end of a longer, softer piece that forms the main body of the blade and projects from the plane. This piece of edge steel is extremely hard, and appears to be high in alloys, as it does not sharpen easily. I have never seen a blade constructed in this manner; I bought an extra one when I had the chance (**Figure 1-15**).

ANATOMY OF A CHINESE PLANE

It was not long ago that even seeing, let along buying, a Chinese plane was a rare thing. Now, not only is the classic style used throughout China and Southeast Asia available, but the market includes high-end Australian-made versions, as well as a number of regional styles.

The classic style of cabinetmaker's plane is typically used to plane tropical hardwoods and so has a high blade angle. A set of prep, true, and finish planes would have angles of 55°, 60°, and 65° respectively. Because of the high-pitch angles, the plane usually relies on a tight mouth opening for controlling tearout, though sometimes a token chipbreaker would be supplied. The mouth opening usually is faced with a brass piece to reduce wear.

Some of the regional models have the cross handle let into the top and screwed to the body and may have an oxbow shape, rather than having a hole in through the body for the handle, a minor difference. Another regional difference, including planes from Taiwan, is a lower, wider proportion, reminiscent of Japanese planes, but with sweeping ergonomic curves to the body. The blade assemblies on many of these look like Japanese-blade assemblies, as well, with a wedge-shaped metal chipbreaker under a metal cross pin. However, the chipbreaker in these planes really does wedge the blade in place, as the blade itself is not wedged into the body the way the Japanese plane blade is. I have not worked with these, so I do not know if the result is a compromise in the ability to adjust the position of the chipbreaker or in the effectiveness of the wedge to hold the blade in position. If this design is successful at both of these (I'm not sure if this is a traditional design or a new hybrid), then it is a stroke of genius. One of the advantages of the Japanese plane is the ability to easily adjust the chipbreaker back and forth for different types of cuts. This can be done because the blade is wedged independently of the chipbreaker. In this Chinese plane, the blade adjustment is dependent on the chipbreaker's position, and adjusting the chipbreaker too far one way may affect whether the blade will hold its position.

In the classic Chinese-style plane, the blade edge is positioned very near the center of the length of the sole, making entering and exiting the stroke about as balanced as it can be.

The main reason I use Chinese-style planes is their high blade angle and the effectiveness of that angle on tropical hardwoods. The central placement of the cutting edge is an added bonus. Many of the regional styles of Chinese planes are being sold with 45° blade angles and an alloy-steel blade cut from stock. As such, they have no real advantage over most other planes, other than perhaps price, and preferable ergonomics.

Figure 1-15. The blade on this Chinese plane has a hard piece of edge steel, about an inch long, brazed to a longer piece of soft steel to form the blade.

CHAPTER 2

SHARP

BLADE STEEL

One of the advantages of using the traditional style of wooden handplane is that there are arguably a wider variety of types of steel available for this style of blade than any other. The roughly 7" (17.8cm)-long blades are available parallel or tapered, "cut" (that is, with a slot cut into it for attaching the chipbreaker with a screw) or uncut, contemporary or antique, and all these types are available in any of the steels ever made for cutting wood (and some steels intended for cutting other things!)

Choices. Here we have (from top): A Hock 1¾" (4.4cm)-wide A2 cryogenically treated blade for a jack plane; a Moulson Brothers 2" (5.1cm) antique cast steel blade for a smoother; and a 2⅝" (6.7cm)-wide Clifton hand-forged blade from a jointer plane. Note the discoloration on the chipbreakers of the jack plane and jointer plane blades (I left these on specifically for the photo): these are the result of the heat of the cut vaporizing the oils in the wood. It cleans off easily and the metal is not heat-stained, but this is still quite a lot of heat!

This is important because different woods respond differently to different steels. Also, the different tasks a plane is expected to do can often be done better when the steel is matched to the work (more on this in Chapter 4 on page 64). Having different types of steel to choose from gives the woodworker the ability to match the best steel to the wood and the task being performed, greatly improving results and increasing efficiency (and reducing frustration).

At first glance, steel seems a simple, cold, and aloof material, but those qualities disguise its complexity. Like wood, steel has grain, structure, and movement. It can even have a bit of personality—or a lack of it. Blade steel, especially forged blade steel, is alive with all of the energy the smith put into making it and the fire used to shape it. A woodworker should understand and appreciate the individuality of blades, learn what they do, and apply this knowledge for greatest effect. Understanding the complexities of the steel used for the cutting edge helps you make decisions about the tools and techniques essential for effective, efficient work. This chapter clarifies some of these complexities.

BASIC BLADE CRITERIA

The woodworker needs the edge on the hand-tool blade to do three basic things: get sharp, stay sharp, and re-sharpen easily. These three qualities usually exist in balance with one another. Increasing one may decrease one or both of the others. In many applications, however, one quality may be most important, and the right blade choice depends upon understanding the strengths and weaknesses of the different steels.

There are additional considerations when selecting a blade. The first consideration is the type of wood being cut. Softwoods and some softer hardwoods prefer an edge that is very thin and very sharp. Some steels can actually be made sharper than others, to a thinner bevel, and still hold an edge. As the wood gets harder, however, the steel's toughness becomes increasingly important. Secondly, edge requirements vary according to the job. A blade required to remove a lot of wood—especially if it is hardwood or tropical hardwood—will need an edge that holds up well under the high heat build-up and impact that accompany vigorous use. The harder the wood, the more important the toughness of the steel.

STEEL GRAIN

There is a standardized chart that refers to the average grain size within a steel. The numbers range from 00 to 14, with 00 being the largest (about 1/50"), and 14 the smallest (about 1/10,000"). Manufacturers normally use fine grain size 7 or finer for the steel used in tools.

SHARPENING VERSUS RE-SHARPENING

I use *re-sharpen* here rather than *sharpen* or *sharpenability* because re-sharpen properly evokes the time and repetition involved that the other two words do not. I believe many woodworkers (myself included) do not keep their blades sharp enough, and I want to encourage them to change their habits. Many woodworkers believe sharpening is like cleaning the house: do it once and you are good for the week, or at least for the next few days. However, in reality, if you are using your plane all day, you will need to re-sharpen many times that day. Re-sharpening becomes the nuisance chore that keeps you from doing woodworking until it is done. *Easy* has a different meaning when it is done 20 times (or more) a week instead of just once.

ANATOMY OF STEEL

The key to understanding edge steel is in its anatomy. For the needs of the woodworker, three characteristics define steel's anatomy—grain, structure, and hardness.

Grain

For woodworking hand tools, the grain of the steel is the most important characteristic of a blade. Ordered, repetitive arrangements of iron and alloy atoms in a crystalline structure comprise steel. The crystals can be small and fine or large and coarse. They can be consistent in size (evenly grained) or vary widely, with odd shapes and outsized clusters in among the rest. The steel's grain affects how finely the blade sharpens and how quickly it dulls. Generally, the finer and more consistent the grain, the more finely it sharpens, the slower it dulls, and the better the blade performs.

Grain is a function of the initial quality of the steel used, the alloys added, and how the steel is worked or formed. In addition to the average size of the crystals, the initial quality of the steel may include impurities, called *inclusions*, which may persist throughout refining. Inclusions add large irregularities to the grain. Irregularities sometimes are used to good effect in swords and perhaps axes, but except for the backing steel on laminated blades, impurities are a detriment to a plane blade. Sharpening impurities out to the edge causes them to break off easily, causing chipping and rapid dulling of the edge. The dirtier the steel, the more rapidly it dulls. Fine chipping will not affect the performance of an edge used for chopping wood: depending on the inclusion, it can add tensile, shock-resisting strength to the blade. For fine woodworking, such as planning a surface, though, even fine inclusions prevent sharpening the blade fully and shorten the edge's life.

Alloys change the texture of the grain. They may be part of the steel's original composition (though usually in small amounts), or added in a recipe to increase the steel's resistance to shock and heat. Alloys often coarsen the grain, so there is a

THE IDEAL EDGE

The edge requirements for cutting different materials vary widely. The most obvious example is the edge required on a kitchen knife. Meat and vegetables are cut by the sawing action of drawing a coarse edge through them. A properly sharpened kitchen knife has what under a microscope would look like a series of small saw teeth, which result from sharpening it with an 800- or 1200-grit stone. If you are skeptical, sharpen your best kitchen knife like a plane blade with a #8000 stone and try to cut a potato. It will stop cutting halfway through and jam: the knife is sharp enough to cut transparent shavings in wood, but it will not cut halfway through a root vegetable. Shaving is another one: a razor is somewhat coarsely sharpened so its edge is a series of fine "teeth." These teeth are then polished with a very fine stone and strop. The teeth snag the hairs and the polish on the teeth allows them to cut the hair. It should be sharper for good woodworking. The lesson is that demonstrations of sharpness using other materials and claims of qualities originating in other trades and uses, such as industry or surgery, are not particularly useful in evaluating a woodworking blade.

Conceptually, for a blade to be perfect for woodworking, it must be possible to polish it down to single-crystal uniformity across its entire edge, with the crystals all lined up neatly, oriented the same direction, all very small and of the same size, equally hard, and tightly bonded to one another so they will not break off. A cutting edge is comprised of several types of crystals greatly different in size and hardness grouped together so that clusters tend to present themselves at the cutting edge, and therefore tend to break off in clusters, leaving voids and dull spots. The finest blades, however, have the qualities enabling something approaching the ideal edge.

trade-off. While the edge of an alloy blade may be more durable, especially under adverse working conditions, it may not sharpen as well as an unalloyed blade. To shear wood cleanly, no other attribute of an edge is more important than fineness.

Structure

Structure, the second most important aspect of a woodworking blade, results from changes in the original composition of the steel because of heating it and changing its shape with a hammer (or rollers), often called *hot work*. Heat causes the crystals of the steel to grow. Hammering steel when it is hot causes its crystalline structures to fracture and impedes growth as the grains fracture into smaller crystals. Before being hot-worked, the crystals of steel are randomly oriented, and frequently inconsistent in size. Through forging (repeatedly re-shaping with a hammer while the steel is hot), the grain aligns and knits together in the direction of the metal flow. Proper forging increases grain structure consistency. When exposed at the edge through sharpening, crystals consistent in size and orientation break off one at a time and dull the blade, rather than breaking off randomly in big clumps. The consistency of the crystals allows for a sharper blade that stays sharp longer.

Three techniques are used in preparing steel for woodworking tools: hammer forging, drop forging, and no forging. Hammer forging, where repeated hammer blows shape the steel, is the most desirable because it aligns the grain particles (or crystals) of the steel. It is a time-consuming, skillful process and therefore expensive. If improperly done, hammer forging stresses the steel, reducing, rather than increasing, reliability. With the general decline in hand-woodworking skills during the last century, and the increased reliance on power tools, the discriminating market that would appreciate the difference forging makes has shrunk considerably. As a result, hand-forged tools are not commonly manufactured or available in the United States.

Drop forging verges on die cutting. A large mechanized hammer called the punch drops on the heated blank, smashing it into a die (mold), giving the tool blade its rough shape, often in just one blow. For tools that vary considerably in cross-section, this method may be more desirable than grinding or cutting from stock, because the heat of grinding or cutting can cause some minor negative alteration in the grain structure at those areas. Drop forging imparts a marginally more consistent structure than a blade cut or stock ground, because the steel often elongates in the process resulting in some improvement in the crystalline structure alignment.

Drop forging is preferable to no forging at all. No forging is an over-simplification because all tool steel receives some hot work during reshaping. Bar stock is hot-formed by rolling or extruding the ingot into lengths of consistent cross section. The process rearranges the crystalline structure and the crystals tend to align in the direction of the flow as the steel lengthens. However, the arrangement is not very refined compared with the structure resulting when steel is hot-worked further at the forge. Modern Western chisel blades are frequently drop-forged (though some new premium chisels are being ground from A2 bar stock). Modern Western plane blades, even many after-market premium blades, are usually ground from unworked, rolled stock.

Hardness

Hardness is a major selling point in the advertising of woodworking tools made from various types of steel. However, as explained earlier, grain and structure are the most important factors in the performance of a blade. A plane blade soft enough to shape with a file (for instance, made from a piece of a good, old handsaw blade) will give excellent results if the fineness of its grain allows it to be sharpened well and its structure allows the edge to break off finely and evenly. I knew an old boat builder who preferred plane blades made from good quality saw blades. The blades made it easy for him to file out nicks when his plane hit unexpected metal in the boat structure.

At the other end of the hardness spectrum is carbide, used on power tool blades. Hard and brittle carbide is unsuitable for the body of the tool blade, because it would shatter. While carbide is extremely hard, the particles are also extremely large. Although they do not break off easily, when they do, they break off in clumps so big they are nearly visible to the naked eye. Carbide also cannot be made nearly as sharp as steel. A sharp steel saw or router blade cuts much more cleanly than a sharp carbide blade. Unfortunately, the steel dulls quicker than the carbide, especially when subjected to the glues in plywood and particleboard.

DISSTON SAWS (AS DESCRIBED IN *KEEPING THE CUTTING EDGE*)

"...Disston saw steel was heat treated in the plant and was harder than competitive saws. We rolled our own saw sheets on a sheet mill so we could control the direction of grain within a sheet, enabling us to set the teeth at that hardness without their breaking. Disston saws were of a hardness that read 52–54 on the Rockwell C scale, and competitive saws were 46–48—about 10–15% softer than Disston's. They did not know the secret of how to roll a new saw sheet so the teeth would not break during setting at that hardness..."

From a letter written by Bill Disston, great-grandson of Henry Disston, to Harold Payson, as excerpted in Payson's book, *Keeping the Cutting Edge: Setting and Sharpening Hand and Power Saws* (Wooden Boat Books, 1988).

Hardness must be in balance with the intended use of the tool. High-impact hand tools, such as axes, should be softer than plane blades. Otherwise, the edge fractures quickly under the pounding an ax takes. The blades of fine tools for fine work can be very hard, but if their hardness exceeds the ability of the steel to flex without breaking at the microscopic edge, the tool will be next to worthless.

The Rockwell C (Rc) scale measures the hardness of woodworking blades. This is a unit of measurement determined by the impact of a ball-shaped point into the steel measured in terms of the depth of the resulting impression. Japanese saws (harder than Western saws) are roughly in the 50–58 Rc range. This is on the cusp of what a file will cut. Decent plane and chisel blades are in the range of 58–66 Rc range. Only some finely wrought steels work effectively in the upper-half of this range, principally high-quality hand-forged Japanese blades, and some high-alloy steels. In carbon steels, Rc 66 seems to be a limit above which the edge breaks down too rapidly in use, though I have heard of a Japanese master blacksmith who has made it a personal goal to develop steel that will hold an edge at about Rc 68. However, his experiments have not been available commercially.

HARDENING, TEMPERING, AND ANNEALING

The hardness and ductility (the extent to which it can be stretched or bent without breaking) of steel depends on its exact carbon-to-iron ratio and its thermal processing. Different temperatures are associated with different crystal structures, or phases, of the iron and carbon atoms. When steel with a carbon content above 0.4% (the minimum amount required for steel to harden) is heated beyond its critical temperature of around 750°C, it enters what is called the *austenite phase.* Austenite has a crystal structure that opens to allow the carbon atoms present to combine with the iron.

When austenite is cooled very quickly (by quenching) its structure changes to a needlelike crystalline form called *martensite.* Martensite locks in the carbon atom, *hardening* the steel. In this state the steel is at its hardest and is under a great deal of internal stress and quite brittle. The more carbon the steel had to begin with, the more of it will be martensite and the harder it will be. As the carbon goes over 0.8%, however, the steel does not become any harder but rather grows more brittle. In order for the steel to be useable as a blade, it must be softened to reduce the brittleness to a workable degree. The process is called *tempering.*

Tempering is a compromise, meant to balance hardness and ductility, and is definitely a judgment call made by the one doing the tempering, based both on experience and the intended use of the blade. To temper a blade, after hardening, the blade is reheated; this time to a lower temperature, perhaps 175°C (depending on the type of steel and the blade's intended use), and quenched again.

There is a third process, done after the blade has been hot-worked to shape, but before hardening and tempering, and that is *annealing.* Here the blade is heated red-hot and allowed to cool **without** quenching. This softens the blade and removes stresses that may have resulted from its being hot-worked. Usually at this point, the blade is then ground to final (or near final) shape—easily done, since it is now soft—and then hardened and finally tempered.

In summary, grain, structure, and hardness are the characteristics of tool steel important to the woodworker using hand tools. Other tool users may emphasize other characteristics—primarily because they are working in other materials or using other methods. The cutting of wood fibers is a very particular application with very specific requirements. The right combination of grain, structure, and hardness—and method—provides good results.

TYPES OF EDGE STEEL

Steel for hand tool blades can roughly be divided into two categories: carbon steel and alloyed steel. All tool steels contain carbon, which makes it possible to harden the metal. Processed from iron and iron ore, carbon steel contains at least 0.5% carbon, and traces of other elements. Alloyed steel is carbon steel with small amounts of other elements added to improve performance under certain conditions and for certain purposes. While manufacturers of steel have specific guidelines with regard to the percentages of alloys used in their steels, and each recipe is identified with a name; manufacturers of woodworking tools, at least until recently, usually chose to ignore the nomenclature, choosing instead to give a broadly descriptive or generic term for the steel that may encompass a group of dozens of different steels of widely varying recipes and characteristics (such as "tungsten vanadium") based on how they perceived the market. As it turns out, there are quite a few steels with tungsten and vanadium each widely varying in their percentage—and performance characteristics. This is in direct contrast to contemporary knife makers who are quite specific about which steel they are using in their blades, such as 12C27 or 440C. Recently, hand tool makers have been a little more specific about what type of steel they use for their blades, such as O-1 and A-2, but this is by no means consistent. If you already have a plane and want to know what kind of steel the blade is, you can put it on the grinder and look up the resulting spark pattern; this will give you a good indication of its type. Of course you can also use it and see if it performs as you want it to, in which case it may not make any difference what type it is. If you're buying or replacing a blade the following should give you some guidelines for your purchase.

Carbon steel

Carbon steel is the longstanding workhorse for use in woodworking hand tool blades. Carbon steel's qualities ideally meet the demands of hand tools for woodworking. When manufactured properly, carbon steel sharpens optimally, holds a sharp edge, and re-sharpens easily—the three basic requirements of a woodworking blade. In addition, its manufacture can be varied slightly to accommodate different woodworking tasks. Many variations exist, based mostly on the quality of ingredients and manufacture, how much it has been hot-worked, and what incidental alloys may be included. With a blade manufactured anytime since World War II the quantity of alloys present may be more than incidental but not necessarily mentioned because of marketing decisions. Before the World Wars, the quality of the steel was largely due to where it was mined, and how well it was processed. And even today there can be considerable variation in quality within a known recipe, even some variation batch to batch.

Figure 2-1. A cast steel blade is usually marked "Cast Steel" or "Warranted Cast Steel."

An important steel that you will find in the vast majority of antique blades made before World War II (though far less common by that time) is *cast steel*. In the 1740's a clockmaker named Benjamin Huntsman discovered that the common steel they were using (called the *cementation process*) could be further refined by being put in clay crucibles, reheated, and by adding a special flux, could have the remaining fine particles of slag removed, further purifying the steel. Brewed in small tightly controlled batches, cast steel, also called *crucible steel*, is high quality and highly predictable. It is an expensive process developed when steel was more of a craft than a manufacturing method. As the Bessemer process, first developed in 1856, continued to be perfected, ever larger, cheaper, and more consistent batches of steel became possible. As the number of demanding craftsmen dropped, along with their market, particularly during the Great Depression, so, too, did the necessity for cast steel. With World War II and

ALLOY INGREDIENTS

Carbon added to iron makes it harder and more wear resistant. Carbon content of about 0.5% to 0.6% is about the lowest amount found in tool steel. The low carbon steel is used for hammers, blacksmith tools, etc. A carbon content of about 0.8% makes a steel file hard (about Rc 56-58). Carbon above that level does not increase the steel's hardness, but raises its wear resistance. A carbon content of 1.3% is about the highest. The highest-carbon steel is used for razors, engraving tools, etc. A carbon content of about 1.05% is a good average—hard with good wear resistance, and yet is not fussy or sensitive to heat.

Tungsten, added in small quantities, can impart a tight, small, and dense grain structure and the ability to attain a keen cutting edge. It also enables steel to retain its hardness at higher temperatures and has a detrimental effect on the steel's forgeability. A tungsten content of 4% (with 1.3% carbon) is so hard it is difficult to grind with an emery wheel.

Manganese makes steel sound when first cast into ingots, and easier to hot roll or forge. Practically all tool steel has at least 0.2% of manganese. Steel can contain up to 0.5% manganese before it is considered alloy steel.

Silicon facilitates casting and hot-work. It usually is used in combination with manganese, molybdenum, or chromium. All steel has 0.1% to 0.3% silicon. Steel with 0.5% to 2% silicon content is considered an alloy.

Chromium increases the hardness penetration of the steel. A thick bar of plain carbon steel will be hardened to a depth of only 3⁄16" (5mm) from its face during heat treatment. Adding chromium allows the bar to harden all of the way through. Because most woodworking blades are less than 3⁄8" (1cm) thick, it is not really an issue for woodworkers. Chromium increases the steel's wear resistance under impact and heat, but does not necessarily increase its hardness. Steel with chromium content of 4% and higher is called high-speed steel.

a changing world economy, cast steel all but disappeared and is now produced in only very small quantities (**Figure 2-1** on page 31).

While there is some variation in performance, and probably, as well, the incidental percentages of alloys contained depending on the specific ore used, cast steel, with its fine grain, takes and holds an edge ideally suited to the demands of fine woodworking, often far superior to most steels available today. For use in a traditional style handplane I will usually choose a cast steel blade over a modern blade.

Cast steel blades are always laminated: cast-steel is too hard, susceptible to shock, prone to cracking during use, and expensive to use alone in a blade. Instead of compromising the edge's hardness by tempering the steel, a thin layer of it is forge-welded (laminated) to softer steel that has more tensile strength. The combination is better able to absorb shock without breaking (**Figure 2-2**).

The backing steel for a laminated blade is low in carbon, softer, and more flexible. Here impurities in the steel can be an advantage. Wrought iron was often used in the 1800s; with a carbon content of 0.02% to 0.08%, it was just tough and malleable enough. Also having a fair amount of inclusions, which in the grain structure appear as strands, similar to the glass in Fiberglass, the impurity increased the steel's flexibility and resistance to breaking—both desirable qualities. The production of wrought iron declined after the 1850s, however, and it is no longer made. But many low-carbon steels are suitable for backing steel, and it is certainly less critical to the performance of the cutting edge steel.

Another option is the "plain" carbon steel blade. The steel is usually not identified and could be one of a few different steels (there are roughly 80 carbon steels, though only a few would be used for plane blades); they could be from what is often called the "10xx" series of steels, of which 1095 is often seen, and possibly 1075 or 1080 and others (the last two digits infer the amount of carbon in the steel). These steels are generally not held to real tight specs, so there is some variation in content and quality, but generally they make very serviceable blades. They could also be one of the water-hardening steels, W1, W2, W3, or even oil-hardening O1, which begins to be on the cusp of an alloy steel. These all make good blades, but unless claims are made to the contrary, contemporary blades are usually cut from bar stock as it comes from the manufacturer with no additional hot work done to improve its structure. Unworked plain carbon blades have not reached their full potential and when compared with a good hot-worked blade may result in disappointing performance. In addition, while many premium after-market blades advertise a higher degree of hardness than competitors do, unless the blades are forged, they will not have the improved grain structure resulting from additional hot work (**Figure 2-3**).

Figure 2-2. A polished bevel on a cast-steel blade reveals the lamination of the two steels; the dark area across the edge of the blade at left is the edge steel, while the lighter area is the softer backing steel. At right is an unlaminated modern blade ground from bar stock.

Figure 2-3. I thought these blades from a set of planes from Thailand were low quality, cut from bar stock, until I sharpened one of them and saw the lamination. They have given good service, though the chipbreaker was not usable.

Alloy steel

Alloy steel was developed by and for industry, mostly in the mid-20th century, to cost-effectively produce large numbers of precisely engineered parts as might be used in cars—and nearly everything else we use now. I suspect the demands of World Wars I and II pushed development of alloys. While an alloy steel blade can be useful in some handplanes and woodworking hand tools, makers use cheaper mass-manufacturing processes mostly to imitate (with generally limited success) the quality blades previously achieved through skilled hot work of high-quality carbon steel.

Carbon steel has a number of shortcomings in industrial production. It hardens only to a depth of about 3⁄16" (5mm). Pieces of thick cross section do not harden all of the way through and their internal structure remains different from their surface structure. The differences compromise virtually any large machine application. As well, the hardening process to produce this less-than-adequate structure requires quenching the red-hot steel in cold water. The shock of quenching usually distorts the object, and is at least unpredictable. If, after considerable time and effort milling a piece precisely to within a tolerance of several thousandths of an inch, the last step compromises the design tolerances, the product is rendered unusable. Lastly, when carbon steel is used for cutting tools to make other objects, especially out of metal or steel themselves, the speed of the cutter (or the object in relation to the cutter, as on a lathe) will overheat the blade, soften it, and cause it to lose its cutting ability within seconds.

Industry discovered adding small amounts of alloys eliminated many problems. The addition of chromium, for instance, allows steel of large cross-section to be hardened all the way through. Chromium and other alloys also produce steel that can be hardened in an oil bath, which is less shocking than water, and thus reduces dimensional distortion. Even better, some combinations of alloys allow the steel to harden in air, a slower, less-shocking process resulting in virtually no distortion. Many alloys produce steel that can be red hard; that is, even when heated by the friction of the cut to red-hot, the steel will not lose its hardness, obviously very desirable in the manufacture of metal-cutting tools.

Eventually, a large number of recipes evolved to produce many different steels for a variety of conditions. However, as the requirements of manufacturing metal parts for cars are different from those for woodworking hand tools, few alloy steels are useful to woodworkers. A small number are worth looking at and are regularly promoted to woodworkers.

The main difficulty when deciding whether to use alloyed steel is that adding alloys usually coarsens the steel's grain and structure. Cutting wood cleanly and efficiently requires a fine blade edge. Coarsening the grain and structure of a hand-tool blade reduces its effectiveness. Casual use of the few alloy steels used in hand-tool blades will not show much difference between them and unalloyed blades. However, there is a difference, and it is more obvious in some woods and applications, which suggests the blades have special usefulness different from unalloyed carbon-steel blades.

Alloy steels are particularly suited for hard-use conditions. While they may not get as keen an edge as a finely wrought carbon-steel blade, their capacity for keeping their edge is excellent. As a result, they are a viable choice for spokeshaves, jack planes, and carpentry chisels, where the stress of deep, repetitive cuts, grit, adhesives, and impact all take a toll on the edge. The steel does get sharp and may be a good choice for versatile tools such as the block plane, which may chamfer edges, remove glue, shape the edges of

FORGEABILTY

Because they remain hard while red-hot, many alloy steels cannot be hot-worked (forged) or forged only with great difficulty, and must be ground to shape. Many of the varieties, though, would not benefit from being forged.

plywood, and smooth various surfaces, all on the same project.

Because alloyed steels cannot achieve the sharpness of carbon steel, I believe they are more suited to harder hardwoods, particularly tropicals, than to softwoods and softer hardwoods. Softwoods require a keen edge, though as the types of wood being worked increase in hardness and density, the importance of edge toughness increases. Tropical hardwoods require a demanding combination of keenness and toughness in equal proportions.

As to the third requirement for blades for woodworking hand tool, alloyed steels require different sharpening methods, increasingly so as the alloy content grows. The greater the alloy content, the less effective are water stones and oilstones, necessitating a diamond stone or paste. The technique and the amount of time is about the same once the different abrasives are employed.

Some of the more common alloy steels woodworkers encounter are the generically named chrome vanadium and tungsten vanadium; also PM-V11, occasionally D2 and M2, and more commonly O1 and A2. In the latter two, the *O* stands for *oil hardening*, the *A* for *air hardening* (O1 and A2 are two of only a few oil- and air-hardening steels that actually have an O or A in their name). The numbers complete the name of that particular steel.

Chrome vanadium and tungsten vanadium often are clearly marked on German plane blades as well as some others. Both chrome vanadium and tungsten vanadium are workhorses, not given to much subtlety, and often prove quite durable. They are well suited to the heavy work horned planes often perform. While chrome vanadium and tungsten vanadium are suitable for many miscellaneous tasks around the shop, both are coarser grained and make fine, tearout-free shavings in many woods difficult to achieve (**Figure 2-4**).

Figure 2-4. Blades of alloyed steel are often marked, but not consistently so.

A2 steel blades have gained prominence as the apparent answer to both the manufacturers' desire for affordable quality and consistency, and the woodworker's interest in satisfactory performance. A2 steel is more finely grained than chrome vanadium and tungsten vanadium blades, and rival their durability. Additionally, higher-end blades are cryogenically treated. In theory, the cryogenic process hardens the blade similar to heat-treating by causing the growth of carbides (crystals that cause steel to harden) but without enlarging

Figure 2-5. Blades of A2 steel are usually marked. The one above at top was cryogenically treated and is labeled as such.

Figure 2-6. The blade from this small Chinese-style plane at left is high-speed steel, as is the blade from the finger plane next to it. The traditional-style blade at right has a piece of high-alloy steel brazed on the end of a longer blank.

the crystal structure, as can happen during heat treatment. Actual evidence this is happening is inconclusive, and anecdotal evidence from woodworkers suggests it is difficult to tell any difference between cryogenically treated and untreated blades. Regardless of whether they are cryogenically treated or not, the sharpenability of the blades varies by manufacturer. I have one blade I sharpen on waterstones while another requires diamond stones. You will have to discover what works best for your blades **(Figure 2-5)**.

A2 blades promise performance across a spectrum of tasks and difficult woods, and may become the new industry standard (though we'll have to wait and see if it's supplanted by the new PM-V11). Aiming toward a least common denominator, however, compromises performance at both ends of the spectrum. Fine smoothing in softwoods and many hardwoods is not as effective with an A2 blade because it does not take a thin bevel well (25° or less), and a blade with higher alloy content better handles heavy work in tropical hardwoods.

PM-V11 is one of a group of new steels made using powdered metal technology. The PM stands for powdered metal and I assume the V11 stands for 11% vanadium, which is quite high. The technology results in a steel of very consistent grain size. This along with its high alloy content has, according to testing and many reviews resulted in a steel that outlasts virtually all the other steels commonly used for plane blades, and is, in addition, easy to sharpen. It would seem to be an ideal all-around blade steel. The jury is out, though, on just how sharp you can get it, though it would seem for most uses—sharp enough.

D2 and M2 show up now and then, though often identified only as high speed steel. Both these are very high in chromium (11-13% and 3.75-4.5% respectively) with M2 having over 6% tungsten as well. They exhibit classic alloy steel characteristics: extremely durable edge, but they don't get very sharp and they are very difficult to sharpen. For most uses these steels are not suitable for plane blades.

O1 tool steel is another alloy blade now available. O1 has one-tenth the chromium of A2. I have not worked with O1 (that I know of!). I suspect its lower chromium content will make it easier to sharpen and probably (depending on quality) will take a keener edge than A2. Because it has some tungsten and vanadium in it, it will probably show greater endurance in shaping tasks than most carbon steels.

I have tungsten vanadium blades in my jack planes and A2 in my block planes, and they perform well. I have a high-alloy blade in my traditional Chinese smoothing plane, which has a very high cutting angle. I use the Chinese smoothing plane for tropical hardwoods with good results. However, for my best smoothing planes, from which I expect tearout-free performance in softwoods and Northern hardwoods, I prefer a good quality cast steel blade.

High-speed steel

Further yet out on the scale of alloy steels are high-speed steel (HSS), which has chromium, vanadium, tungsten, and others (but mainly chromium) added in relatively high percentages. HSS is essentially the same steel used in drill and other power-driven bits, and is very hard and tough. Industry originally developed HSS to work at red-hot temperatures while remaining hard enough to maintain its cutting edge. For the woodworker, there are two main problems with the use of HSS, the same problems associated with the alloy steels, only multiplied several times over. The first is the difficulty in sharpening. While alloy steels are difficult to hone on the more common sharpening stone, HSS is next to impossible. A diamond stone or diamond paste is a necessity, which actually is more a nuisance than a problem. The second problem with HSS is it does not get as sharp as carbon steel or even alloy steel. The grain of HSS is coarser than alloy steel—so it has limitations.

HSS has found favor among woodturners. A lathe tool, especially when aggressively used, can build up a lot of heat, causing a carbon-steel blade edge to degrade fast. However, arguments in favor of both steels exist here as well. A carbon-steel tool used with rhythm and sensitivity at the lathe will be sharper starting out, and will shear cleaner longer than a HSS tool. Developing and maintaining a more refined technique (shearing rather than scraping, in this case) in order to produce higher quality work using more finely suited tools is the challenge all woodworkers face as they advance in the craft.

Its only possible use in plane blades would be in very high blade-angle planes (60° and above) used on tropical hardwoods. Here the edge could be sharp enough for this near scraping cut and the durability would be a definite asset. I have seen modern Chinese-style planes use HSS blades and the blades in other traditional Chinese planes also appear to have high alloy content. Coupled with the heat generated by the hardness and abrasive quality of the woods, HSS could make sense here (**Figure 2-6**).

MY RECOMMENDATION

Unless you are dissatisfied with the performance of the blade you currently have in your plane I wouldn't change it. If after you've used the plane for a while, and you find the longevity of the edge disappointing for the use you're giving it, or you are unable to get tearout-free results with a well set-up plane I would consider replacing the blade as follows: first of all, I think cast steel blades can usually be used for all tasks, as they traditionally were. This is unless it is a cast steel blade you're dissatisfied with. In this case you can try to get a better cast steel blade (there is some variation) but that's going to be a roll of the dice, though they do remain pretty affordable. Or you can try different blades as follows:

- For planes used for heavy stock removal, a good tungsten- or chrome-vanadium blade or a PM-V11 blade (I have not been impressed with A2 for stock removal).
- For general purpose work probably a PM-V11 blade (I say this with the reservation that I haven't used this steel extensively) or an A2 blade.
- For fine smoothing of softwoods and hardwoods probably O1, a cast steel blade, or a laminated Japanese Stanley-style blade; with A2 and then PM-V11 being used as the wood gets harder and the blade angle higher.

The option to choose a blade of one type of steel or another is one of the great advantages woodworkers have today. Understanding the qualities of each in the face of contradictory claims and explanations allows us to choose one over another and expedite the work. Knowledge and practice allows us to match the blade to the tool and the tool to the work.

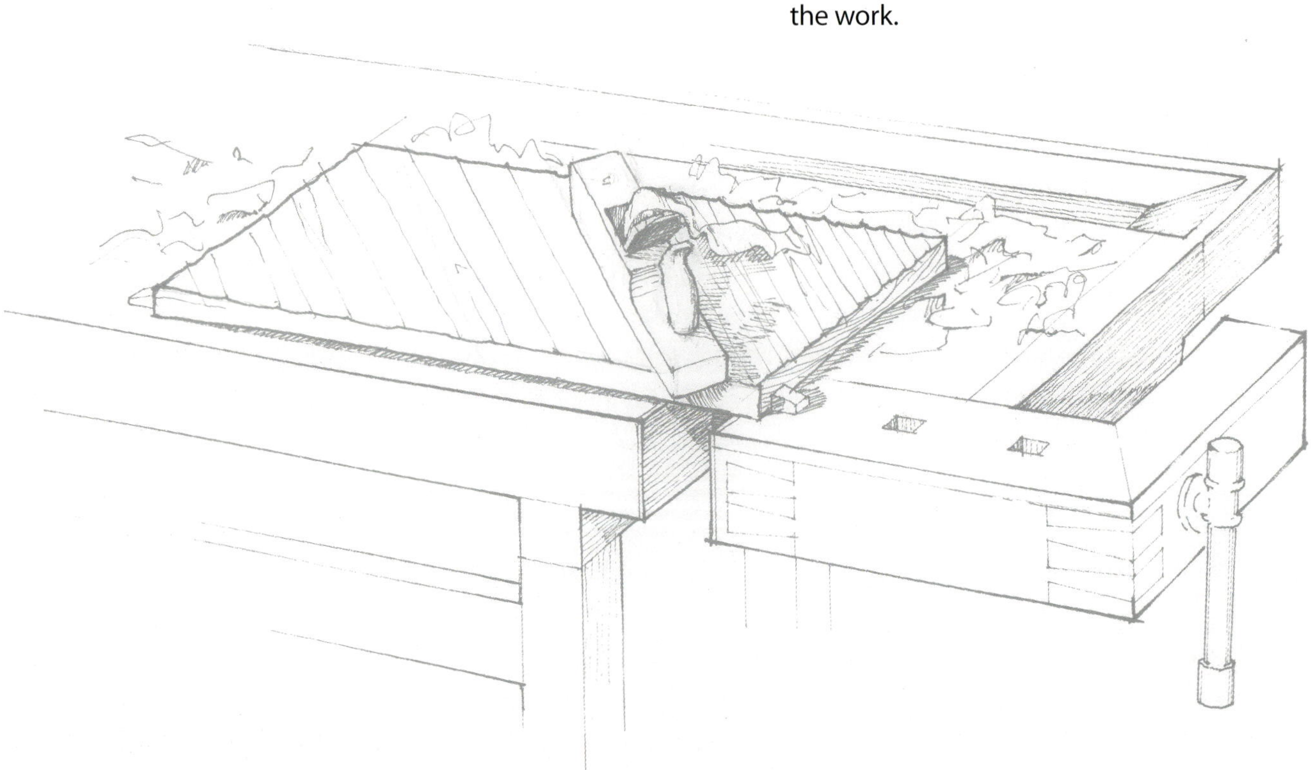

ULMIA
Made in German

CHAPTER 3

HOW A PLANE WORKS

THE SIX TACTICS USED TO ACHIEVE BEST PERFORMANCE

This chapter discusses in detail the anatomy common to all handplanes—and the techniques for optimal quality and efficiency they make possible—both individually and in their interaction with one another. Later chapters demonstrate how these techniques were traditionally employed in various combinations to dimension, join, and smooth lumber by using the jack, jointer, and smoothing planes; and how a modern user can put his or her own combination of techniques together to achieve fast and effective results. The information here is fundamental to setting up, tuning, modifying, and troubleshooting your plane.

All planes, including this Razee-style jack plane, use the same anatomical tactics to produce efficient, quality work.

The core techniques for efficient, effective performance involve six common anatomical features:

1. Angle of the blade to the work. Using planes with blade angles suited to the wood or to the task increases a plane's reliability and efficiency.

2. Clearance of the mouth through which the shaving passes. Little understood and often abused, a suitable mouth opening controls, if not eliminates, tearout.

3. The use of a chipbreaker. A relatively recent invention that nearly eliminates tearout while increasing a plane's versatility.

4. Angle of the blade's bevel. Not having the correct blade bevel angle causes many headaches.

5. Shape of the blade edge. The re-sharpened edges of a plane's blade are not all straight—in fact, few of them are.

6. Length of the plane body and width of the blade. The two have a relationship to each other and define a plane's intended use.

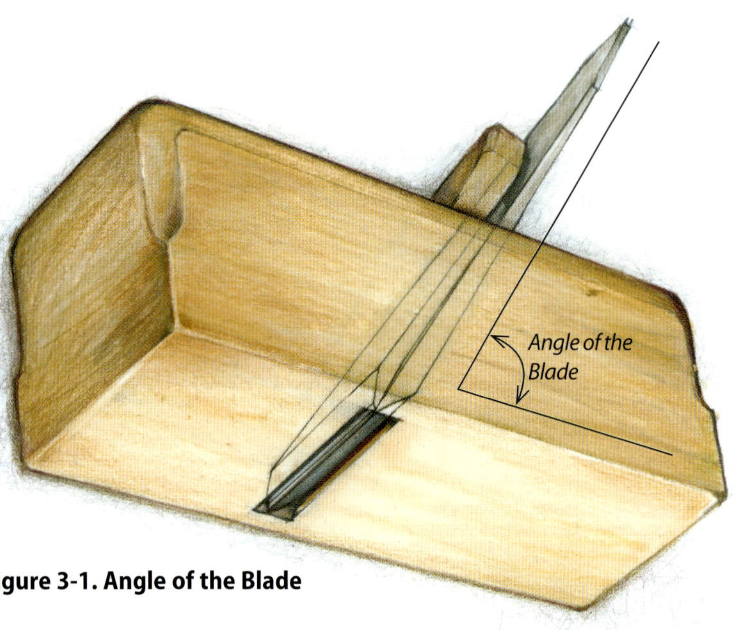

Figure 3-1. Angle of the Blade

1. THE ANGLE OF THE BLADE

Most woodworkers take this aspect of the handplane for granted because it is built into the plane and the availability of new planes with different blade angles has been limited (**Figure 3-1**).

The response of different woods to different blade angles is not necessarily pronounced, except with extremely hard and extremely soft woods. But step away from the middling ground to more demanding projects in difficult woods, and matching the blade angle to the work becomes a powerful asset leading to better and more consistent results, and more efficient work.

Traditional blade angles

Looking at old traditional tools, you can see that using planes with different blade angles (or *pitch*, as it is called in Britain; see **Figure 3-2**) was a common practice. Variations in blade angles among traditional tools are large and obvious, varying according to the woods usually worked by that trade, and within a range of angles according to the job that plane had to do. The difference in blade angles between a classic Chinese furniture plane working rosewood and a traditional Japanese carpenter's plane working cedar, for instance, is striking—and instructive.

The best blade angle

The inference of studying the traditional tools of different trades, and a fact borne out in practice, is that softer woods take a lower cutting angle than the harder woods; conversely, the harder the wood, the higher the angle. This is not always true, but it is a good starting point. I would add: use the lowest cutting angle that remains effective, for two reasons: the lower angle shears wood fibers rather than scrapes them, producing a better surface; and the lower angle also involves less work as the shearing cut presents less resistance than the scraping cut.

It is, of course, often somewhat more complex. A number of factors interplay with this rule of thumb. First, softwoods, hardwoods, and tropical hardwoods each respond differently to the cutting action of the blade.

Softwoods require cutting, not scraping. The higher cutting angles that, in hardwoods, produce successful compression failure (Type-II chips, as per Bruce Hoadly in *Understanding Wood*) will only tear the fibers in softwoods, causing the chip to crumple into a bunch (**Figure 3-3** on page 44). A scraper, for instance, will shape, but not actually smooth, softwood. The thinness of the edge and its sharpness is particularly important in softwoods.

Hardwoods are somewhat on the cusp between softwoods and tropical hardwoods. Hardwoods often respond well to a sharp low-angle blade, but smoothing is also possible with just a scraper. The variety of grain structures and hardness within hardwoods suggests using a variety of cutting angles.

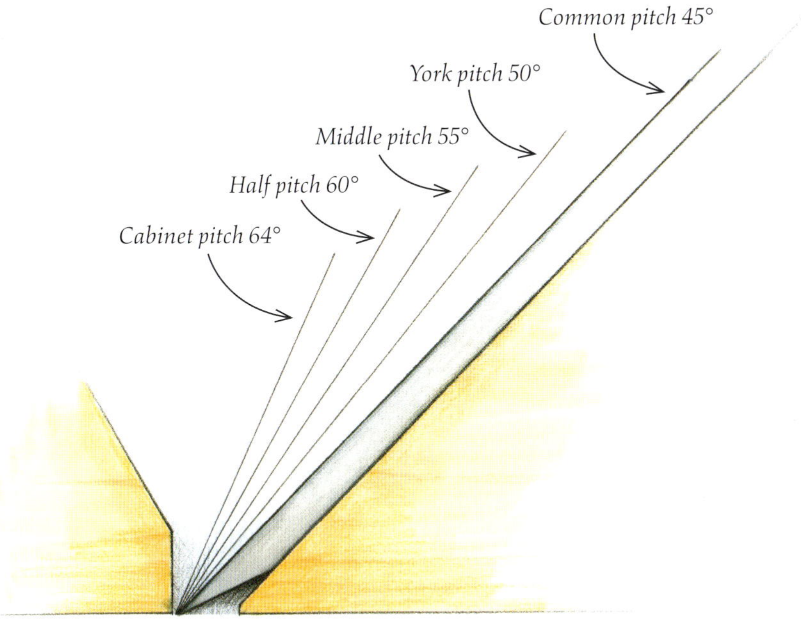

Figure 3-2. British Nomenclature for Common Blade Angles (Pitch)

USE THE LOWEST EFFECTIVE CUTTING ANGLE

The lower the angle, the cleaner the shear. The higher the angle (increasingly above 47½°), the more it cuts like a scraper. At an angle around 75° or 80°, the tool is best regarded as a scraper.

As a general rule of thumb, the plane-blade angle for softwoods varies from 35° to around 45° with the lower end working best. Blade angles for hardwoods run the gamut from about 40° to 55° and higher, though the majority works well in the 45° to 50° range. Tropical hardwood blade angles range from about 50° to over 65°.

Low-to-medium blade angles work well, though higher blade angles are sometimes safer and more predictable, producing less tearout with less adjustment, maintenance, and sharpening.

Figure 3-3. Blade Angle and Wood Species
Within the range for each wood, the lower angles are generally for preparatory planes. The higher angles are for smoothing planes.

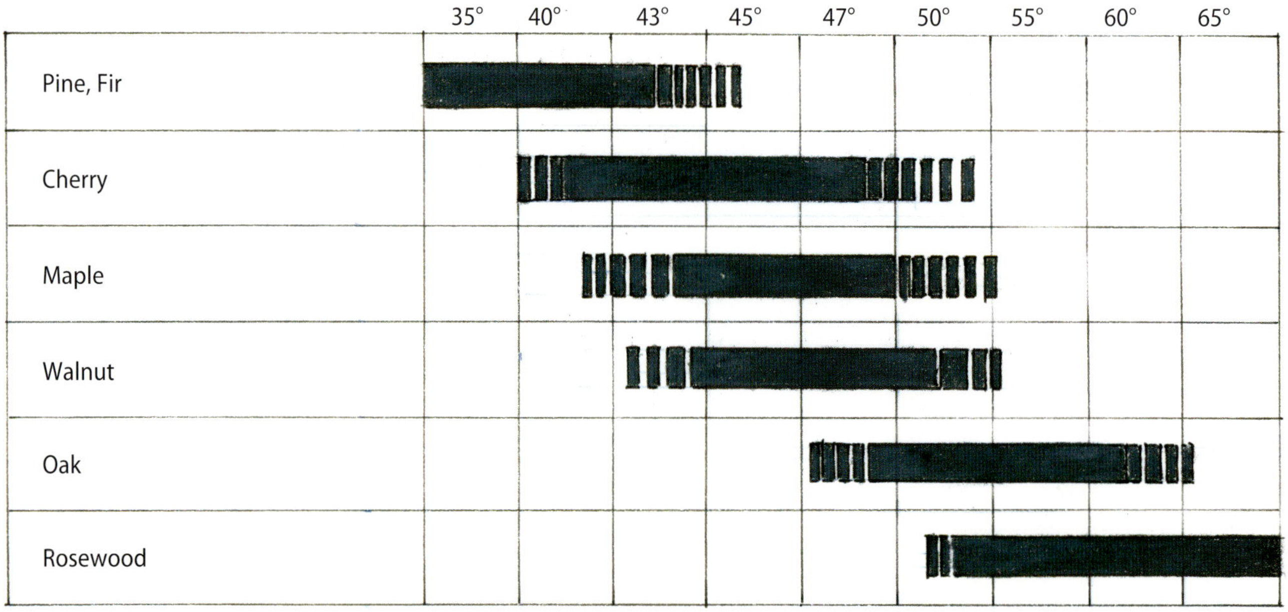

MOLDING PLANES

The practice of using higher blade angles on molding versus smoothing planes for hardwoods suggests two things:

- increasing blade angle increases *reliability* of the cut; and
- increasing the blade's pitch above the normal range reduces cut *quality*.

Increasing the blade angle is the default for reducing tearout on a molding plane.

Many molding planes use pitches in excess of the normal range—often as high as 64°—in smoothing planes for the same woods. Experience with molding planes confirms that while this might produce a surface with minor roughness, it largely avoids more disastrous forms of tearout. A reduced-quality cut was the better choice for the eighteenth-century craftsman who used these tools, than a higher quality cut punctuated with deep tearout. Look at the alternatives to eighteenth-century craftsmen.

The goal of smoothing work for the eighteenth-century craftsman was to achieve an acceptable surface straight from the plane or scraper, and to absolutely minimize the use of glasspaper. Glasspaper, the precursor to sandpaper, was usually made by the craftsman himself, by pulverizing an expensive piece of glass, and sieving and sifting it onto paper coated with hide glue. It worked slowly, wore out quickly, and was effective only for polishing—not removing anything more than minor imperfections. The craftsman aimed for a surface from his molding plane that required only minor, if any, glass papering. Moldings produced by high-pitch molding planes would be acceptable.

To further reduce demands on planing and increase the chances of getting an acceptable surface, craftsmen carefully selected molding stock for straight grain and even texture. Also, moldings were often used in millwork that was painted, or of such size (or height) as to further obscure a less-than-polished surface.

The resulting surface, though, is not as smooth or clear as with a lower-angle cut.

Tropical hardwoods respond well to scraping, conversely tearing out disastrously at low and intermediate blade angles. Traditional blade angles for tropicals often are quite high—at what would be a scraping angle in a softer wood. Despite the high angle, the plane blade leaves a clean-cut surface with good clarity (**Figure 3-4**).

Additionally, there is a great deal of overlap of which angles work well in a particular wood. Often the same angle seems less effective from one board to another in the same species, or even from one part of a board to another. Because of such variations, most woodworkers use more conservative angles—slightly steeper but within the acceptable range—for more predictable results and little or no tearout.

Finally, you will find some blade angles cannot be used when cutting some woods. It is not that they do not cut well, but that they nearly do not cut at all. Pine, for instance, seems to crumple as the blade angle increases over 45˚. Results can be disastrous with some tropical hardwoods at even the intermediate blade angles.

Blade angle and the task

Studying traditional tools also shows the cutting angle of a plane blade depends upon the task being performed. Because a lower-angle blade presents less resistance in cutting than a higher-angle blade with its scraping cut, planes used for shaping or preparing stock tend to have lower angles. Lower-cutting angles are less fatiguing because the plane requires less effort to

Figure 3-4. A set of Chinese cabinetmaker planes, front to back: jointer with a 55° pitch; intermediate smoother with a 60° pitch; smoother with a 65° pitch. The size of the intermediate smoother varies from woodworker to woodworker. Sometimes it is about the same size as the jointer but with a higher pitch and finer setup. Sometimes it is about the size of a Western jack plane, as shown here.

push. At this stage in the work, stock removal is more important than smoothness, which can be accomplished with succeeding planes. Traditionally, craftsmen use several planes to take a board from initial surfacing to final smoothing. Each succeeding plane had a slightly steeper pitch, usually finishing with a plane the craftsman determines has the optimal angle for the work produced (See **Figure 3-1** on page 42). (For more on this see Chapter 4 and "Dimensioning Stock" on page 78.)

Custom blade angles

If you utilize wood you suspect would work more easily or predictably with a blade angle different from the planes you have access to, you should make your own. If you have not made a plane of your own, it may sound intimidating. Do not let it be. A woodworker of intermediate skill can readily make a traditional wood plane. With a little extra effort and time, a novice can make one as well. The trick is to know the simple techniques. This book contains plans and instructions for building a full set of traditional western bench planes that can be modified according to your specific needs. (See Chapter 8 on page 152.)

Making your own planes expands your options. You can customize the blade angle as well as match the blade steel to the work, choosing from a variety of contemporary parallel and vintage tapered blades in a variety of steels.

Alternatively, you can still find many antique traditional planes at very reasonable prices. The blades in these are often very good laminated cast steel. The range of blade angles is limited, but often outside what is available in a newly manufactured plane. To get a sense of what you are looking for, see "Setting Up a Traditional Wooden Plane" on page 118.

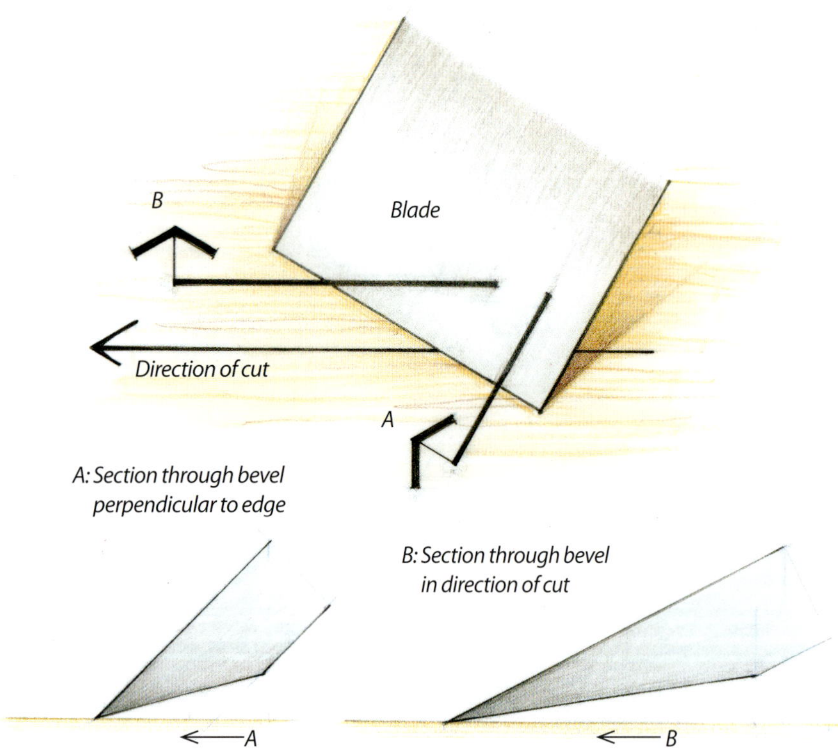

Figure 3-5. If the blade is skewed when planing, the effective bevel angle (as presented to the wood) is smaller than the actual ground bevel.

Another way to get a custom blade angle, particularly if it's an emergency, is to back-bevel the blade. This is where you put a second bevel on the topside of the blade, opposite to the main bevel. This is usually a small bevel, maybe 1⁄32" (0.8mm) or less wide, established by honing rather than by grinding. I would do this only for the occasional piece. If you find yourself working repeatedly with woods that require a different angle, it will be more efficient to make a plane to that angle. This is because when you work a lot with a plane, you have to re-sharpen frequently, sometimes every 15 to 20 minutes, depending on the fineness of the work. Repeating a finely angled back-bevel becomes a problem (which can usually be solved by a precisely set sharpening jig—you're not going to do it freehand), but meanwhile that little back-bevel is growing larger and larger. This also negates the ability to use the chipbreaker for any further tearout control. In addition, back-beveling may require the bevel to be reground: as the bevel angle becomes larger, that is, more blunt when the back-bevel is added to it, it reduces the blade's cutting action. When you finally want to remove the back-bevel, you have to grind that now much larger back-bevel away to restore the original edge, losing a lot of steel and a lot of time. You may want to just dedicate that blade to that angle and get another blade to use for regular work. On the other hand, back-beveling can be an efficient solution for less-frequent plane users or for those occasional situations that really do not warrant the time required to make or set up a plane specifically for that task. (If you are interested in exploring this topic further, purchase the booklet *Double Bevel Sharpening* by Brian Burns.) (See "Bevel Angle" on page 54.)

Skewing the plane in use is another way to vary the blade angle. Craftsmen who plane a lot do it instinctively in response to the feedback from the wood. They may do it over the whole board or only those sections of it that respond better to the technique. Skewing the plane effectively lowers the blade angle, and presents a thinner bevel to the wood **(Figure 3-5)**.

It works sometimes for these reasons, but if you've ever used a wood spokeshave with a cutting angle of only the bevel of the blade (22°–30°) you know it is prone to disastrous tearout. I think it is usually successful more because you are approaching a section of difficult grain from a more successful direction, which may be different from the general direction of the grain of the board. I usually skew the plane only to change the angle of attack. Keeping the blade sharp usually works better. Nor would I use this tactic as a substitute for a plane built with the correct blade angle.

A surprising amount of tearout at any angle is avoidable by having an extremely sharp blade. Here is where you start to notice the difference between what is just sharp, and what is extremely sharp. Your first clue comes in the midst of working: your plane, a finely set smoother, still cuts effectively but occasionally leaves some tear out. You stop and sharpen it and the problem areas of tearout cut smoothly again. The only thing you changed is the blade sharpness. It makes a difference. I have lower-angle blades that often work better than higher-angle blades in a wood I know prefers a higher cutting angle, only because the quality of the blade is better—it just gets and stays sharper.

2. MOUTH OPENING

Controlling the shaving as it passes through the opening in the bottom of the plane is probably the second-most basic technique for controlling tearout, but one that is not well understood **(Figure 3-6)**. Restricting the throat opening **(Figure 3-7)**

Figure 3-6. Mouth Opening

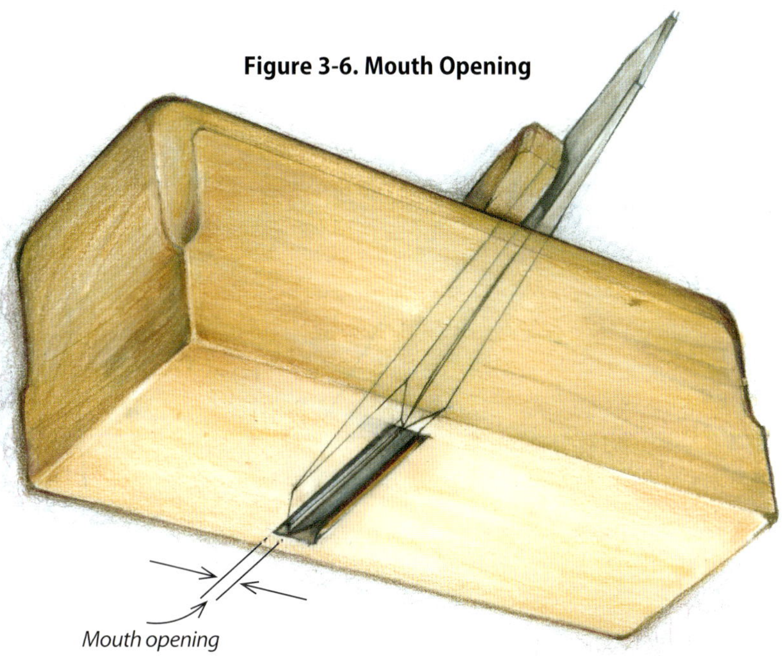

Figure 3-7. Unrestrained shaving splits out ahead of cut, causing tearout.

Figure 3-8. Shaving restrained by a tight mouth opening prevents shaving from lifting ahead of the cut, reducing or eliminating tearout.

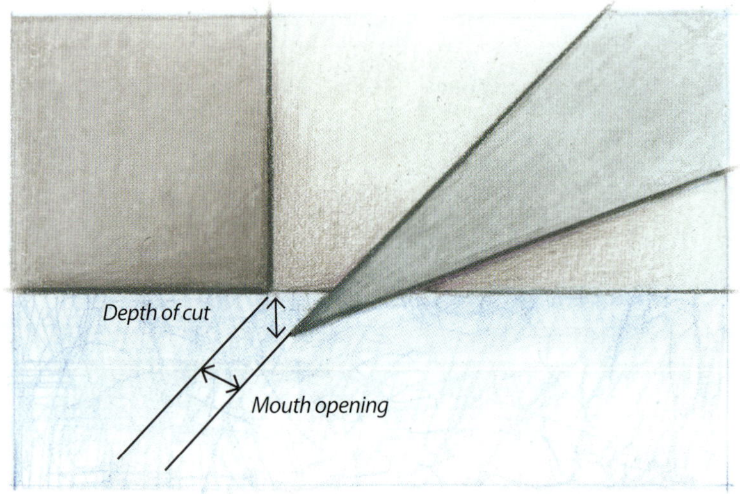

Figure 3-9. For maximum effectiveness against tearout, the mouth opening is equal to the depth of cut. In the real world, the mouth may have to be ever so slightly larger, but definitely no less, than the depth of cut.

Figure 3-10. A mouth opening or bevel angle that is too small can cause the edge to flex.

works to reduce tearout (**Figure 3-8**) by compressing the wood fibers immediately in front of the blade, thus keeping them from splitting out ahead of the cut (**Figure 3-9**). While it is an effective tactic, it has become a less popular one for a number of reasons.

For one, the amount of openness is a dynamic factor, affected by the combination of blade angle, chipbreaker bevel angle, and escape angle of the throat.

The result of such complexity is easy to misjudge, and can be frustrating. If the mouth is too small for the cut, the shavings jam in the throat, which can damage the edge of the mouth and sometimes the blade. Restricting the chip at the mouth of the plane definitely increases stress on the blade, as both pressure and heat build. The increased downward pressure on the blade due to the chip being constricted as it passes through the mouth—made even greater at the higher blade angles—increases the importance of the correct bevel angle, as the blade edge is liable to flex (**Figure 3-10**). When this happens, it flexes deeper into the cut, taking a slightly thicker chip. The result is one of three things: tearout, a chattering cut (as the blade flexes back and forth), or a chip too large for the opening, which causes the chip to jam.

Closing the mouth down also increases the wear on the edge of the mouth itself. For maximum effectiveness, the edge of the mouth should be crisp. Sharp is even better. The increased pressure from constricting the chip rounds the edge over pretty fast, and the rounder it gets, the less effective it is. Ideally, the material at the mouth of a finish plane should be at least as hard as brass. For that reason, many old wood planes that incorporate a restricted mouth opening employ a piece of brass, iron, or hardwood which is let into the sole of the plane to close the throat opening (**Figure 3-11**).

Increased heat build-up at the mouth is palpable. The oils in the wood being planed vaporize and condense on the top edge of the blade, causing a superficial discoloration of the blade just above the edge (**Figure 3-12**).

Though work-hardening of a plane blade seems like a woodworking myth, when you see evidence of this kind of heat, you begin to think that perhaps some change in the steel might be occurring. Increased heat build-up speeds deterioration of the edge. I believe this is one of the main reasons Chinese planes, which have a high-angle blade (more heat-inducing) and a narrow throat, tend to use a higher alloy steel in their blades (see "Alloy Ingredients" on page 32).

The interrelationship of the mouth opening to the other anatomical tactics is dynamic. The effectiveness of restricting the mouth opening varies according to the blade angle. While effective at lower angles, it seems more so at higher blade angles (50°-plus), and practice confirms it. The chipbreaker, however, seems to be less effective on higher-angle planes and increasingly effective as blade angle drops below 50°. On planes with angles greater than 55°, I rely on a small mouth opening alone to control tearout.

Without an adjustable mouth, finish planing is the only task you can do with a plane so configured because the mouth is too narrow for other work. You will need more planes because a single tool will not do a variety of tasks as designed. I believe you will find the setup and maintenance of a fine finish plane does not lend itself to the plane doing less-refined tasks, mouth opening or not, intended versatility or not. Fine-finish planing is demanding and having dedicated planes set up for it is a time-saver.

Figure 3-11. The mouth on this old coffin-sided smoother—repurposed as a spoon-bottom smoother—has been closed down with a brass piece let into the sole.

Figure 3-12. You can see the brown discoloration from heat build-up on the face of the blade, right; it follows the silhouette of the bottom edge of the wedge.

Adjusting the mouth opening

Woodworkers have developed a number of different ways to match the mouth opening to the work. The first

Figure 3-13. This is the sole of the Ulmia reform smoothing plane with its adjustable throat plate. It is adjusted with two screws: one on top that loosens the plate, and one in front that moves the plate forward or backward.

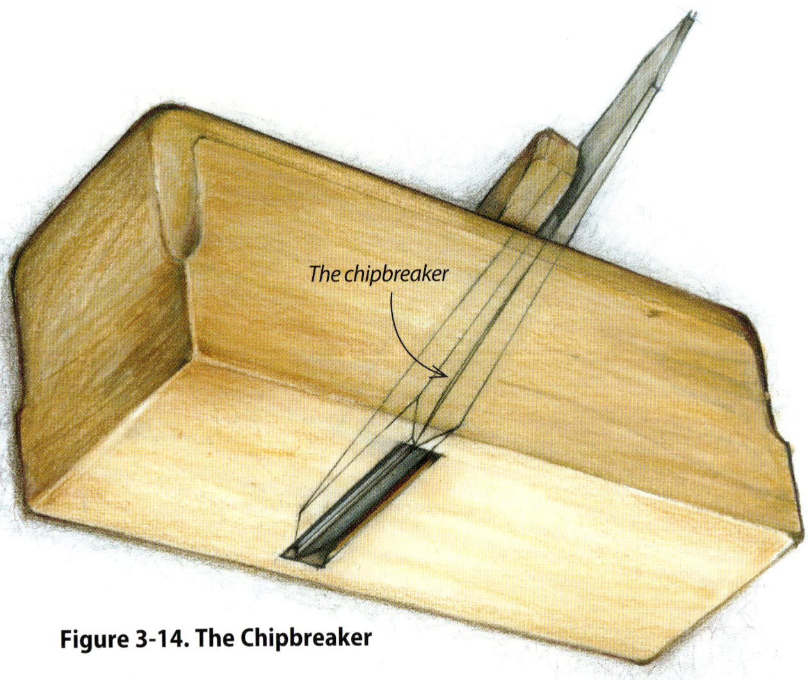

Figure 3-14. The Chipbreaker

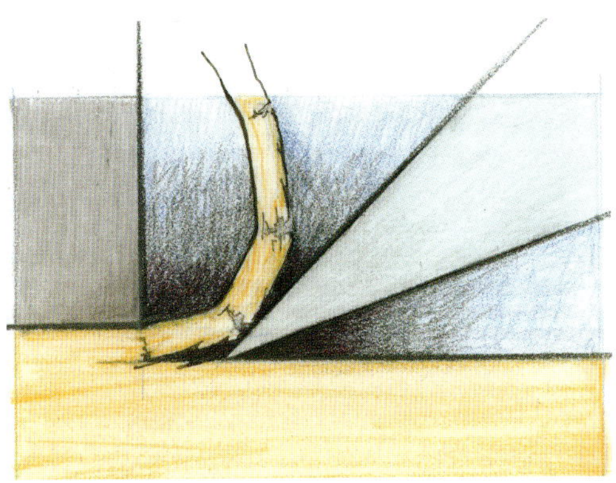

Figure 3-15. As the shaving rides up the blade, it can lift and split out ahead of the cut.

is to have different planes dedicated to different tasks, each with a matching mouth opening. If you are doing a lot of such work, it is the most efficient method. A second method is to alter the plane's mouth by inserting a piece of metal or wood to close the opening. Insertion repairs a plane with a worn open mouth or modifies the mouth for a different use (see Chapter 8 on page 152).

The best method for adjusting the mouth is the sliding mouthpiece, set into the sole of the plane in front of the blade; this is a very effective, quick, and easy method for adjusting the throat while the blade remains firmly bedded **(Figure 3-13)**. These can be found on the German reform (improved) wooden planes, and instructions for retrofitting vintage plane as well as installing a movable throat plate on a new plane are presented later in the book (see Chapter 8 on page 152).

3. CHIPBREAKER

The chipbreaker **(Figure 3-14)** is a 300- to 400-year-old invention that has increased the reliability of the handplane in getting consistently smooth results. The chipbreaker accomplishes this through one main mechanism and some secondary ones. The primary mechanism for improving consistency of the cut gives the piece its name. By sharpening the bevel on the chipbreaker and placing it directly behind the cutting edge **(Figure 3-15)** the chip is broken backward before it has a chance to lift and split ahead of the cut **(Figure 3-16)**. This has proven to be a highly effective method of reducing tearout, especially when coupled with a small mouth opening at lower-to-medium blade angles.

There are at least three distinct shapes of chipbreaker. One, typical on older, wooden planes, Japanese planes, and now Lie-Nielsen planes, consists of a large flat bevel ground at about 25° (measured when mounted to the blade), with a secondary, smaller bevel that does the work (**Figure 3-17**).

A second shape, seen on both new and old manufactured planes, is similar in profile, only slightly rounded, rather than beveled (**Figure 3-18**).

The third shape, most often seen on the Stanley/Bailey planes, is a bulbous, almost semicircular curve near the blade edge (**Figure 3-19**).

The first shape is probably the most versatile, because the large, low bevel provides more clearance for the shaving broken by the smaller bevel. Rounded chipbreakers constrict the throat more, resulting in a greater chance the shavings will jam. (See "Plane Geometry, A Summary" on page 57.)

The second type, slightly rounded, will often work satisfactorily, but if you have problems with jamming, consider filing the rounded shape to a flat secondary bevel (assuming you are left with enough material not to weaken the chipbreaker itself). I would try this fix before opening the throat angle.

The third type, with its bulbous rounding, perhaps meant to provide better pressure distribution under a lever cap, often takes up too much room to allow chips to pass through a narrow throat. It also won't work with a wedge

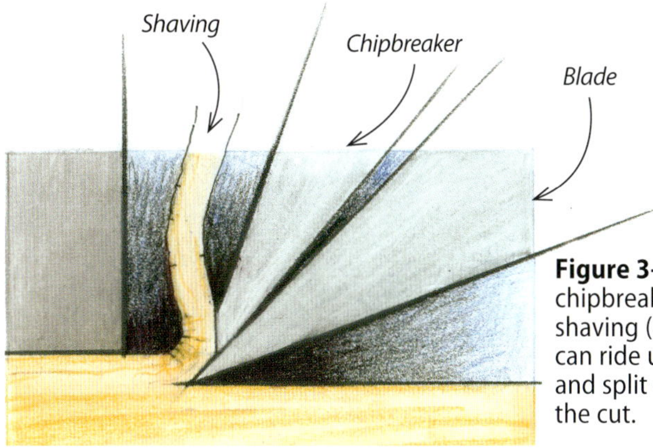

Figure 3-16. The chipbreaker breaks the shaving (chip) before it can ride up the blade and split out ahead of the cut.

Figure 3-17. Flat Bevel-Style Chipbreaker with Secondary Bevel

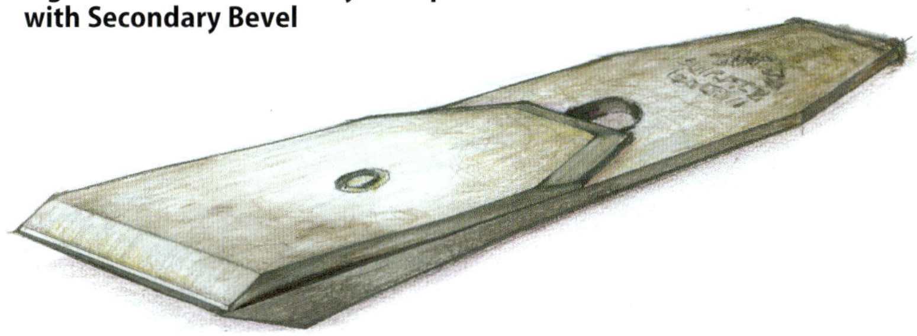

Figure 3-18. Rounded-Style Chipbreaker

Figure 3-19. Stanley-Type Chipbreaker.

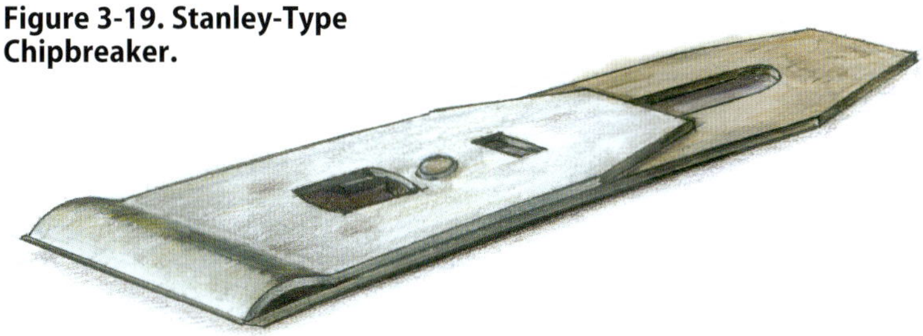

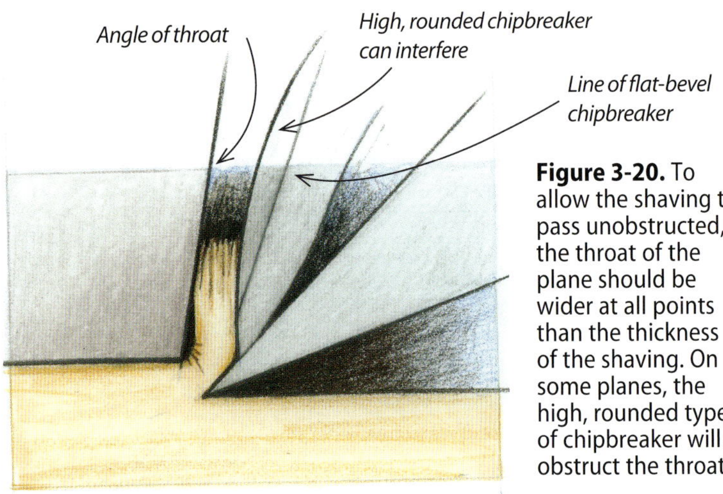

Figure 3-20. To allow the shaving to pass unobstructed, the throat of the plane should be wider at all points than the thickness of the shaving. On some planes, the high, rounded type of chipbreaker will obstruct the throat.

HARD CHIPBREAKERS

Chipbreakers really need to be made of hard, good steel, of a quality to match that of the blade. If you're really using them hard—in a position tight to the cutting edge—they are subjected to a lot of impact and heat. They will dull and need to be re-sharpened over time, and if they are not, they may begin to trap chips. I have seen soft chipbreakers get a multitude of tiny dents from just the impact of the shaving. I also have seen the discoloration on the edge from when the oils in the wood vaporize from the heat of the cut. I have also used blades with chipbreakers so soft, they dull and trap chips before the blade gets dull. Having a hard chipbreaker reduces maintenance and improves reliability.

For instance, good quality Japanese planes have chipbreakers laminated with a hard steel edge similar to the main blade. Sometimes on the lesser-quality Japanese planes, the chipbreaker is only hardened and tempered, not laminated. One might think this is excessive, but it is not.

and so is not an option for planes that use a wedge to secure the blade. It can be made to work with a lever cap, though its bulbous shape still can be a problem with chip clearance **(Figure 3-20)**.

In the Sta-Set, a new two-part chipbreaker by Clifton, the lower part where the chip is actually broken removes and reinstalls without unscrewing the main body of the chipbreaker from the blade. This is a great time-saver when sharpening. You have to be careful, though, when using waterstones, because water can get between the main body of the chipbreaker and the blade, and cause rust. The Sta-Set is rounded, though low, in profile. It fits flat to the blade, rather than arching above it, and is quite a bit thicker than most modern chipbreakers, adding considerable stiffness to the blade **(Figure 3-21)**.

The use of a chipbreaker does introduce some interesting dynamics into the functioning of the blade. Screwing the chipbreaker to the blade firmly enough to ensure tight contact bends the blade into an arc. When used with a heavy, handmade tapered blade fixed with a wedge, this was an advantage. It nearly guaranteed the blade would contact the bed at the heel (right behind the bevel), the most important place, and at the top. This eliminated the need when the plane was made to custom-fit the bed of each plane to the varyingly thick blade and simplified any fine-tuning of the blade bed by the user as well. I have even seen the bed of an old plane cut concave to guarantee this fit **(Figure 3-22)**.

Relieving the bed this way is a less successful strategy with thin modern parallel blades, however, as they are not stiff enough. This strategy relies on a thick blade, assisted by an equally massive chipbreaker. Tapered blades are nearly ¼" (6mm) at their thickest part; together with the chipbreaker the assembly is almost ⅜" (1cm) thick. Many contemporary blade/chipbreaker assemblies together are barely the thickness of an old tapered blade by itself, not much more than ⅛" (3mm). However, high-end contemporary blade makers are now offering assemblies that total around ¼" (6mm) thick greatly improving your chances of being able to eliminate blade chatter.

Another type of chattering happens because the bevel angle is too small (and thus the material immediately behind the edge is too thin). Some woodworkers say the chipbreaker can correct this situation by *pre-tensioning* the cutting edge. However, I would not rely on the chipbreaker to correct for a too-small bevel. It is far better to give the edge its proper bevel angle. (See "Bevel Angle" on page 54.)

Figure 3-21. The Sta-Set chipbreaker with its edge-piece removed so the blade can be sharpened. Reassembly does not require readjustment, as the part of the chipbreaker that is screwed to the blade has an interlocking groove and a small pin that aligns with a matching hole in the edge-piece. The edge-piece is then held in place by the lever cap.

Setting the chipbreaker

I think the main advantage of the chipbreaker is to increase a plane's versatility. Setting the chipbreaker down close to the edge reduces tearout and allows a more finished cut. Setting the chipbreaker back allows the blade to be more deeply set to hog off wood. All of this can happen regardless of the throat opening, which on a plane without a movable mouth is built-in. But because backing off the chipbreaker requires disassembly, and a screwdriver, it is not something that can be done frequently or quickly.

Figure 3-22. Section Through an Antique Wooden Plane with a Tapered Blade
The blade contacts the blade bed only at the top and bottom, but across its full width.

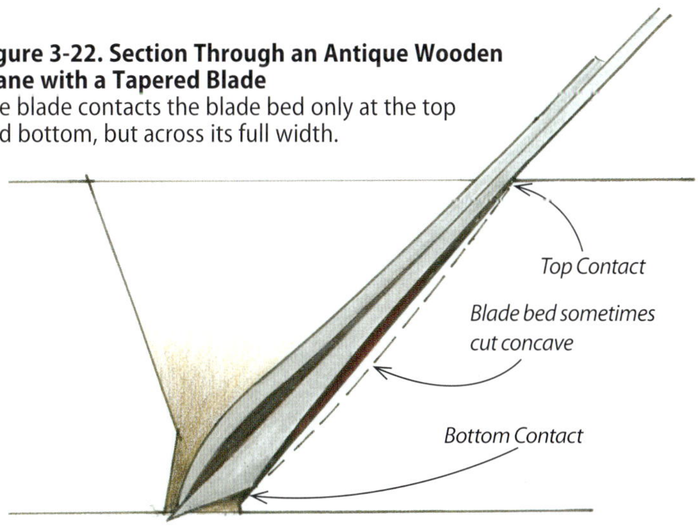

How close should the chipbreaker be set to the edge? Generally, the chipbreaker is set back from the edge a distance equal to the maximum thickness of the shaving you expect to make with that plane. This is also usually equal to the amount of curve honed into the edge of the blade. (See "Shape of the Blade Edge" on page 56). You do not want the chipbreaker set below the corners of the blade. For the finest finish work, I set the chipbreaker down until there is only the barest glint of light left on the top (back) of the blade. This is much less than

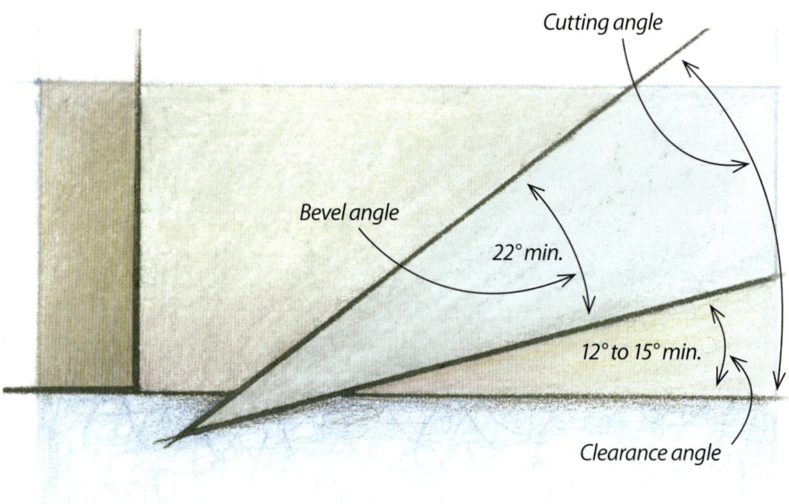

Figure 3-23. Practical Minimum Bevel Angle and Clearance Angle

Figure 3-24. Shape of the Blade Edge

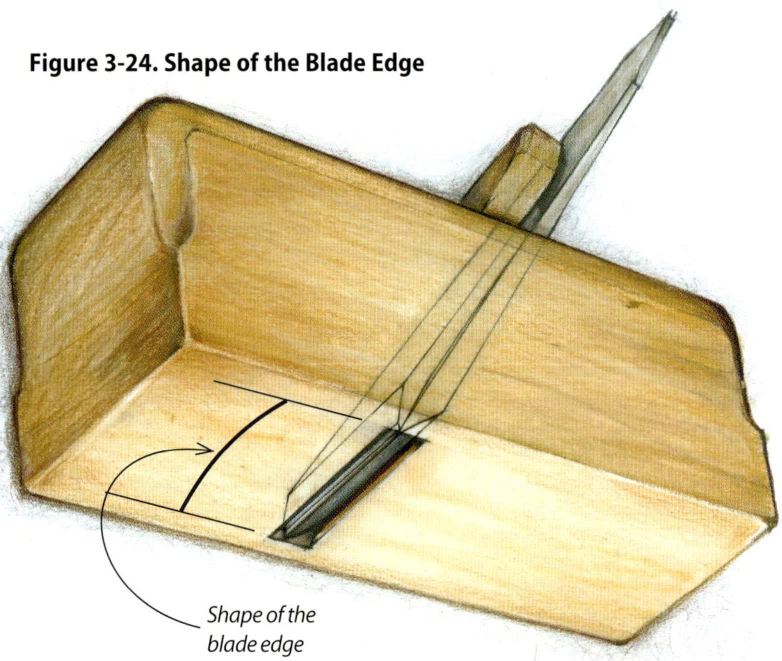

1⁄64" (0.4mm); only that fine line of light tells me there is still some blade exposed. For the adjustment to work, the chipbreaker must be very well prepared (see "Prepare the Chipbreaker" on page 121) or the chips will jam.

For coarse work, the chipbreaker can be set well back, though it is usually not necessary to set it back much more than 1⁄16" (2mm). On planes used to prepare stock, such as the jack, the chipbreaker is usually set back a little more than the arc of the blade edge.

4. BEVEL ANGLE

The bevel angle is the angle to which the blade is sharpened. Most blades leave the factory with a 25° or 30° bevel angle. To bring a plane to its finest performance, the bevel angle may well need further attention (**Figure 3-23**).

If the bevel angle is too small, the edge flexes under the load, bending down until the chip releases, and then springing up to its original position (See **Figure 3-9** on page 48). It may do this repeatedly, resulting in chatter. Or, the blade may flex under the stress of cutting the shaving,

THE CORRECT BEVEL ANGLE

There are limits and ranges you can use as rules of thumb in correcting the bevel angle. First, the minimum clearance angle on a bevel-down blade should be about 12°, though 15° would be better. The parameter will limit the size of the bevel angle on low-angle planes. For instance, if you have a plane with a 35°-cutting angle, the bevel angle of the blade is going to be limited to a maximum of 23° (35°–12°=23°). The practical lower limit of the bevel for most blades is about 22°—any smaller and the blade usually crumples at the edge in common use. And, as well, some blade steels such as A2 may have trouble giving good service at such a small bevel angle. Also, the bevel angle varies according to the bedding angle of the blade; the steeper the bedding angle, the greater the bevel angle should be. For instance, a plane with bedding angle of 40° could have a bevel angle of 22°; 25° to 28° would probably be more serviceable; a 45° plane would have a bevel angle of 25° to 30°. A plane with a bedding angle of 55° could have a bevel angle of 30° to 32°, to perhaps as much as 35°. A bedding angle of 65° could have a bevel angle of as much as 38° to 40°.

HONING A HOLLOW-GROUND BEVEL

An argument against hollow grinding is that it thins the metal immediately behind the edge and produces a bevel angle that is too small. This happens because even though the edge is honed at the proper angle, the steel right behind that honed edge that should support it has been removed—hollowed out to the curve of the grinding wheel. If you were to draw a tangent to the curve of the grind in the area immediately behind the honed edge, you would see this is a much smaller angle than the honing angle, and could allow the blade to flex. (See Chapter 5 "Sharpening Plane Blades" on page 92 for a discussion of the types of bevel configurations.

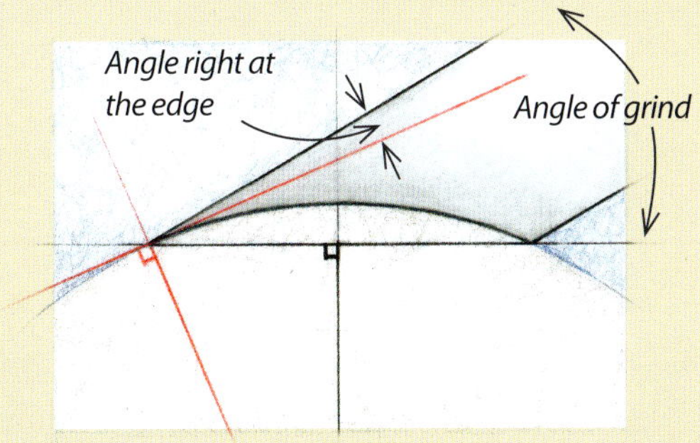

Figure 1. The angle near the edge on a hollow-ground blade (shown here exaggerated for clarity) is much less than the overall angle to which the blade has been ground. On a ⅜" (1cm)-thick blade, such as a Japanese blade, ground to 30° on a 6" (15.2cm)-diameter wheel, the angle is roughly 7° less at the edge than the angle of grind, resulting in about a 23° edge angle—close to the minimum. With a 25° grind, the difference is even greater and results in an edge angle of less than 18°.

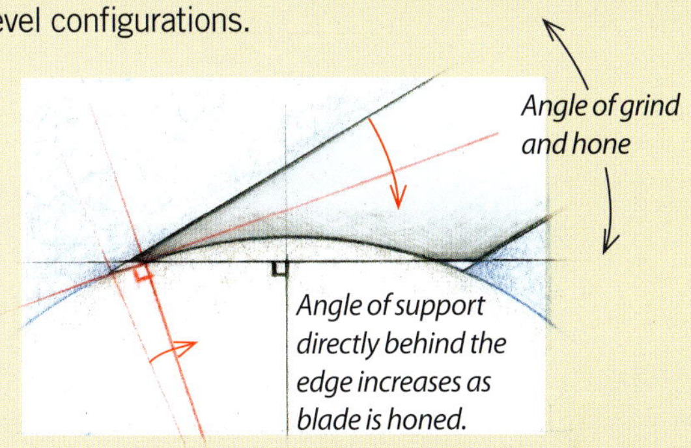

Figure 2. As the blade is honed, the hollow decreases with each sharpening, and the angle directly behind the honed edge increases. Eventually, when the bevel has been honed flat, it equals the grind angle

especially if it hits a harder part of the board, diving down into the wood and cutting a chip thicker than it was set for. If the plane has a very fine mouth, instead of springing back up, the thicker chip may jam the mouth. Therefore, even though the plane is otherwise finely tuned, the mouth can continue to jam with chips.

As a rule of thumb, the bevel angle should be as small as will cut without chattering. Higher angles and a restricted mouth opening will place increased stress on the blade edge, causing it to deflect in use. Increasing the bevel angle will alleviate this. The objective is to increase the bevel angle only enough to eliminate chattering. Any more increases resistance and may reduce the smoothness of the cut. Begin with the factory angle

HOW AN EDGE DULLS

To understand why you would want the bevel angle as small as possible, study how an edge dulls. The gradual effect is that the edge rounds over. If the bevel angle is too large, the worn edge retreats from the work and the main bevel begins rubbing, which prevents the edge from contacting the work. This is exacerbated by the natural tendency of the wood to spring back slightly after the cut. The larger the bevel (on a bevel-down blade), the less the clearance angle to the work, and the sooner the action happens.

(sometimes it will already be ground to a greater angle on the higher-angle planes) and see how it performs. If you suspect it is too small and diagnostic checks as described in the "Troubleshooting" on page 146 indicate that is the problem, then increase the bevel angle until you achieve the desired performance.

FACTORY-GROUND BLADE ANGLES

Japanese blades often come sharpened to 22°, even on higher-angle planes. This is very small and may be a source of flex or exceptional wear in planes with higher bedding angles. European tradition suggests sharpening blades to 25° for softwoods and 30° for hardwoods. In some high-angle smoothing planes, especially those with a small throat, even 30° may not be enough. My traditional Chinese plane came with the bevel angle sharpened to over 35°.

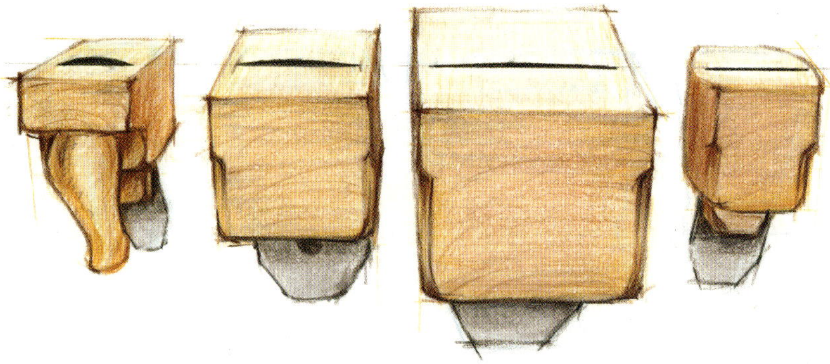

Figure 3-25. The progression of the curvature of the blades of a set of traditional Western planes, used in order from left to right, rough lumber to smooth. On the far left, the blade of the scrub plane has a curve of ⅛" (3mm) or less; next to it, the jack plane blade has a curve of 1⁄16" (2mm) or less; the jointer plane blade a curve of 1⁄32" (0.8mm) or less; and the smoothing plane blade a curve of less than several 0.001" (0.025mm).

5. SHAPE OF THE BLADE EDGE

Shaping the blade edge (**Figure 3-24** on page 54) is a traditional technique also not well understood today, but one that greatly increases the effectiveness of the handplane. The basic concept is: roughing and shaping planes have blades of significant curvature across their width; truing planes have a slight curvature, less than that of the roughing-out planes; and smoothing and finishing planes have blades of decreasing curvature, the final plane used having a nearly straight edge. In theory, on all three planes, the curvature equals the maximum thickness of the planned shaving (**Figure 3-25**). The tactic is effective for a number of reasons. On all planes, it keeps the corners of the blade from digging in and tearing up the wood at the borders of the cut. On roughing-out planes properly used diagonally to the grain, it reduces tearout, the amount of effort required to push the plane, and chip jamming at the most likely spot—the corners of the blade. On finish planes, it eliminates steps or ridges between each cut, producing a smoother surface. On jointer planes, the slight curvature can speed up jointing edges and strengthen the resulting edge joint (see "The Jointer Plane" on page 69).

A few planes should have a straight edge, most notably rabbet planes. In addition, any plane used on a shooting board should have a blade with a straight edge (see Chapter 4, beginning on page 64).

PLANE GEOMETRY, A SUMMARY

The interrelationship between blade angle, mouth opening, chipbreaker, throat angle, and bevel angle is dynamic **(Figure 1).** When constructing or tuning a plane, keep the interplay in mind and adjust each element according to the other. Single-bladed planes, of course, do not have a chipbreaker. Planes with a chipbreaker are sometimes called double-iron planes.

Figure 1. Definitions

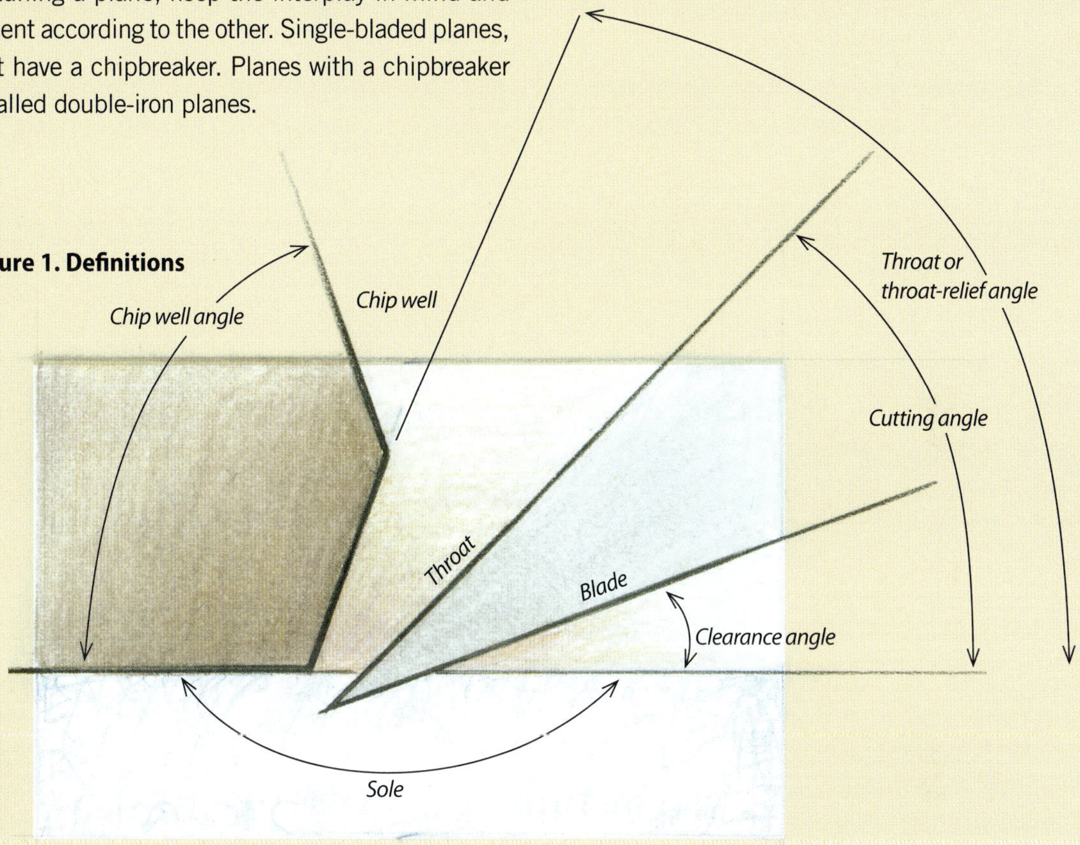

PLANES WITHOUT A CHIPBREAKER

On planes without a chipbreaker, the mouth opening should be the same size or perhaps slightly larger than the thickest shaving you intend to make with that plane. On roughing-out and dimensioning planes, the opening could be 1⁄32" to 1⁄16" (0.8mm to 2mm) or greater **(Figure 2).** (The scrub plane has a throat of about ¼", or 6mm.) On intermediate smoothing planes, a mouth opening of 0.01" (0.25mm) or less is expected **(Figure 3).** On your finest finish planes, the mouth opening could be just several thousandths of an inch **(Figure 4).**

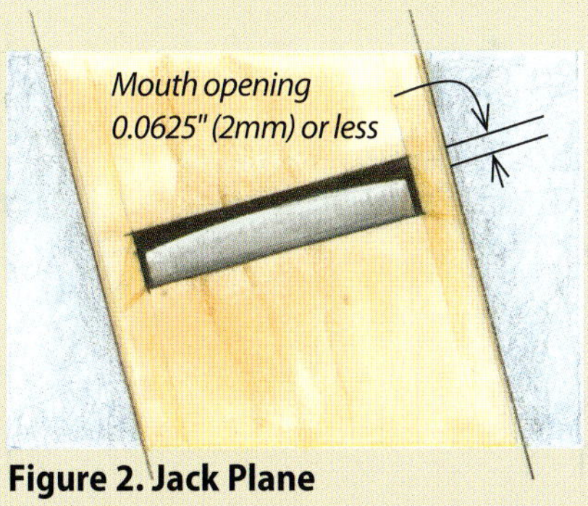

Figure 2. Jack Plane

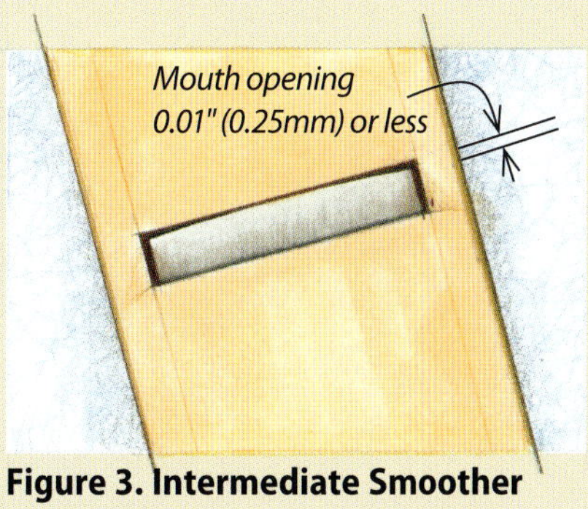

Figure 3. Intermediate Smoother

Figure 4. Finish Smoother

PLANE GEOMETRY, A SUMMARY (CONTINUED)

The angle of the throat opening need be only 15° to 20° greater than the cutting angle, but usually not less than 70° **(Figure 5).**

You want to keep the throat angle as small as possible because as the plane wears and the bottom is trued repeatedly, the mouth opens **(Figure 6)**. Keeping the angle as small as possible slows this process and delays mouth repair. If your plane has a movable mouth plate, you avoid the problem.

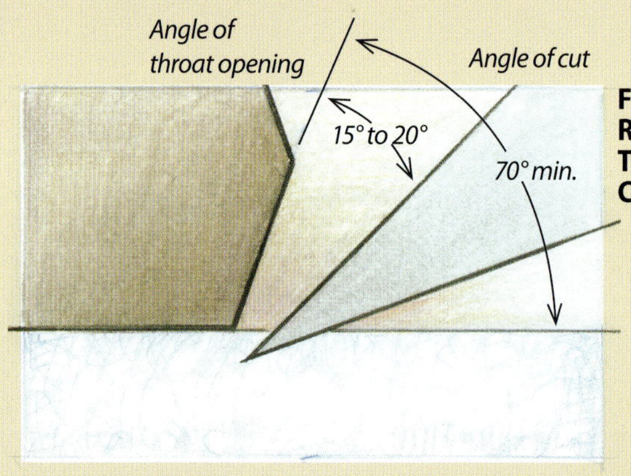

Figure 5. Relationship of the Throat Angle to the Cutting Angle

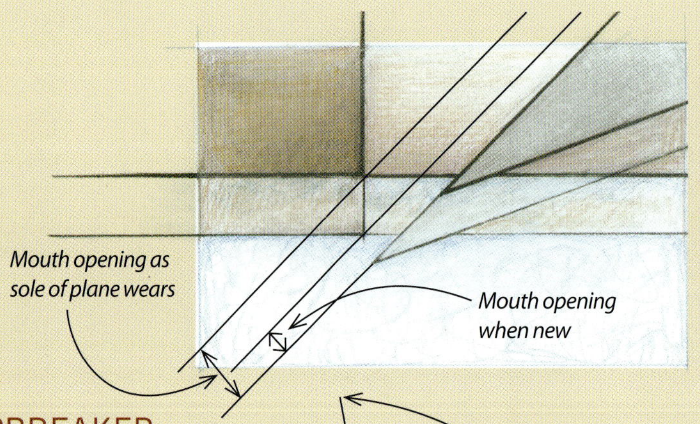

Figure 6. As the sole of the plane wears and is flattened repeatedly, the mouth opening gradually increases in size.

PLANES WITH A CHIPBREAKER

Sharpen the working edge on a chipbreaker so it is 90° to 100° to the sole when mounted in the plane. Use the higher angle on low-blade-angle planes, the lower angle on high-blade-angle planes **(Figure 7).**

For maximum reduction of tearout, the chipbreaker should be set back from the edge a distance equal to about the thickness of the shaving to be cut. Depending on the curvature, the setback often equals the sweep of the blade. Of course, the chipbreaker should not be set below the bottom of the plane **(Figure 8).**

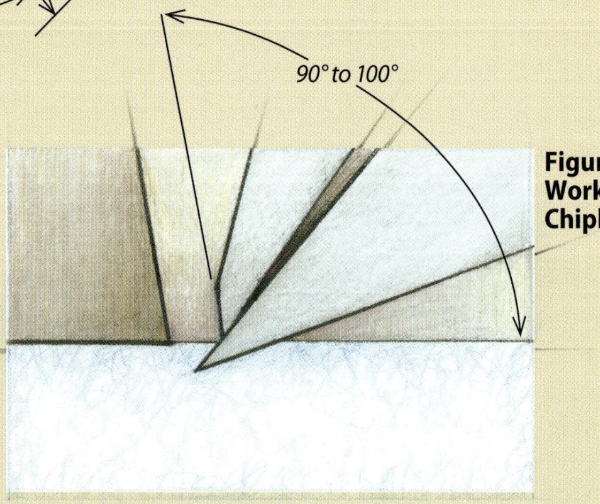

Figure 7. Angle of the Working Bevel of the Chipbreaker

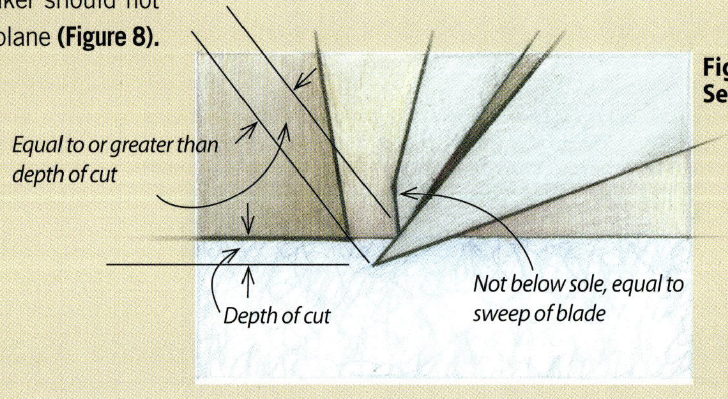

Figure 8. Chipbreaker Setback

At all points, the opening for the shaving to pass must be greater than the thickness of the shaving itself. To maximize the effect of a small mouth opening in combination with a chipbreaker, the throat angle must be equal to, or preferably greater than, the combined angle of the blade and chipbreaker bevel, or between 90° and 100°—maybe slightly more **(Figure 9).**

Any more, however, and the edge of the mouth can become too thin, wearing extremely quickly and sometimes even flexing under the pressure of the constrained shaving, causing the shaving to jam the throat. As the sole of the plane flattens, the mouth also wears open quickly.

A plane set up with the smallest mouth opening and tightest chipbreaker setting can make only the finest, thinnest of cuts. For smoothing planes requiring more versatility, especially in the low-to-intermediate blade angles, it is more practical to rely mostly on the chipbreaker to eliminate tearout, with the mouth opening in a supporting role. Such a strategy allows a reduced throat angle that will slow the gradual enlargement of the mouth opening as the sole is conditioned. The mouth opening would be no more than 1/64" (0.4mm). Clearance for the shaving through the throat must be maintained, however.

Because the throat angle in this setup is not parallel to the working edge of the chipbreaker, the high point of the chipbreaker is where the shaving tends to jam **(Figure 10)**. Have the edge of the chipbreaker ground with a second, main bevel of about 25°, with the working edge shaped to a microbevel of about 1/32" (0.8mm), rather than the more rounded profile seen on many chipbreakers. In preparing the chipbreakers, be certain they are not rounded over more than their original shape. It is easy to stroke the top of the chipbreaker when preparing the edge with an overextended rotating motion that increases the curve, steepens the angle, and constricts the chip.

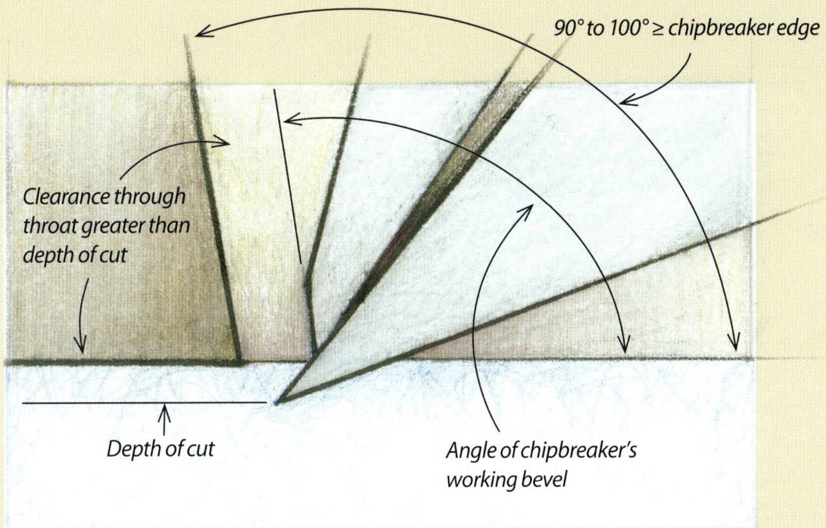

Figure 9. The Angle of the Chipbreaker's Working Bevel

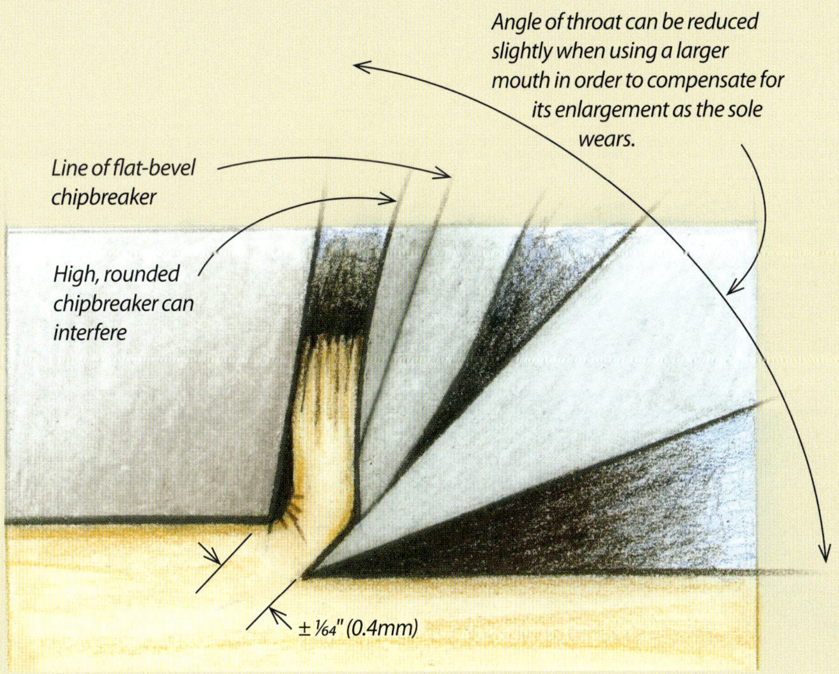

Figure 10. To increase a plane's versatility, especially in planes with a blade angle of 47½° or less, it's more practical to rely on the chipbreaker than the mouth opening to reduce tearout. On a smoothing plane, however, you'll still want a mouth opening of about 1/64" (0.4mm).

Figure 3-26. Length of Plane Determines Function

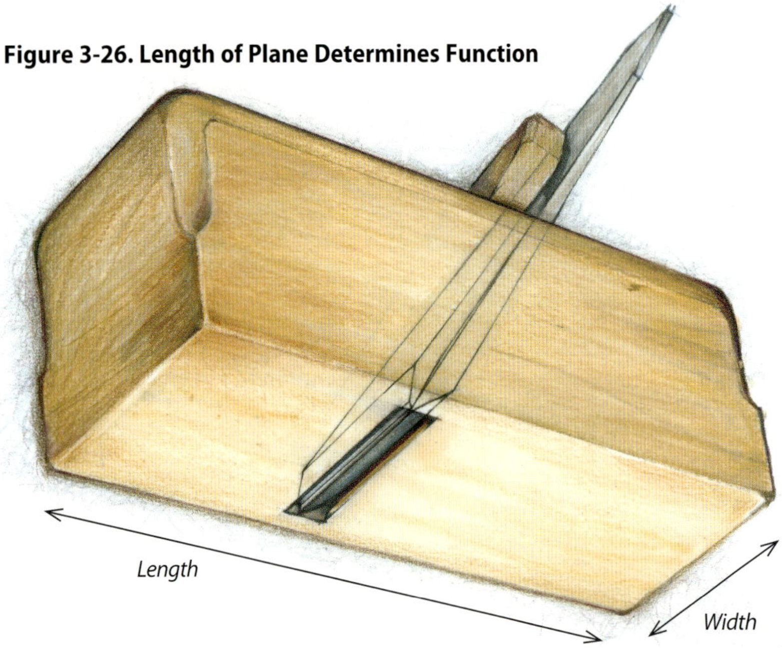

Figure 3-27. Longer planes bridge the low spots, cut the high spots, giving a truer surface.

Figure 3-28. Even though you can see the blade is adjusted to a cutting depth, it may be held off the work and prevented from cutting by the amount the sole is out of true.

6. LENGTH OF PLANE/ WIDTH OF BLADE

The length of a plane determines its intended function (**Figure 3-26**).

Long planes true (straighten) surfaces. Their long length bridges low spots with the blade cutting the high spots down and lowering all surface points to the same plane (**Figure 3-27**).

Intermediate-length planes handle initial stock preparation. A longer plane for truing often follows, or they follow a longer plane as a preparatory plane (utilizing a blade edge with less curvature) before finish smoothing. Appropriate setup and blade shape accompanies either use.

The shortest planes are for final smoothing. They are short for the opposite reason truing planes are long—to follow the low spots. Because of the fine tolerance of their setup and use, variations in the surface of only a few ten-thousandths of an inch may cause the plane to skip over the low spots. On difficult woods, setting the blade deeper to cut to these low spots is not an option because a deeper setting may cause tearout. Shortening the plane's length helps reduce this bridging**.**

A corollary to the length of the plane is the configuration of the bottom of the plane. Western tradition has the bottom of all planes dead flat. However, what is flat? Is within 0.01" (0.25mm) good enough? 0.001" (0.025mm)? 0.0001" (0.0025mm)? In addition, on what areas on the bottom of the plane would the variation be allowed?

The plane must be as flat as the finest shaving you expect to make with that plane. If you intend the plane to produce shavings only 9 microns thick, as sometimes happens in Japanese planing competitions, then the bottom of the plane must be within 9 microns of flat; otherwise, the blade may be held off the work by the bottom and will not cut (**Figure 3-28**). If you are making a cut 1⁄16" (2mm) thick with a jack plane, then the bottom needs to be only less than 1⁄16" (2mm) out of flat (though it will work better if it is flatter than that). If you are heading for very fine work, this can be a daunting proposition conceptually; practically, it is downright frightening. To flatten 16 square inches to within 9 microns, and keep it there despite wear and variations due to heat and humidity, is meticulous, nearly perpetual work. (See "Configure the Sole" on page 127 for more on truing soles.)

In response, the Japanese have a practical answer to flattening the bottom of a plane, one I use on all of my planes. The concept is only two (or three or four, depending on the type of plane or its intended use) areas need to be in a flat plane: the width of the sole, and about ¼" (6mm) long. All other areas are relieved so they do not contact the work or need constant attention (**Figure 3-29** on page 62). This simplifies *flattening* and maintaining the sole of the plane (**Figure 3-30** on page 62). The contact areas are then configured for the use intended for that particular plane: dimensioning, truing, or smoothing, as the shape of the wood being planed will mirror the way the bottom of the plane is shaped.

THE PROPORTION OF LENGTH TO WIDTH

In the full-size planes, a truing plane ranges from about 18" to 30" (45.7cm to 76.2cm). Both preparation and intermediate smoothing planes range in length from about 13" to 18" (33cm to 45.7cm). Smoothing planes range in length anywhere from 6" to 12" (15.2cm to 30.5cm). None of this is set in stone, however. It is up to the crafter to decide the best use for planes of particular lengths. Ultimately, the decision may have more to do with blade shape and bottom configuration than length. Additionally, I have seen Japanese planes with 2¾" (7cm)-wide blades and a plane-body length of little more than 6" (15.2cm). A plane disproportionately short for its width of blade can be useful for planing difficult pieces of wood. It allows a fine setting of the blade while still reaching into the slight hollows left from the preparatory planes.

The proportion of plane length to blade width used in full-size planes can also be scaled down to the smaller planes used in smaller-scale work—6" (15.2cm) smoothing planes, for instance, with 1½" (3.8cm)-wide blades. In addition, preparatory, truing, and smoothing planes of proportional lengths can be useful for curved work. Later chapters go deeper into the topic.

To facilitate rapid stock removal, the contact areas of dimensioning planes are relieved in the area following the blade perhaps 0.01" (0.25mm) (**Figure 3-31** on page 63). Truing planes will have all contact areas along the length of the plane in a line, to ensure stock being planed comes out straight. Smoothing planes will have the contact area behind the blade slightly relieved—usually less than the desired thickness of the shaving (approximately 0.005" or 0.125mm)—both to help maintain flatness and to enable a very finely set blade to contact the work. (See the various "Configuring the Sole" sections in Chapter 7

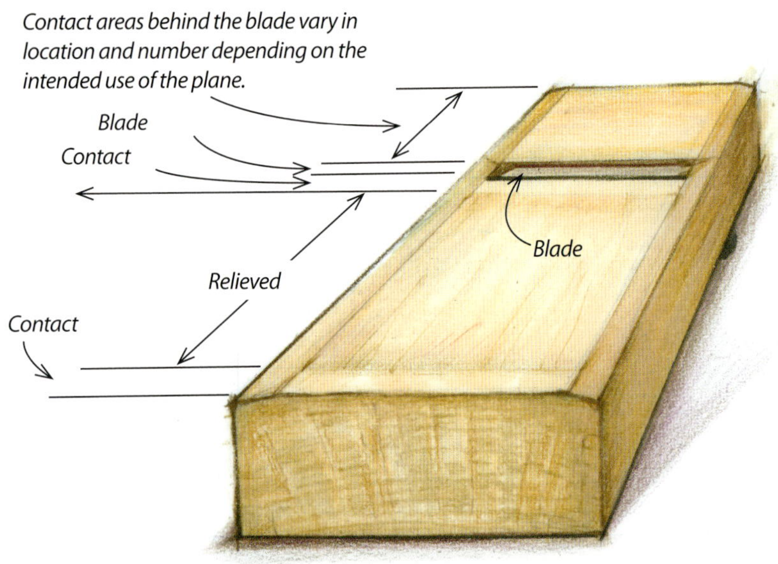

Figure 3-29. The sole of a Japanese plane is traditionally relieved in strategic areas to simplify maintenance.

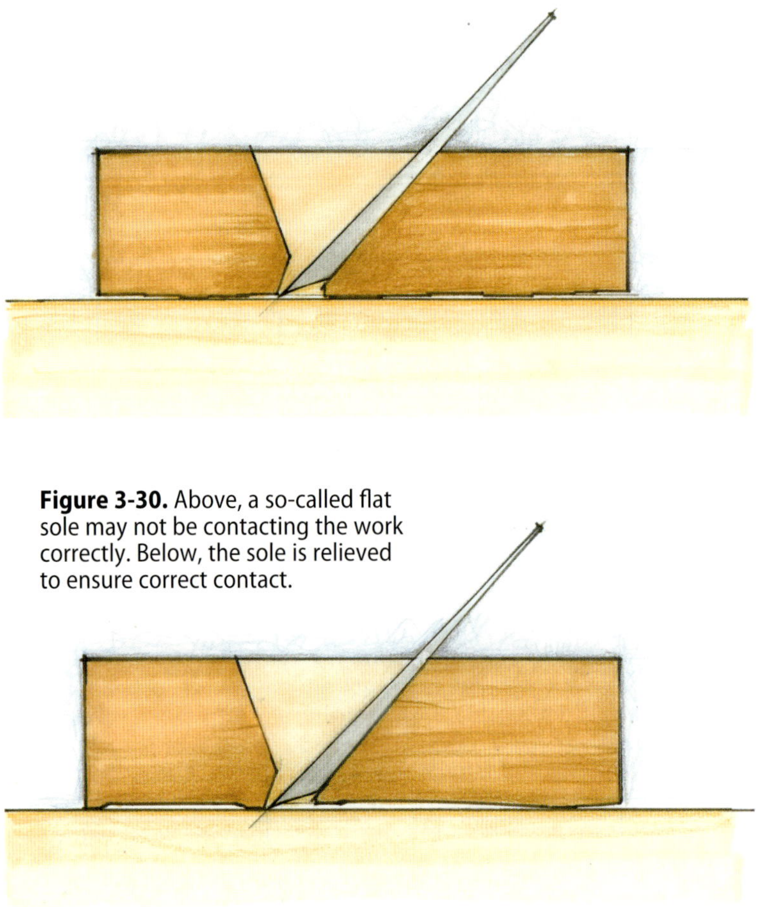

Figure 3-30. Above, a so-called flat sole may not be contacting the work correctly. Below, the sole is relieved to ensure correct contact.

that cover setting up each specific type of plane.)

The width of the blade (and the plane) also varies according to the intended use of the plane. The blade of the truing plane (the longest plane) also tend to be the widest, about 2⅜" to 2¾" (6cm to 7cm) wide. This helps produce the flattest surface. Planes for stock preparation, such as the jack, have the narrowest blades, usually from about 1¾" to 2" (4.4cm to 5.1cm). Because they are used to remove large amounts of wood, a wide cut would be too much work. Smoothing planes tend to be wider than the stock-removal planes, but just how wide is pretty much up to the crafter. The wider the blade, the less pronounced the faint scallops, which are a result of the faint curvature of the blade edge. However, a wider blade involves more setup, maintenance, and work to use. Smoothing planes, especially for hardwood, are in the range of 2" to 2⅜" (5cm to 6cm) wide, though 2¾" (7cm) is not unheard of.

And remember…

There is an additional aspect of effective plane work that tends to be overlooked—the sharpness of the blade. No planing operation will be very effective unless the blade is sharp. This becomes unavoidably apparent during demanding finish-planing operations. While you can continue to push a dull plane with increasing effort and increasing tearout when roughing down a board (the change is so gradual, the blade often is dull before you notice it), on a demanding finish-planing operation, unless the plane is exquisitely sharp, results will be immediately disappointing—no waiting.

Beginners often find sharpness difficult to judge. It is often a fleeting thing, seemingly there one moment and gone the next. As your wookworking skills grow, you will become more demanding of your tools and accept only true sharpness. You will learn that some blades do not get as sharp as others. There are nuances of difference in the concept of sharp. Without a blade sharp enough for the task, however, all other strategies for effective planing fail.

Figure 3-31. The jack plane may have its sole slightly relieved behind the blade to facilitate access to a rough surface when first preparing a board.

CHAPTER

4

TRADITIONAL USE: THE BENCH PLANES

JACK, JOINTER & SMOOTHER —AND A COUPLE MORE USEFUL PLANES

Bench planes perform three basic functions in woodworking: shaping and dimensioning lumber, truing and preparing pieces for gluing, and smoothing surfaces. The correct application of the anatomical tactics discussed in Chapter 3 is critical to effectively performing these tasks. Because each task requires a significantly different combination of tactics, traditionally a different plane was developed and used for each: the jack, the jointer, and the smoothing plane. They are visually distinguished from each other primarily by their length relative to the width of their blade, and by the shape of the blade's edge. Varying the other tactics as well maximizes work efficiency.

The triumvirate of traditional Western wooden bench planes: jack, jointer, and smoothing.

Figure 4-1. Razee-Type Wooden Jack Plane
Razee Planes have the body cut away behind the blade and alongside the handle.

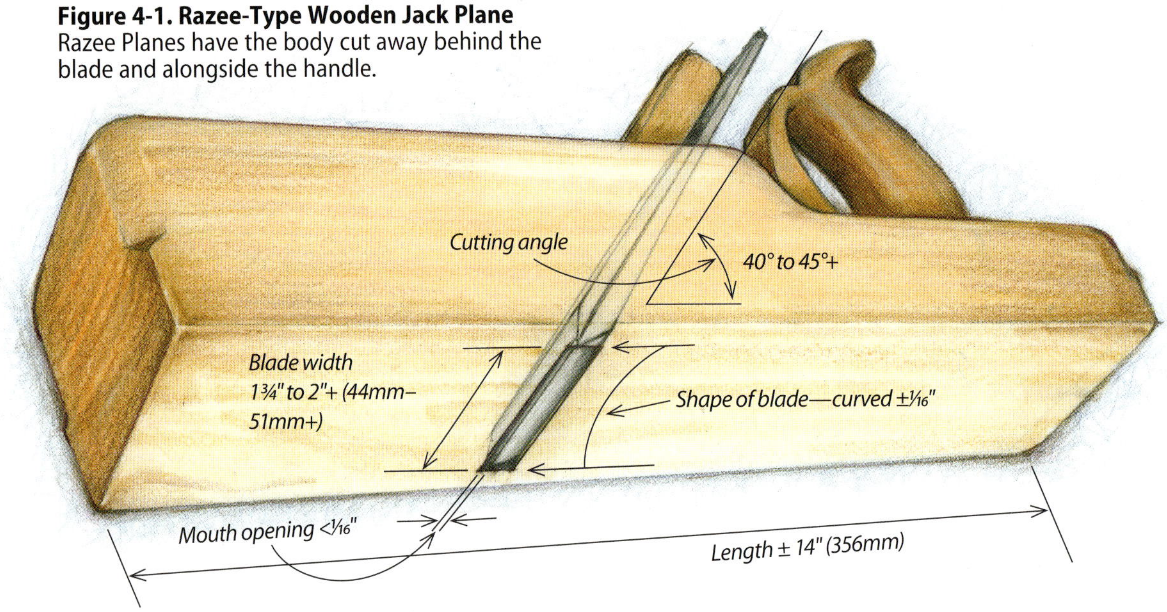

I informally call these three types of planes the *triumvirate*—from the old Roman phrase *the three who jointly rule*. Additional planes assist these and fill various particular needs, as will be explained in subsequent chapters. However, these three planes are basic and, for centuries, have formed the core of the broad spectrum of handplanes. While you may only occasionally dimension lumber or true an edge with handplanes, understanding the form and anatomy of the jack, jointer, and smoother, and how they have traditionally worked, allows you to effectively select, use, and modify handplanes in your own work.

THE JACK PLANE

Most closely identified with shaping and dimensioning lumber is the jack plane **(Figure 4-1)**. It is traditionally used to remove a fair amount of wood quickly to bring a piece to rough shape and dimension after being rough-sawn, split, or hewn from the log. It usually is in the neighborhood of 14" (35.6cm) long. For rapid stock removal, and to reduce tearout and resistance, the edge of the blade sharpens to a curve, projecting as much as 1/16" (2mm) **(Figure 4-2)**.

The chipbreaker, if used, is set well back from the edge—about 1/16" (2mm). You really don't need a chipbreaker on a jack plane if all you do is use it for heavy stock removal, but having a chipbreaker gives you the option of setting the plane up for more delicate work **(Figure 4-3)**. In addition, to minimize effort in using the plane, the blade is narrow, usually about 1¾" (4.4cm) to 2" (5.1cm), and set at the lowest angle among the three planes of the triumvirate. In the European tradition—generally for hardwoods—the blade angle is as low as 40°, though 43° or 45° is more common. As well, 47½° and 50°, intended for particularly hard wood, are also found, as are planes with an even higher angle. In working with tropical hardwoods, the blade angle generally is 50° to 60°. In softwoods, 35° and 40° are used. Configure the sole straight or slightly convex over its length, with the contact area behind the blade relieved perhaps 0.01" (0.25mm). Because this is a rough plane and makes a deep cut, maintenance of a flat bottom is less critical and these planes are often found badly worn.

The jack is a real workhorse. Before the common availability of power tools, the jack did the bulk of the dimensioning and surfacing in the woodshop, often resulting in knee-deep shavings by lunchtime. Except when working on edges and narrow pieces, you push the plane along the grain diagonally resulting in the curved blade making a nice *downhill* shearing cut with the grain, reducing both effort and tearout in all but the most difficult-grained woods. (See "Dimensioning Stock" on page 78.)

In a way, we all start with the jack plane. We commonly purchase and use a single plane for a long time to shape, dimension, and smooth work—the job of the jack. As your skills improve, you become more demanding and look for more specialized tools to address specific tasks. Nevertheless, the traditional use of the jack in the multi-step process of stock preparation remains relevant. Stock that is too large for your equipment need not intimidate you. Proper use of the jack and the others in the triumvirate makes such work go quickly. In addition, understanding the jack allows you to choose aspects of its anatomy for customizing other planes for other purposes. If you know why the blade curves, for instance, you can decide whether your use requires a blade with curvature, and if so, how much. From experience with the jack, you can reference how big a throat opening or chipbreaker setback should be, or what sole configuration another plane requires. You can modify planes of different sizes for shaping or preparing pieces not going through the jointer or planer. Your work becomes faster, more efficient, and not limited by your power tools; only by your imagination, resourcefulness, and willingness to experiment.

Figure 4-2. Jack Plane Mouth Opening

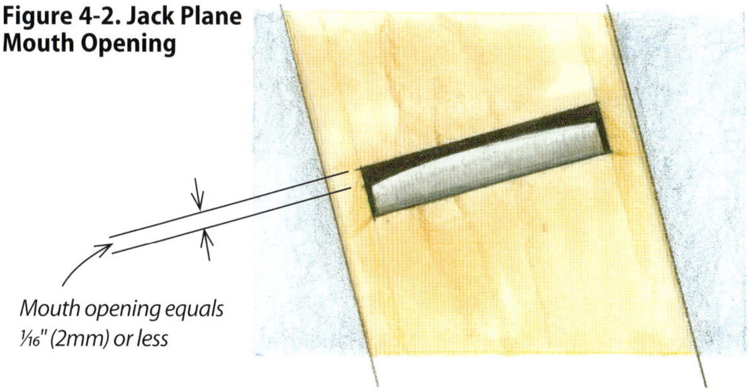

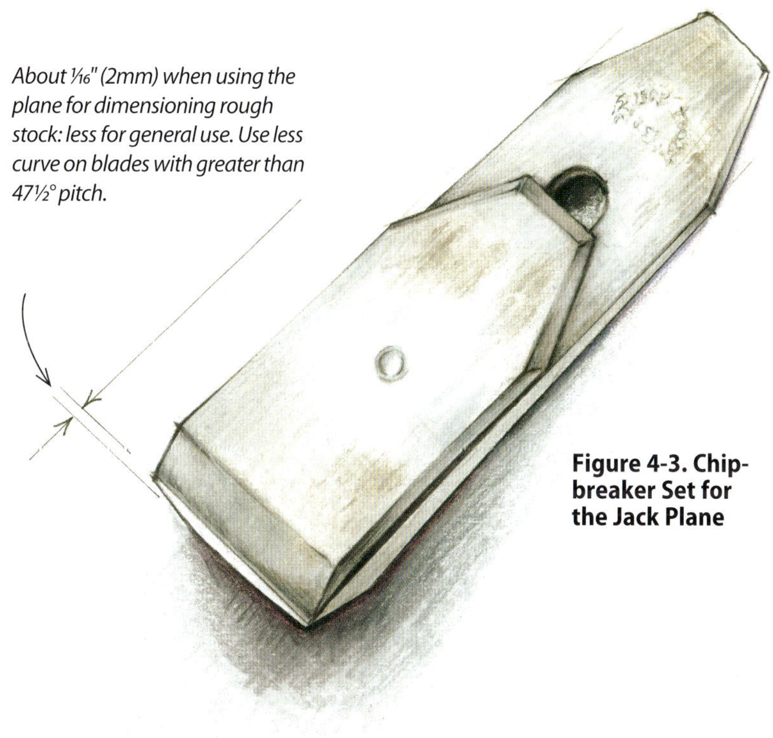

Figure 4-3. Chipbreaker Set for the Jack Plane

THE FORE PLANE

In a time when most stock was prepared by hand, another plane was often used: the fore plane, 14" to 17" (35.6cm to 43.2cm) long. It was often set up like a jack plane, with significant curvature to the blade, and was generally used to prepare larger stock or rough down a long edge in preparation for shooting it with the jointer or long plane. Its actual setup would vary with the craftsman's particular needs. The fore plane could also be followed by the try plane, about 22" (55.9cm) long and used to prepare an edge for trial fitting (thus its name) before being finally shot true with the jointer or long plane.

Figure 4-4. The English pattern jack (left), and the German-style horned plane (right), are lighter and more comfortable than their metal cousins.

What to look for in a jack

Traditional wood jack planes, both vintage and new, are a good choice for these tasks because of their weight, ergonomics, and low friction soles (**Figure 4-4**). It is advantageous, though not critical to have a blade mechanism that quickly and easily adjusts the blade as work progresses. It is often necessary to retract the blade as the work becomes smoother, and then readjust from one piece to another. I have a Primus jack horned plane that I find very comfortable for heavy work, and its precise adjustment mechanism allows me to go back and forth rapidly to accommodate changes in the wood and progress in the work. The horned plane, however, is only about 10" (25.4cm) long, which works fine, but if Primus' English pattern jack at 15½" (39.4cm) long was available at the time I bought the horned jack, I might have chosen it over the shorter plane. The traditional wedged jack is much slower to adjust back and forth, though once I got used to it, it went faster than I would have initially imagined.

Because you are removing a lot of wood, which subjects the blade to heat and stress, a blade of alloy steel is a good choice for a jack plane (see Chapter 2 for a discussion of steel). However, if you are using an older plane with a laminated blade in good shape, you should change it only if you are dissatisfied with its performance.

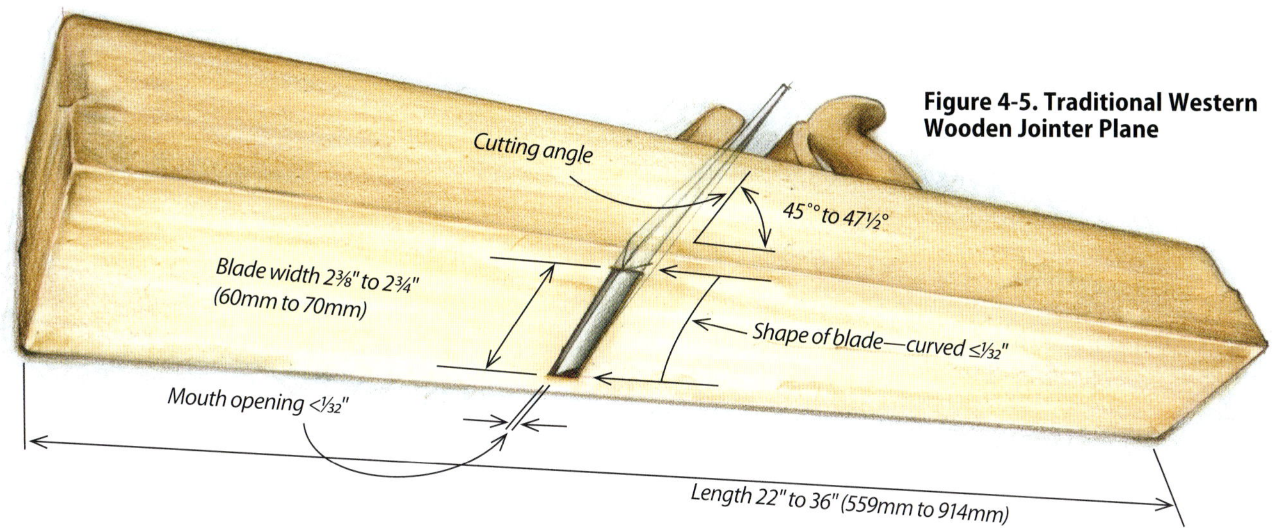

Figure 4-5. Traditional Western Wooden Jointer Plane

THE JOINTER PLANE

After generally straightening and roughly dimensioning the stock with the jack, you use the jointer (**Figure 4-5**), a long, wide plane, to remove the roughness left by the jack and to true surfaces and edges in preparation for final smoothing. Today, the jointer plane in the Bailey style is only 22" (55.9cm) long (the Stanley #07). In the past, longer planes of 24" to 30" (61cm to 76.2cm), up to 36" (91.4cm) and more were used, and can still be found. The plane's long length and greater width—the blade is usually 2⅜" (6cm) to 2¾" (7cm) wide—results in a flat surface overall. Its wide blade, traditionally sharpened to a gentle curvature of about 1/32" (1mm) or less (perhaps even less if you are edge-joining very thick boards)—takes out the ridges left by the coarsely set jack, and aids in squaring board edges (**Figure 4-6**). The chipbreaker is set back from the blade edge the distance of the thickest shaving. The blade angle is intermediate, usually higher than the jack, but less than the smooth plane, to reduce tearout and the effort needed to work the plane, which often makes thick shavings (**Figure 4-7** on page 70). Old wooden jointers typically had a cutting angle of 45° to 47½°. The sole is trued dead flat or may be relieved slightly in strategic places to simplify keeping it true.

What to look for in a jointer plane

What you want in your jointer depends on its planned use. The majority of woodworkers today will use the jointer only for shooting an edge, and for this, stability and low maintenance are priorities. For this reason, the Stanley-type plane has been the first choice among woodworkers for several generations. If you do a lot of surface prep with a jointer, however, you ought to consider a wood-body jointer. The plane is lighter, the wood sole offers less resistance than an iron one, which is particularly noticeable when making the repeated cuts required to surface a board. In addition, you can sometimes find these with higher blade angles than the Stanley, for use in the harder woods; or you can make a plane to your preference (see "Making Traditional Wooden Body

Planes" on page 166). When working with the tropical hardwoods you may encounter considerable difficulty with tearout because of the lower blade angles found on most jointers. If you are working a lot with these woods, you may want to fabricate a plane with a high cutting angle, or use a Chinese-style jointer.

A carbon blade such as 01, a laminated blade, or light alloy blade such as an A2 or PM-V11 blade is a good choice here, unless you are using a very high angle blade for tropical hardwoods, in which case chrome vanadium or tungsten vanadium blade is a good choice.

TRYING, LONG, AND JOINTER

We classify any plane 20" to 30" (50.8cm to 76.2cm) long as a jointer plane. Up until about the 1870s, however, three distinct planes occupied this range: the trying (or try) plane, 20" to 22" (50.8cm to 55.9cm) long; the long plane, 24" to 26" (61cm to 66cm) long; and the jointer plane, 28" to 30" (71.1cm to 76.2cm) long. After 1870, use of these planes began to diminish, as did the distinction between them.

Figure 4-6. Jointer Plane Mouth Opening

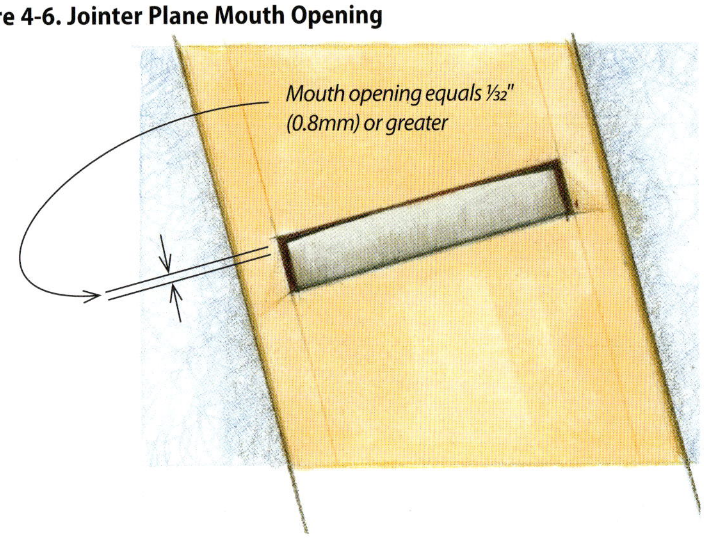

Can you get by without a jointer plane?

You probably can work without a jointer plane, but for the best quality work, only good tools, well maintained and properly operated, will accomplish something comparable. And even then you have to evaluate the quality of the surface made by these machines. Glue-line ripping saws and well-maintained and accurate power jointers (large enough for the work) are adequate for good quality (and quantity) work. But for work we expect to outlive us, the fineness of the glued edge must be attended to. So let us look at this edge in detail.

Under a microscope, the ripped or sawn edge looks torn. Even with the best blades, there is some scoring, some small

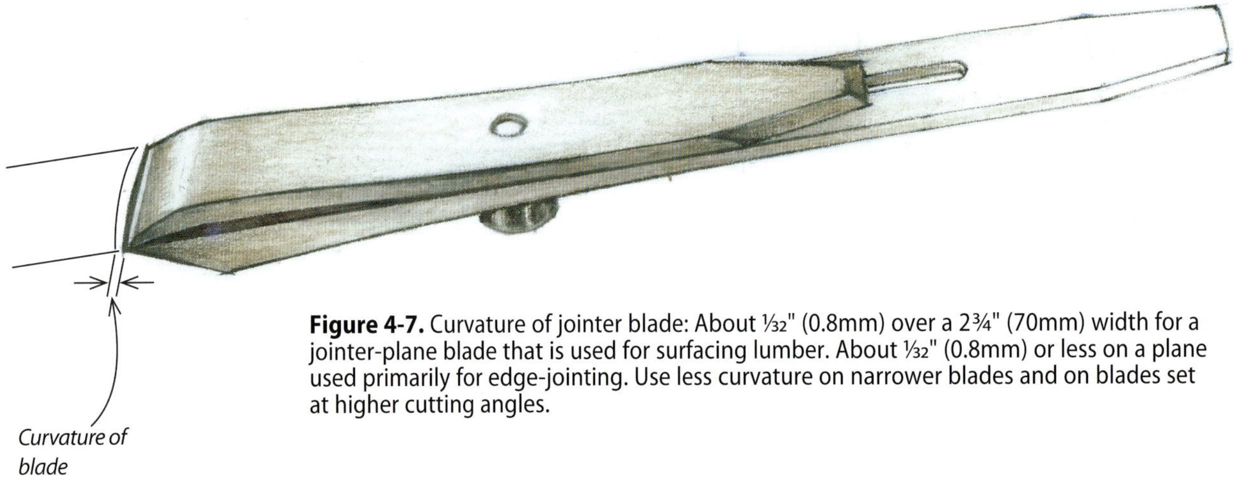

Figure 4-7. Curvature of jointer blade: About 1⁄32" (0.8mm) over a 2¾" (70mm) width for a jointer-plane blade that is used for surfacing lumber. About 1⁄32" (0.8mm) or less on a plane used primarily for edge-jointing. Use less curvature on narrower blades and on blades set at higher cutting angles.

irregularities. Most glues bond best when the fibers are cleanly sheared, and the surfaces closely mated. A sawn surface compromises both of these qualities. However, most modern glues are gap-filling to the extent necessary between two well sawn surfaces and provide strength in excess of the wood itself, so for good quality work, sawn surfaces can be adequate if done well.

However, I believe the true longevity of this joint is in question. Edge-glued planks, such as in a tabletop, are under tremendous stress over the years and have no mechanical advantage (such as a mortise-and-tenon joint does) to resist the stresses—they depend solely on the strength of the glue. If you have ever seen a 200-year-old tabletop, you know what I mean. If the cupping of the planks has not opened the joints, then differential moisture from the seasons or central heating has opened the joints at the ends. We place a great deal of faith in our modern glues, and they appear to be miracle workers. Hide glue and the other protein glues have been around since before the time of the pharaohs, so we know pretty much how they react. However, our modern glues are only one or two generations old, and while testing assures us they are durable, the testing only mimics our best guesses and cannot possibly include all the variables. We do not actually know how they will react in the long term.

Our responsibility as woodworkers is to understand wood movement, to take into account the reaction of the wood during the gluing process as well as afterwards, and to give the glue the best conditions under which to function. We can design the piece as best we can and select the wood for optimal structural functionality (as well as grain appearance), making sure the wood is dry and has reached equilibrium with its environment. We can prepare the joint, finessing it for gluing. To do this, tradition recommends the mating edges be planed to a slight concavity over their length, so that clamping them together produces slightly increased pressure at the ends. This concavity is less than a paper thickness when two boards are put together. As the glue dries and gives off moisture at the ends of the joints first, the pressure equalizes and the joints at the ends will not open up. This finessing also increases the longevity of the joint as seasonal changes in temperature and humidity affect the open pores of the end grain first and the rest of the plank lags behind. This differential movement over the length of the plank also stresses the glue joint. The slight pressure created by planing a bit of concavity along the length of the joint helps keep the joint together. A machine cannot do the subtle shaping; it is done by skilled hands with a jointer plane, by a crafter who understands his material.

I conjecture as well, that the slight concavity across the *width* of the joint resulting from the blade being sharpened

THE CORRECT BLADE SHAPE

While the amount of curvature of the edge is at the discretion of the woodworker, it is important that a sweep to the edge tapers off the corners of the blade because it allows you to adjust the edge of the board being planed to square while the plane itself remains in solid contact with the work (see "Techniques for Shooting an Edge" on page 89). The edge of a jointer-plane blade is not sharpened straight unless it is used with a shooting board.

to a curve contributes to the longevity of the joint. The resulting surfaces puts slightly more pressure at the outside edges, combating both the initial stress from the glue drying from the outside in as well as differential movement from the outside of the board responding more quickly to seasonal changes. However, this is only a conjecture, and would be more difficult to verify than what experience over the years has shown to be true about planing a bit of curve over the length of the board.

This kind of care, precision, finesse, and craftsmanship is what sets the skilled woodworker, the conscientious studio furniture maker, apart from the manufacturer.

SMOOTHING PLANES

The smoothing plane (**Figure 4-8**) has the widest variety of sizes of any of the planes. Length may vary anywhere from 4" or 5" (10.2cm or 12.7cm) to around 12" (30.5cm). Blade width may be from 1¼" (3.2cm) to 2¾" (7cm), or even greater. Planes outside of that range tend to be called something else, though they may be used for smoothing. Generally, the ratio of plane length to blade width tends to be 4 or 5 to 1, sometimes even less. Selecting the right plane depends on the size of the work and the difficulty of the grain. The general rule is small planes for small work, wider planes for wider work, and longer or larger planes for longer work. The craftsman makes the choice based on his experience.

The blade is sharpened either to a shallow curve not exceeding the depth of the blade set (a few thousandths of an inch) or dead straight with the corners slightly rounded off. Both techniques prevent the blade corners from digging in and leaving steps in the work, undesirable because this is the last plane to be used, and the resulting surface must be defect-free. The chipbreaker is set right down to the edge, back only as far as the thickest shaving for which the plane will be set (**Figure 4-9**). Blade angles can be the highest of all the planes of the triumvirate.

Ideally, the smoothing plane should be as wide as possible—as wide or wider than the jointer. This will result in a flatter surface because though perhaps only a few thousandths of an inch deep, the resulting cut is basically a shallow trough. The wider it is in relation to its depth, the less perceptible it will be. There should also be a progression in the blade widths of the planes of the triumvirate, progressing from the jack (the narrowest), to the jointer (wider), and

Figure 4-8. Traditional Western Coffin-Sided Smoothing Plane

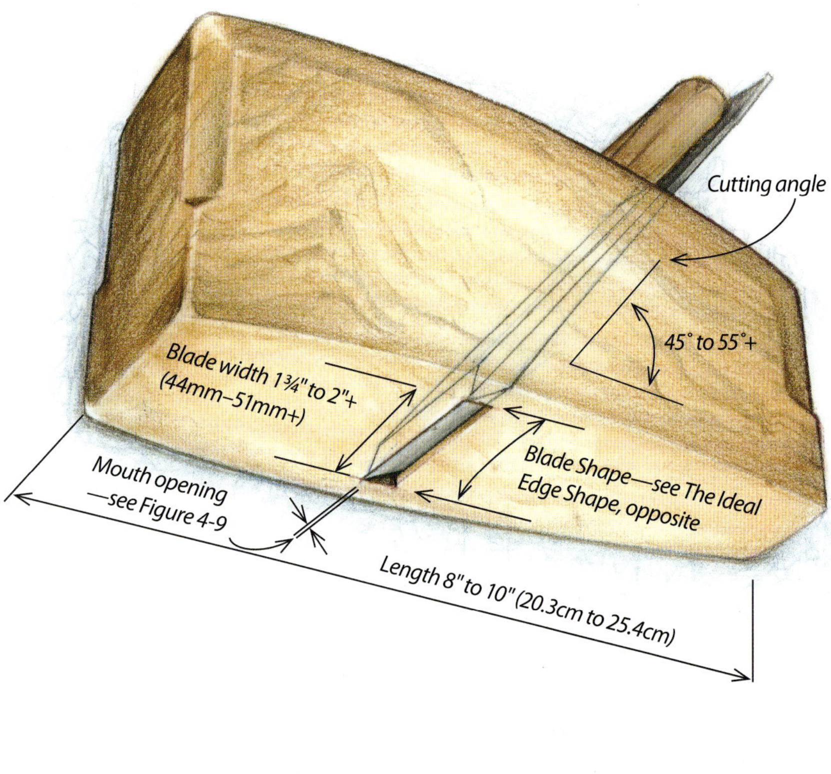

then the smoother (the widest). However, in reality this ideal relationship of the smoothing plane to the jack and jointer is difficult to maintain when working with harder woods.

Because the cutting angle of the smoothing plane is the highest of all the planes and the blade is cutting its full width (unlike the jack, and often the jointer plane, which often are not set to make a cut the full depth of the sweep of their blade), the amount of resistance to the cut is very high. A wide blade, though making a very shallow cut, will have greater resistance than a narrow blade. On hard woods, this can mean that for all but the lightest cut, smoothing wood will be hard work. For this reason, I believe, European smoothing planes traditionally have blades 1¾" (4.4cm) to 2" (5.1cm) wide, even though jointers traditionally are much wider than that, with blades 2⅜" (6cm) to 2¾" (7cm) wide. Because of these factors, generally, I would tend to limit blade widths on planes with cutting angles of 50° and greater to 2" (5.1cm) or less.

Short planes can be particularly useful in smoothing difficult woods. Smoothing planes do not have to stick to the common proportions of width to length. The converse of the functional shape of the jointer plane applies: while the length of the jointer trues a surface by bridging the hills and valleys, a very short plane will smooth the surface by following them. The best way to approach difficult woods, after leveling with a jointer, is to prepare the surface with a smoothing plane finely set to true the surface, followed by an even more finely set smoother, of shorter proportion, that follows the surface and smooths any remaining roughness. This procedure is similar to using a *polishing plane*—a small plane about 6" (15.2cm) to 7" (17.8cm) long. The difference is the finishing plane is a full-width plane, equal to or greater than

Figure 4-9. Smoothing Plane Mouth Opening

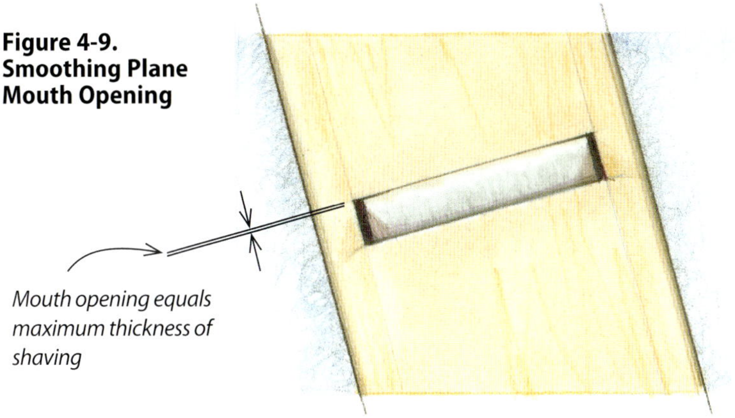

THE IDEAL EDGE SHAPE

Ideally, the edge of a smoothing plane should be straight across, with the ends tapered off to avoid leaving tracks in the work. The taper needs to equal the depth of cut, which may be less than 0.005" (0.13mm). This is most easily achieved by added pressure at each corner when sharpening: five strokes for each corner on the first sharpening stone (in addition to sharpening the main edge), a few more than that on the finishing stone(s) can be enough. The resulting configuration works well, but I could not swear that it looks like the drawing.

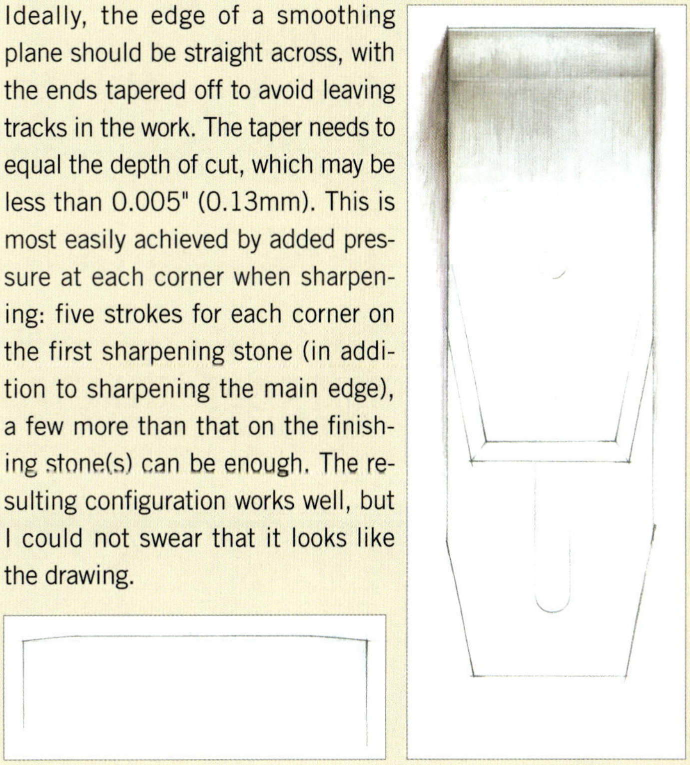

the intermediate smoother. The length-to-width proportions of a polishing plane could be as severe as 2-to-1.

What to look for in a smoothing plane

Blade quality is the most important consideration in selecting a smoothing plane. The other tactics of plane anatomy fall in line after this priority. It must be possible to execute these tactics finely and precisely, and, just as importantly, the settings must be easy to maintain. As to the style of the plane, unlike the jointer, where height above the work is advantageous, giving feedback as to the angle of the plane to the work when shooting an edge, I think it is preferable to be low, close to the work, when smoothing. This position gives greater control and more sensitive feedback. Weight is less of an issue than in other planes, as work is less repetitious and physically less vigorous than with, say, a jack plane. Conversely, I do not believe additional weight improves the quality of the cut itself, though perhaps by personal preference it may give you a greater sense of command in use.

A more expensive plane may get you adjustment that is more precise and more dependable maintenance of fine settings, but unless the blade is of the highest quality, and matched to the work, all of that will mean nothing. In the end, your choice of smoothing plane more than any of the other planes is personal. Whatever your preference, get the best blade for it that you can.

To get the most efficient and effective use of the smoothing plane, you have to use all of the strategies for effective planing. While a nice piece of even-grained wood may be forgiving of sloppiness in the setup of a plane, only those planes that have been precisely set and fastidiously maintained smooth difficult woods. To effectively plane the most difficult-figured woods, the critical tolerances required of blade shape, sharpness, cutting depth, and sole flatness become difficult to perceive. Maintaining the proper balance between the position of the chipbreaker and throat opening in relation to the blade angle is also difficult. However, with practice, you can begin to sense the correct tolerances or what is out of balance in the interplay between particular tactics. This *sense* bears on what we call skill, achieved only by a striving for excellence through practice. Knowing and understanding the tactics is the first step. The next, more difficult step is to know (and be able to perceive) the tolerances involved. That can only be learned through practice.

CHINESE SMOOTHERS

The Chinese-style smoother, despite the great hardness of the woods they traditionally worked, is often as wide or wider than the jointer. Curiously, the smoother is about the same width as the European smoother; the jack and jointer is just narrower, due to the hard work of preparing such hard woods.

WHY A NARROW SMOOTHER?

Making the smoothing plane narrower than the jointer can make setting up and tuning it a little less demanding. A narrower smoother also makes accessing the entire surface of the work easier without annoying and unproductive *skips*. This is especially important with hardwoods because they can be prone to tearout and must be worked with a very finely set blade.

The smoothing plane is the most commonly available plane today, and perhaps the most useful. Whereas machines have largely supplanted the plane in dimensioning and truing lumber, the effectiveness of the smoothing plane is hard to cast aside. For some tasks, it is demonstrably faster, more accurate, and more effective than abrasives in producing the highest quality surface. Its main drawback is that it takes skill and practice to achieve proficiency, and this requires an investment of time and training.

Figure 4-10. At left is a 12" (30.5cm)-long Razee-style panel plane with a 2¼" (5.7cm)-wide blade bedded at 47½°. It works well to prepare the surface for the 8" (20.3cm)-long coffin-sided smoother (right), which has a 2" (5.1cm)-wide blade bedded at 50°.

A COUPLE MORE PLANES

While the triumvirate—the jack, jointer, and smoothing planes—form the core of the bench planes, there are a couple more in the traditional toolbox that I find useful:

The panel plane

The origin of the term panel plane is unclear. One source speculates it originated in a Spiers or Norris catalog, describing a plane 14" to 18" (35.6cm to 45.7cm) long with a 2½" (6.4cm)-wide cutter. While this is the general size of a jack plane, the panel plane, because of its fine, un-adjustable throat and great weight was obviously meant for smoothing, not taking down rough timber. The implication of the terminology in the catalog is that preparing larger pieces, such as panel boards, is the reason for its name, though it was probably set up and used variously, depending on the needs of its owner. Whatever its origins, it is an extremely valuable type of plane, and its use can both speed and improve results in the woodshop (**Figure 4-10**).

If you do a lot of handplaning, you will find it faster to use more than one plane for smoothing. Surfaces straight from the jointer plane or the power planer can have many surface irregularities. The jointer plane, with its scalloped cut, leaves a slightly textured surface. Lumber from the planer often will be surprisingly uneven, usually with some snipe at the ends from before and after it leaves the bed rollers, and often other irregularities, or tearout. When working the surface with a finely set and maintained smoothing plane, irregularities show up as the plane skips over them initially, leaving large areas untouched. Your first reaction is to set the plane deeper, to avoid wasting effort cutting air. This may necessitate setting the blade deeper and, depending on the plane, opening the mouth a little (if it is adjustable) and possibly backing off the chipbreaker.

If you have a screwed-on chipbreaker, you will have to disassemble the plane before you can readjust. In addition, on a surface prone to tearout, you will have to use all of the usual planing strategies to get good results. Once you have the surface leveled, you will have to close the mouth down and reset the chipbreaker and blade. If the surface is particularly difficult, the blade should be fresh from the sharpening stone. If you have already used the blade to prepare the board, you will probably need to re-sharpen it. Getting the proper setting for a fine tearout-free cut takes a bit of finessing, so adjusting it back and forth from one type of cut to another takes additional time.

To avoid adjusting, readjusting, and re-sharpening it is faster to use two and sometimes three planes for smoothing. When preparing parts for a project, I often work through the majority of the pieces with only one plane, experiencing no problems, especially when some of the surfaces are hidden. Prominent surfaces, or ones prone to tearout, may require more care. For these, after smoothing away the milling marks with the first plane, I go over the surfaces with a second, more finely set plane. Sometimes on tougher surfaces, I resort to a third plane. Each plane in the sequence has an increasingly finer set of the blade, as well as chipbreaker and throat settings, and the blades themselves are of increasing quality. The last plane I use has my best blade and is so finely set that it cuts only dead flat surfaces. This plane cuts an extremely fine slice, with shavings like gossamer, leaving a tearout-free surface. However, if the work is not prepared to a sufficient tolerance of flat, it just skips over the low spots.

Initially I used another smoothing plane the same size as the final smoother for this *panel plane*—and often still do—and this works well. However, I found that using a plane larger than my final smoothing plane is often even more effective in achieving the required flat surface. The extra length, with a sole prepared as a truing plane, really levels the surface, and the use of a wide blade (2¼" to 2¾", or 5.7cm to 7cm, depending on the type and size of the wood to be planed) sharpened straight with just the corners honed off as in a finely set-up smoother yields a flatter surface as well. This panel plane is finely set up, so that it cannot make a deep cut. If the surface is too rough coming off the machines, I will use a more coarsely set plane to initially level, and then prepare the surface with the panel plane.

The panel plane has become my workhorse. Often, it is the only plane I use. Because the sole is set up as a truing plane, I know the surface it leaves will be true. In addition, because the throat, chipbreaker, and blade are set up as a fine smoother, it can plane all but the most difficult surfaces. If I have to use a finer plane, I know the surface the panel plane leaves will be flat enough that I will not have to spend a lot of time planing off the high spots until the smoothing plane is able to cut the whole surface.

The panel plane should be 12" to 16" (30.5cm to 40.6cm) long; it depends on the length of your smoothing planes. If your smoothing planes are 8" or 9" (20.3cm or 22.9cm) long, then 12" (30.5cm) should be long enough. If your smoothing planes are 10" or 11" (25.4cm or

27.9cm) long, then a 14" or 16" (36.2cm or 40.6cm) long panel plane will be good. (If the plane is too long, you create work for yourself.) Likewise, the width depends on the blade width of your smoothing plane. If your smoothing planes are 1¾" to 1⅞" (4.4cm to 4.8cm) wide, for instance, a 2" (5.1cm)-wide blade on the panel plane would be good; a 2¼" or 2⅜" (5.7cm or 6cm)-wide blade would be even better.

Blade angle on a panel plane should be the same or a little lower than the plane you finish with. Ideally though, for hardwoods, I think a blade angle of 47½° works well. Your smoothing planes can then be the same or steeper, depending on the wood and your preference. If you have to use more than one plane to get a surface smooth, it is often helpful to use a progressively steeper blade angle as you progress from one plane to another. There are also some hardwoods, such as cherry, that work well in the lower blade angle range. For these, I often use a 43° or 45° plane to finish, with a 40° panel plane to prepare the surface. For softwoods, a panel plane with a blade angle of 40° is useful. However, unlike hardwoods, I have found no advantage to increasing the blade angle on the smoothing planes. Smoothing planes for softwoods can all be 40°; if you encounter difficult grain, it is best to set aside one of your best planes, carefully sharpened and finely set, to be used for the final few strokes after the work has been smoothed by the panel or subsequent smoothing planes.

The scrub plane

The scrub plane **(Figure 4-11)** has a radiused blade, ideal for removing a lot of wood. It is usually about 9" (22.9cm) long with a 1⅛" to 1¼" (2.9cm to 3.2cm)-wide blade. The edge has nearly ¼" (6mm) of curvature. It is used before the jack plane, usually to flatten badly warped lumber in preparation to being trued up. Its anatomy is instructive, as all its features are so exaggerated. The throat is wide, often nearly ¼" (6mm), to clear the heavy chips that it produces. The blade is bedded as low as 40° in order to reduce the resistance to the cut. The blade is radiused not only so the corners will not dig in but to produce the deepest cut with a minimum of resistance. As tearout is not an issue at this stage of the work, it does not have a chipbreaker, although when used diagonally along the grain, it does not tear out as much as you might think, not when you consider how much wood it removes.

Figure 4-11. With its blade sharpened to a pronounced radius, the scrub plane is the first plane to use on uneven or warped stock, because it removes so much wood so quickly.

The scrub plane can be a very useful tool. I would find it hard to insist that it is a necessity today, but it is nice to know it is available. For that occasional wide piece, just perfect for what you have in mind, jointing the face by hand need not be slow or physically daunting—if you use the right technique. If your board is really out of flat, the proper technique includes using the scrub plane. I use the scrub plane only occasionally, and although the jack plane can be used for the same thing, the scrub plane really speeds things up.

While the scrub plane is not fussy in its setup, you will want to pay particular attention to the ergonomics, as you will be removing a lot of wood while holding on to it. I really do not find the Bailey-style grips comfortable at all for this work. Another consideration is the weight. Because the resulting width of cut is less than ¾" (1.9cm) (the blade's curve is that pronounced), many passes with the plane must be made. For this reason, a light plane is advantageous, and so I prefer using wood rather than iron. I cannot see where iron's durability is an advantage here. Besides its weight, its surface friction is much higher, creating noticeably greater resistance to the stroke. The wear on the throat and sole of a wood scrub plane is not enough to compromise its function or to outweigh the disadvantages of iron. As well, I find the most comfortable handles for heavy work to be those on the classic German (wooden) horned plane. I find the ball and tote handles on the iron planes rapidly blistering. As they come from the factory, the horned planes may need some rounding in places, according to how you like the grip, but overall, I find this style most comfortable for this type of work.

Figure 4-12. Examine Your Boards

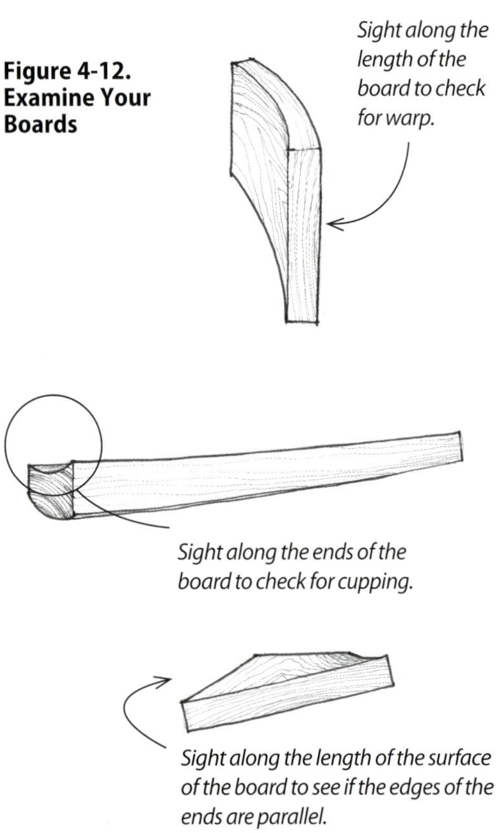

DIMENSIONING STOCK

Before power machinery, this is how woodworkers dimensioned stock nearly every day, sometimes all day. This task was performed this way well into the twentieth century in many parts of the world (and in some parts, I'm sure, still today). As a notable example, the English Arts and Crafts furniture maker, Edward Barnsley, resisted installing power machines in his shop until the late-1950s, believing machines would change the nature of the work and the craftsman's enjoyment of it, and so he continued to surface lumber by hand until that time.

If you have ever done this task before, you will recognize the importance of the variations in the anatomical tactics of the jack, jointer, and smooth planes. Dimensioning stock without the correct setup of these planes is not just difficult—it is nearly impossible. A craftsman certainly could not do this every day, all day, without having developed and understood the required setup for his planes and their sequence of use.

Today, machinery largely spares us the effort of having to bring stock from rough to final dimension by hand. However, sometimes you have to surface boards too large to fit into your machinery. Using these techniques to flatten one side and putting it through the planer increases your versatility, allowing you to use lumber you might otherwise have to pass up. And then there might come the time when, unable to pass up that certain piece of wood even though it fits in no machine you have, you have no choice but to reveal the beauty of that rough board by the final polishing strokes of your handplane. This is how to do it.

Figure 4-13. Winding sticks, one at each end of a board to be planed, will help determine twist in the board. Sight from one end of the board, along the tops of the sticks.

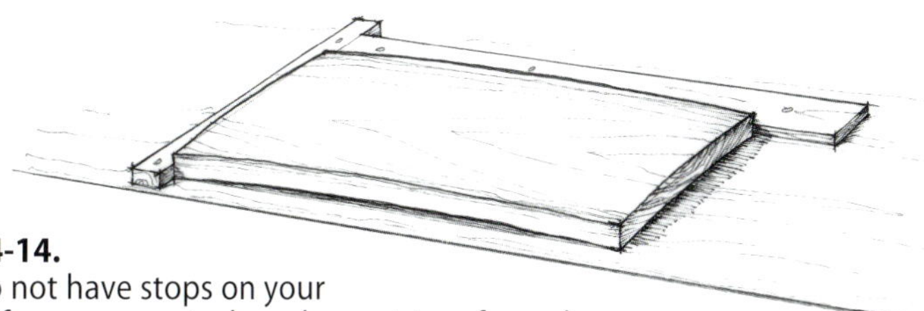

Figure 4-14.
If you do not have stops on your work surface, you can tack or clamp strips of wood or plywood to keep the work from moving around when planing.

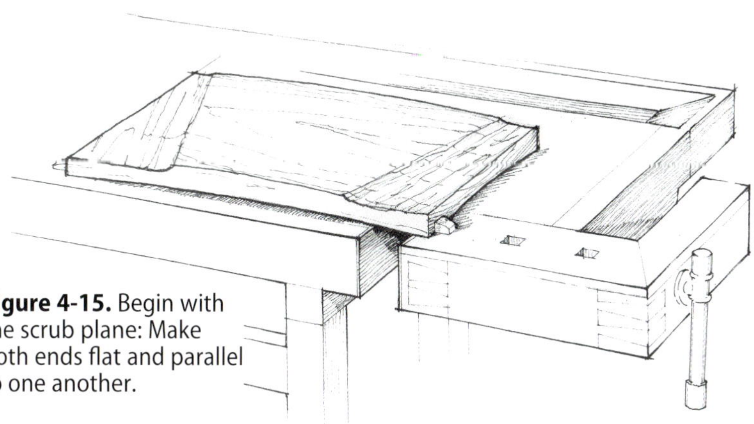

Figure 4-15. Begin with the scrub plane: Make both ends flat and parallel to one another.

Preparing the first face: scrub and jack planes

Before beginning any work, check the piece to be planed for warp, twist, and cupping by sighting down the length and across the width of the board (**Figure 4-12**). If the distortion is subtle, you may have to use a straight edge and winding sticks to determine where and how much it is warped. You can put notes or marks on the board indicating what needs to be done where, if you want, including scribble marks on the high areas to be planed off. This technique is secondary to the frequent checking of the surface with a straight edge, winding sticks, and the information you will get from the shaving the plane makes.

Dog the board onto the bench. You can dog it crown up or down; either way you have to take off the same amount of wood (though it would seem like you're removing more wood crown up, you're not—think about it!) Usually,

Figure 4-16. Check for Parallel

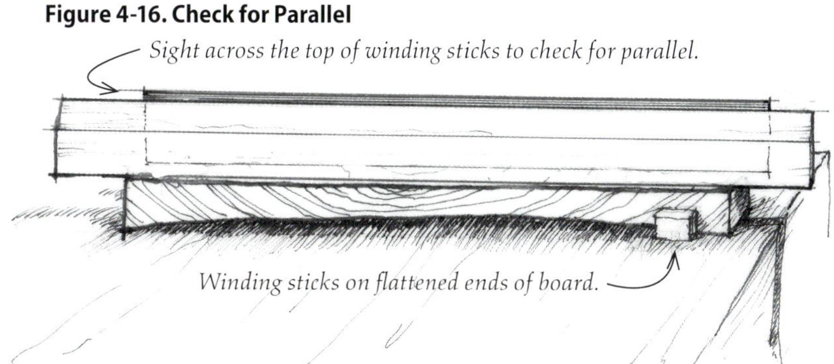

Figure 4-17. Straighten the ends of the boards with the scrub plane and use winding sticks to check that they are parallel.

Figure 4-18. The area in between the flat and parallel ends can now be leveled to match using the scrub plane.

crown-side-up gives better support (you may have to shim one corner as opposed to three) and less chance of splitting out the edges when working. Check for twist and cup with winding sticks (**Figure 4-13** on page 79).

If you do not have a European-style bench with dogs, a work surface with two stops will do: one for the end of the board, and one alongside the board to keep the board from shifting sideways when planing diagonally (**Figure 4-14** on page 79). The stops can be tacked, if you do not mind putting tacks in your work surface, or clamped down. Stops must be thinner than the board, and clamps must be well back so that you do not hit them when planning (wide pieces of plywood clamped from the far side of the bench work well).

Using a scrub plane, flatten the crown of each end. Work on a slight diagonal, with the grain, to reduce chewing up the wood, as happens when working

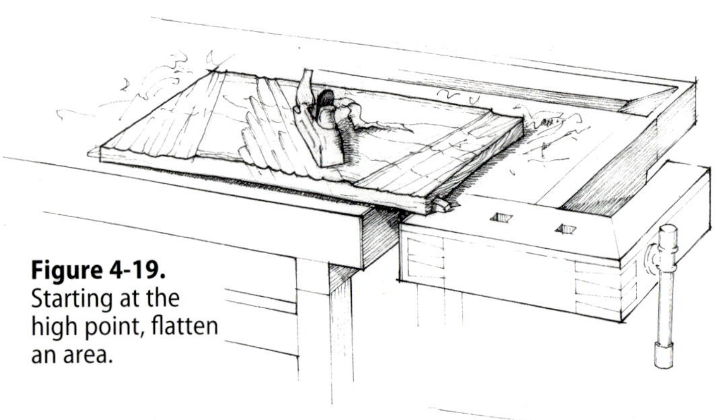

Figure 4-19. Starting at the high point, flatten an area.

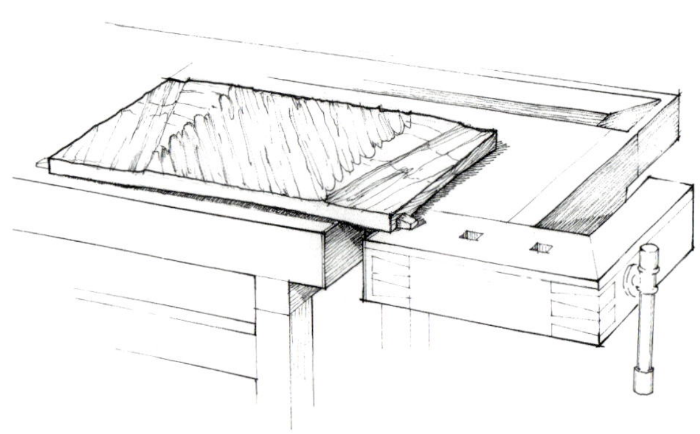

Figure 4-20. Plane the area again, extending it further.

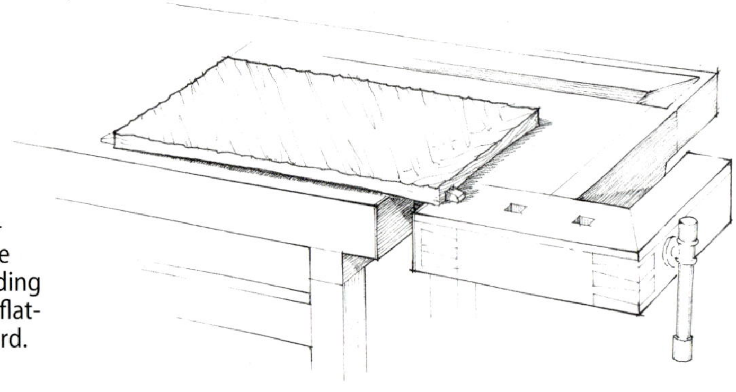

Figure 4-21. Make repeated passes over the area, each time extending it until it matches the flattened ends of the board.

Figure 4-22. Right-Handed Means Start at Left

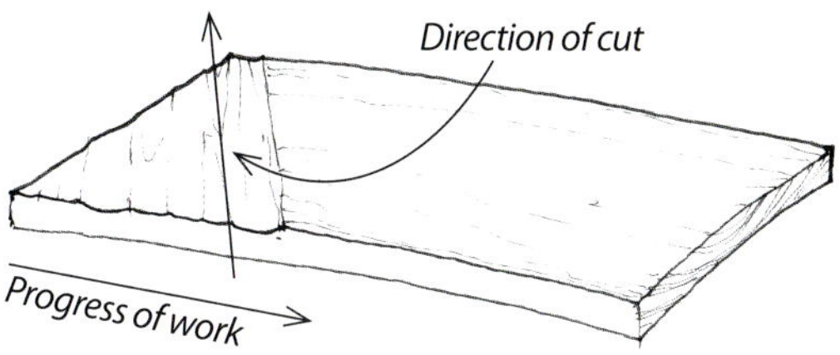

across the grain **(Figure 4-15** on page 79**)**. Depending on the hardness of the wood and how bad the board is, the scrub plane is set to take a cut about ⅛" (3mm) deep or less.

Place winding sticks on the flats at each end **(Figure 4-16** on page 79**)** and check for wind (twist), sighting over the tops of the sticks, and lowering your line of sight until the top edges are brought nearly together **(Figure 4-17)**. The edges should be parallel. If not, plane the high corners down, keeping the ends flat and straight, until the sticks show parallel.

Once the ends are flat and parallel **(Figure 4-18)**, the area in between can be lowered to match. Starting in the middle (high point of the crown) flatten an area. Repeat, gradually extending the flat area **(Figure 4-19)**. Make consistent, full-width strokes slightly overlapping the same amount each time **(Figure 4-20)** and **(Figure 4-21)**.

Plane across the grain on a diagonal (usually about 45°). This greatly reduces tearout and splintering of the far side that can happen when removing this much wood. It will also make the planing physically easier. Always work with the grain: for instance, with the board at your right as you stand at the bench ready to plane (if you are right-handed, most of the time you will plane with the bench to your right), start at the left, or far end, of

Figure 4-23. Plane the rest of the board down to match the now flat and parallel ends.

Figure 4-24. Check the progress of the work frequently with a straight edge.

Figure 4-25. The jack improves the rough texture left by the scrub plane.

WINDING STICKS

Winding sticks can be any two sticks that are rectangular in section and long enough to lie across the work you are checking. The sticks need to be straight and have the two parallel edges. For checking timber, the sticks do not have to be of great refinement: you can literally grab two sticks out of the scrap pile—they don't even have to be the same width—as long as they are straight and parallel. The longer they are, the greater the accuracy in checking for parallel, as the greater length exaggerates the distortion.

If you want a tool of greater sophistication, you can buy wood and metal ones, or you can make you own. When making your own, the principal is simple enough. Pin two pieces of wood together so they can be separated, plane both edges straight, pull them apart, and check them by holding the edges together up to the light. Any error in straightness doubles. If light shines between the edges at any point, put them back together and plane them until no light is visible when they are held against one another. If the pieces are used in the same orientation as when they are pinned together (make a habit of doing this), even if a taper has been planed along their length, it will make no difference, because the pieces will still be parallel to one another **(Figure 1).**

To make a set of winding sticks/straightedges select two pieces of any stable, well dried wood, preferably quarter-sawn (mahogany is a good choice, as is white oak), say about 1½" (3.8cm) wide by ½" (1.3cm) thick by 18" (45.7cm) long. Align the two pieces, drill though both near the ends, and insert dowels through both. Glue the dowels to one side only so they can be pulled apart. It is helpful to bevel the inside edges of the ends so you can get your thumbs in to get them apart. Bevel the faces so the reference edges are about ⅛" (3mm) wide, in order to make them easier to read.

Figure 1. A matched set of wood winding sticks.

the board and work toward yourself, each successive stroke stepped further to the right **(Figure 4-22** on page 81). Continue to extend the flat area until it reaches and is even with the leveled ends **(Figure 4-23** on page 81).

Check at several points for flat and wind with winding sticks. Check the length for straight by sighting along it or using a straightedge **(Figure 4-24** on page 81). Correct areas as needed.

Once the board is relatively flat overall, remove the ridges left by the scrub plane with the jack plane. Work systematically, slightly overlapping each stroke, trying to maintain the flatness left by the scrub plane. Work diagonally as with the scrub plane (**Figure 4-25** on page 81 and **Figure 4-26**).

Confirm you are done with the jack by checking for wind and straightness. Work any high spots. Once the board tests flat and does not rock when put face down on a flat surface, you can put the board face down into the power planer (**Figure 4-27**). You are done with the handwork—unless, of course, you do not have a power planer or one big enough to accommodate this board. In these cases, you will have to change to the jointer plane and continue.

Continuing with the jointer plane

Unlike the jack and scrub planes, the jointer is usually used with the grain (rather than diagonally), at least initially. Again, work systematically, carefully overlapping the strokes, starting at one side of the board and working all the way across and back again (**Figure 4-28**). Try to work all parts of the board equally, planning in the direction of the grain. If you find you have large areas of tearout, reverse the board and see if you get less in that direction.

If you have small areas of tearout, reversing the board probably won't do any good; it's probably a rapid change in direction of the grain and reversing the board will just tear out the other side of the spot where the grain changes direction. If tearout is particularly

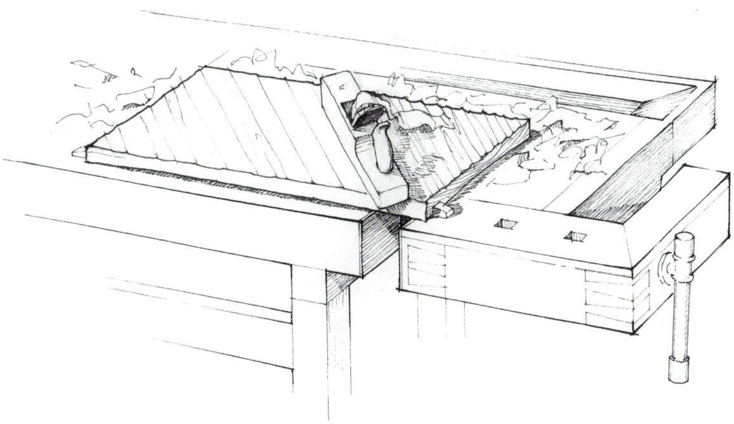

Figure 4-26. Use a jack plane to remove the ridges left by the scrub plane to further refine the surface.

Figure 4-27. The board has been leveled by the jack plane and is ready for the power planer or the jointer plane.

Figure 4-28. The jointer removes the texture left by the jack and brings the board to straight and flat.

Figure 4-29. You can use the edge of the sole of the jointer as a straight edge to check the work.

Figure 4-30. Following the jointer plane, I usually use my 12" (30.5cm) panel plane (included in the set of planes described in Chapter 8) to smooth the surface in preparation for final smoothing.

troublesome, you can back the blade off a bit as the board gets flatter, making a lighter cut (some tearout at this point is acceptable, as the smoother and, if needed, a panel plane will get rid of it).

If tearout is still excessive, once the board is flat, re-sharpen the blade and go over the surface with a light cut to remove what tearout you can. Periodically check the board for flatness. The fastest way is to use the bottom edge of the jointer against the face of the board, tilting the plane up on its long edge and looking for light between it and the board's surface; these are the low spots **(Figure 4-29)**. Low spots will also manifest as places where the jointer skips cutting. Work the entire surface consistently to bring these into line.

If you have a very wide board or panel, you may have to use the jointer across the grain, until the plane makes a shaving at all areas. High areas may have to be worked diagonally, as with the jack. Finish planning with the jointer by planning with the grain until all areas are cut and the face of the board tests flat.

Smoothing the first face

Once the jointer makes a consistent shaving over the entire face and the face tests flat, you can move on to the smoothing plane **(Figure 4-30)**.

Since the cut made by the jointer is comparatively coarse, it may be more expedient to use two smoothing planes, one set coarser to remove the tracks left by the jointer, followed by a fine-set plane to finish **(Figure 4-31)**. Alternatively, you can reset your smoothing plane. If the surface is prone to tearout, it may be best to use a panel plane—a wide and long smoothing plane with the sole set up as a truing plane—to prepare the surface left by the jointer (see "The Panel Plane" on page 75). This will remove much of the tearout left by the jointer while truing the surface even more. The smoothing plane that follows can then be set much finer than it otherwise would be, greatly reducing or eliminating tearout. Sometimes, on difficult pieces, another smoothing or polishing plane may be used after that. This would be your best plane most finely set.

Final smoothing of the first side may be postponed until the second side is ready, to avoid marring the surface of the first while working the second.

Planing the edges and second side

Next, either the opposite face or the two edges are done, at your discretion. If the board is being done entirely by hand, often the edges are done next. This reduces the width, leaving less area to surface (that is, less work), and makes it easier to mark the thickness, as the edge is now smooth and not rough-sawn. If the board is very wide and is to remain close to its rough width, it might be best to surface the second side; the board may have to be cross-planed, and this may splinter out the edges. Do the edges afterward to remove any splintering.

To plane an edge, set the board in the front vise. (If you have a simple planing bench as I have described later and have installed a hook on the front for holding boards when shooting, you can use that.) If the edge is badly out of straight,

Figure 4-31. After the surface has been smoothed and leveled by the panel plane, a finely set smoothing plane, here a modern coffin-sided smoother, is used to remove any remaining imperfections.

Figure 4-32. A fore plane quickly straightens a badly curved edge.

Figure 4-33. Use a jack or fore plane to initially level a badly curved edge, followed by the jointer to finish.

Figure 4-34. A jointer plane finesses the edge left by the fore plane.

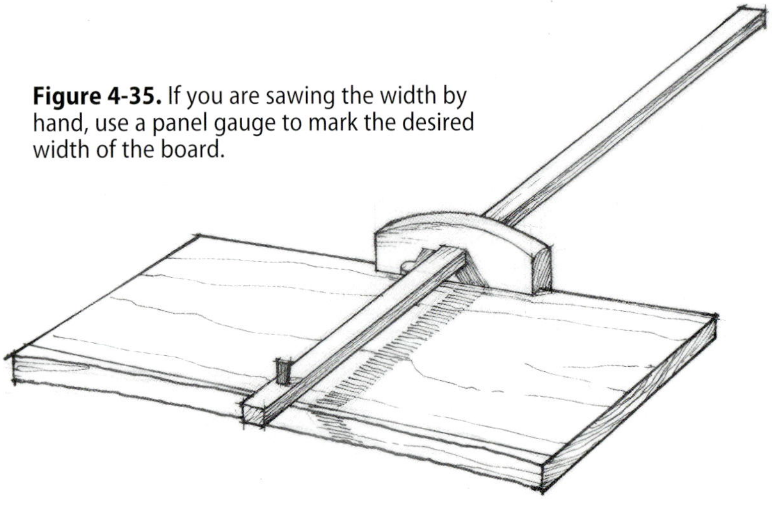

Figure 4-35. If you are sawing the width by hand, use a panel gauge to mark the desired width of the board.

use a jack plane or fore plane to take the high spots off, gradually extending the straight section until it runs the whole length of the board **(Figure 4-32 and Figure 4-33** on page 85).

After the edge has been roughly straightened, shoot the edge with a jointer plane in continuous single passes **(Figure 4-34)**. When the plane makes a continuous full-width shaving, check for square to the flattened face. Correct as necessary.

Once the first edge is done, mark the width with a panel gauge (if you are sawing by hand) and saw the board to width. Cut the width about 1⁄32" (0.8mm) wide if using a table saw, or about 1⁄16" (2mm) wider if sawing by hand, depending how good a cut you can make **(Figure 4-35)**. If you've sawn the board by hand, plane the edge down until you are about 1⁄32" (0.8mm) away from the scribe line. Check for square, correct, and plane to the line. With both edges done, mark the required thickness all around with a marking gauge **(Figure 4-36)**.

Repeat the process used on the first side for the second side, except that the ends do not have to be flattened to test with winding sticks first. Work the entire board, taking extra strokes on the high spots to make the entire second side parallel to the first. Then bring the entire side down to the line **(Figure 4-37)**. This completes the surfacing of the board.

OTHER HANDPLANE PREPARATORY WORK

Few woodworkers nowadays will be faced with surfacing a board entirely by hand. More likely, you will smooth boards that have been prepared by machines, removing snipe and ripples left by the blades. This is usually accomplished by one or two smoothing planes, which can make quick work of machine-made blemishes. Larger pieces would benefit from preparation with a panel plane.

Pieces with difficult grain can be prepared with two planes, the second one set finer than the first to remove any remaining tearout. With tough and hard woods like oak, major imperfections such as snipe can be removed with a plane with a 55° or 60° pitch, followed by a Stanley #80 handled scraper. If imperfections are minor, you can go right to the #80. Follow with a card scraper once over the board. A better plan is to follow the #80 with a Scraper Plane to take out the slight scallops left by the #80. Once over followed by a light pass with a card scraper usually does it.

Some woods can be planed fast and with little difficulty, and the surface left by the plane is stunning. Others not only are difficult to plane but do not seem to be improved by planing. For these, and for pieces that are less critical, such as shelving, handled scrapers followed by card scrapers, with the plane used here and there to remove a bit of material that might otherwise take too long to remove with a scraper, can be the most efficient approach.

SHOOTING AN EDGE

Planing a long edge to straighten it in preparation for gluing is called *shooting*. For most people it is one of the most frustrating tasks in woodworking. However, having a gentle curve honed into the edge of the blade of the jointer

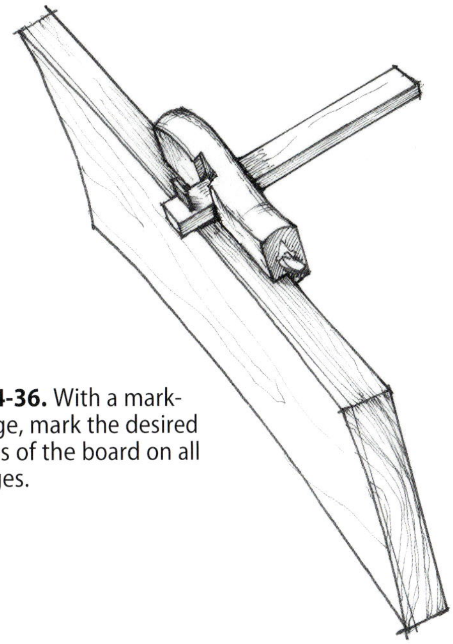

Figure 4-36. With a marking gauge, mark the desired thickness of the board on all four edges.

Figure 4-37. Completing the Board's Surface

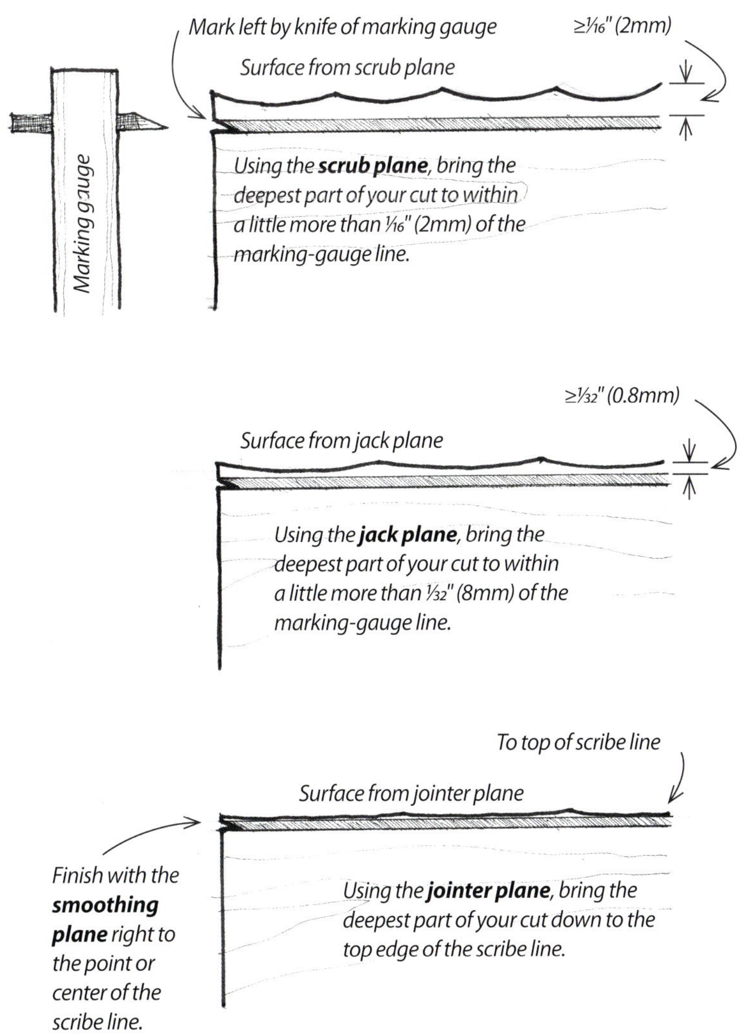

plane can make this task manageable. I like this technique better than others I have tried—and I think I have tried them all. If you are not too set in your ways already, try this one.

Tips for shooting an edge

To plane an edge straight, you must have the focus of your attention and your energy at the cutting edge. The shaving (eventually) must emerge continuous, full width, and unbroken. At first, most of your energy will be everywhere but at the edge, causing tense muscles, cramped hands and shoulder and back muscles, and quick fatigue. Eventually, you will expend energy efficiently, with no muscles tensed except those used to cut the edge, and no wasted motion. You will be able to do this all day and feel better at the end of it than you would have having sat at a desk all day.

Practically speaking, the following things must be done: the stance must be balanced from the start to the finish of the stroke. The work must not be too high or too low. The planed edge at about 34" (86cm) above the ground is good for a person 5′ 8" to 5′ 10" (1.73m to 1.78m) tall; less if you are shorter, more if you are taller. This will allow you to keep both your balance and your focus. The weight on the plane must be on the front at the start of the stroke and the back at the finish, gradually shifting as the stroke progresses.

You can practice holding the front half of the plane at the beginning of the board edge using your left hand only, supporting the weight of the plane cantilevering off the back and then holding the back of the plane with your right hand only, supporting the cantilevered front of the plane off the far end of the board. Now practice smoothly shifting your weight while purposely lifting one hand and then the other as the stroke progresses. Every time your plane accidentally dips off the end at the start or the finish of a stroke, go back and practice this weight shift.

Another technique that is helpful is to use your front hand as a kind of fence by placing you thumb on the top of the plane and keeping two or three fingers under the plane up against the face of the board. This is often helpful and is the most used position, but it doesn't always work if, for instance, you want to move the plane from side to side to take out a twist, or if you have a very hard wood that requires more pressure than the thumb can give; so you should also learn how to control the plane with the usual hand positions as well.

Learning to keep the plane in solid, continuous contact with the work will help you greatly in focusing on the cutting action of the plane. Keep your eye's attention at the throat of the plane, always monitoring the quality of the shaving that emerges.

TECHNIQUES FOR SHOOTING AN EDGE

1. One of the main difficulties in shooting an edge occurs when the edge is out of square. With a straight blade, you have to attempt to balance the plane square to the face, literally on the corner of the board, and plane that narrow edge repeatedly at the same angle.

2. You can, as I have seen recommended, clamp two boards together so that even though they are out of square with their faces, they will have the same angle. The boards are then flipped to be joined and their complementary angles zero each other out. There are two big problems with this method:

3. The first problem is that any error in the straightness will be doubled when the boards are joined. To correct the problem, the boards must be unclamped and checked and re-clamped and planed, and unclamped and checked, maybe many more times. The second problem is the boards have to be perfectly realigned every time they are re-clamped, or the method will not work at all. This is tedious and time-consuming.

1

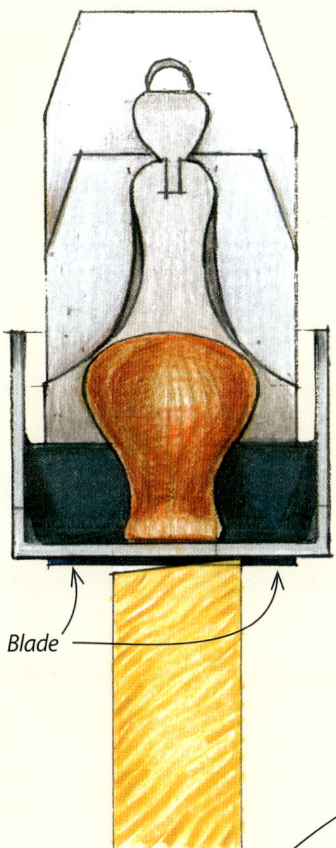

2

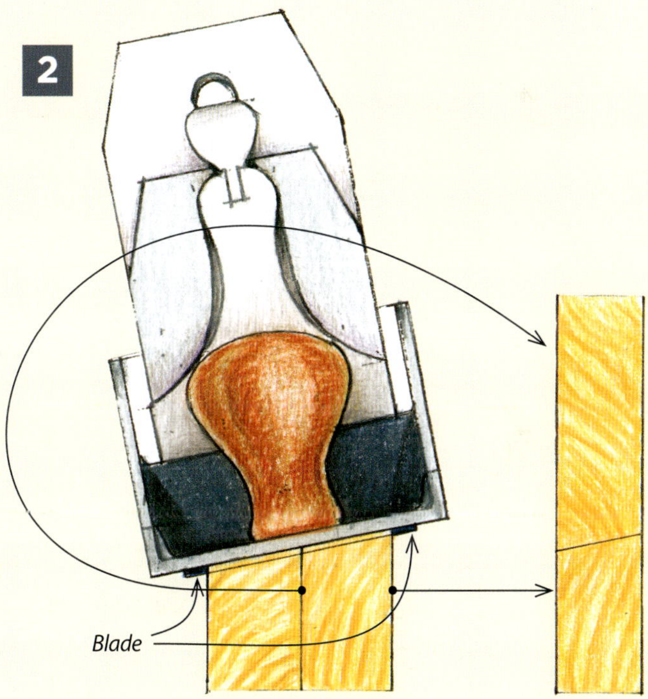

3

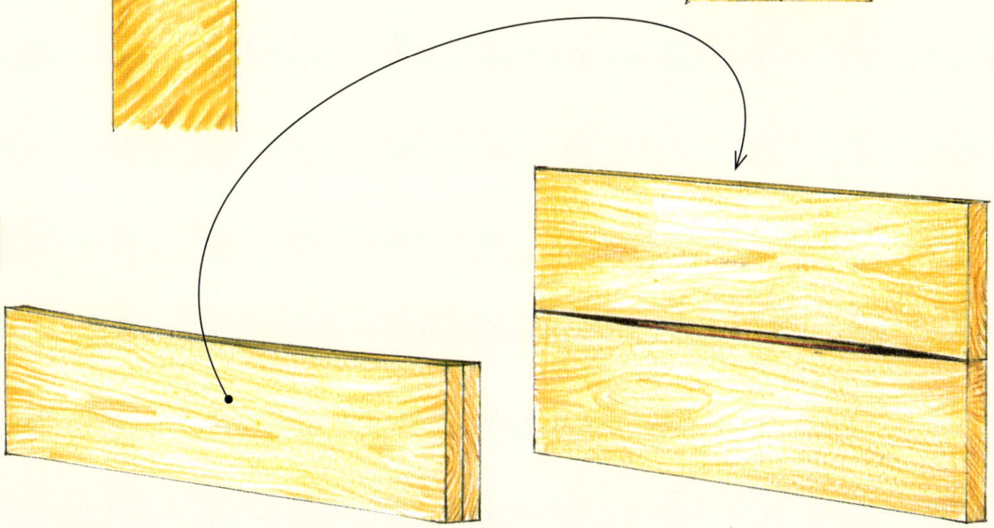

TECHNIQUES FOR SHOOTING AN EDGE (CONTINUED)

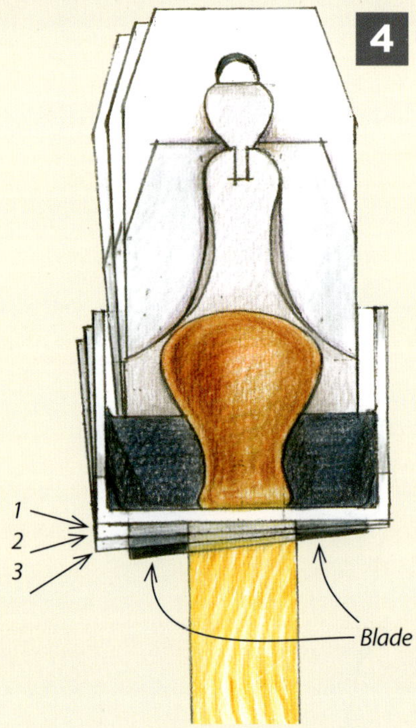

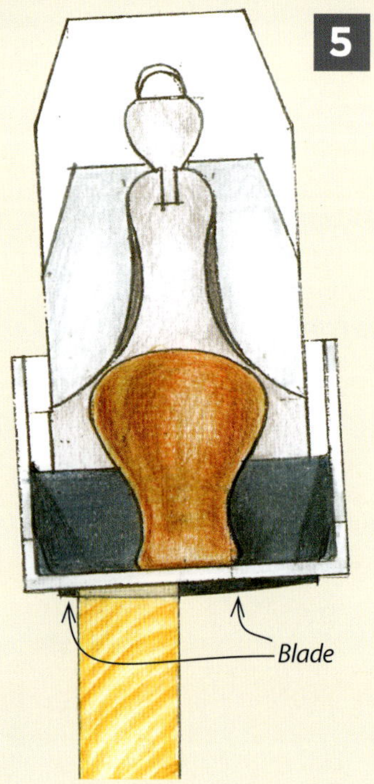

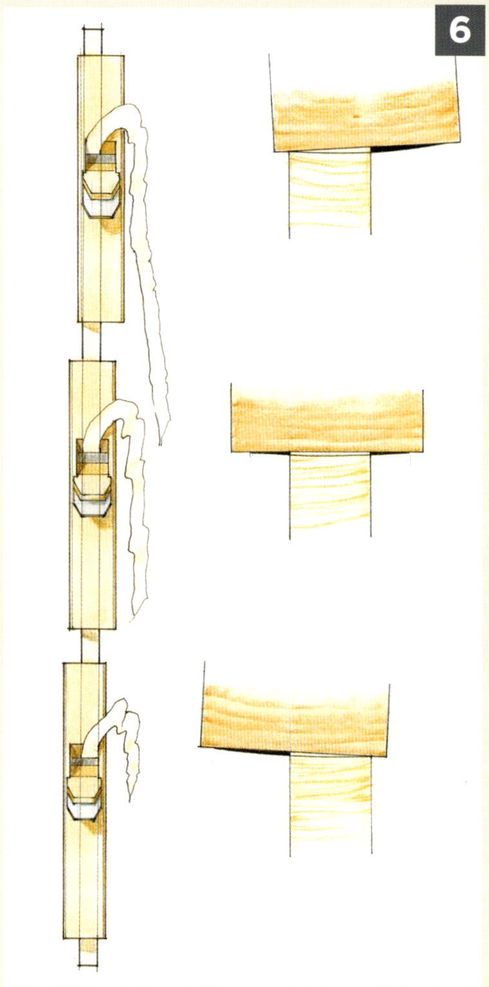

4. You can plane one board at a time, marking them to be flipped after planing so the angle of their edges will be complementary when joined, resulting in a flat panel. While you may find you favor one side or another repeatedly, this technique works consistently only when a shooting board is used. This is because with a shooting board the plane is referenced off its side so the angle planed onto the edge of the board will be consistent from board to board (as long as the blade is not readjusted). Without a shooting board, even if you repeatedly favor one side, this technique has problems. If your plane's straight blade is out of parallel with the sole of the plane, each stroke will increase the error. If you plane one board's edge more than the other, then your angles will not match, and you are back to where we started—correcting the angle on the edge of the board, trying to balance the plane.

5. But if you have a bit of a curve to the edge of your 2¾" (7cm) wide jointer-plane blade, you can set the sole of the plane flat on the edge—you will not have to balance it—and by keeping the plane so that the board is to one side of it or another, you can alter and correct the angle in one or a few strokes. Traditionally, the edge of the jointer-plane blade was sharpened to a curvature of around 1/32" (0.8mm) across its width because the plane was also used to smooth out the scallops of the jack plane as well as shoot edges. Nowadays, the jointer is used principally to shoot edges, and while this much blade curvature may present a useful amount of concavity on the edge of a ¾" (1.9cm) board, it may be a little much on thicker boards. I have been sharpening my blades so that they curve less than a 1/64" (0.4mm) over the 2¾" (7cm) width of the blade. You want to be able to utilize the whole width of the blade, so the projection should be equal to the maximum depth of cut you want to make on the type of wood and width of stock you're working with. If the cut is too deep, it is too difficult to control the cut.

6. Because using the plane to one side of the board or the other effectively lowers that side, you can even take out a twist in the edge by starting the plane with the board to one side of the plane and finishing with the board on the other. After you have checked for square, make a pass down the board with the plane centered on the edge, repeating until a continuous unbroken full-width shaving emerges, indicating that your edge is now a flat continuous plane.

CHAPTER

5

SHARPENING PLANE BLADES

A BASIC SKILL THAT LEADS TO OTHERS

OK, OK. I know anyone who has ever sharpened a plane blade has a firm, perhaps even adamant, opinion about how it should be done. I say, if it is working for you, you do not need to fix it. But in the interest of coaxing new growth out of any woodworker who wants to improve his or her craft, and to give at least a sense of direction to those who are starting out, I throw out the following for your consideration.

The ability to sharpen quickly and well is essential to the craft of woodworking.

I have two goals when sharpening:

- the acquisition and improvement of skills (sharpening and otherwise);
- and getting back to working wood as quickly as possible—with the most effective blade edge.

Sharpening is fundamental to the craft of woodworking. Learning to sharpen fast and effectively lays the foundation for the acquisition of nearly all of the other skills to be required in the craft. It teaches body mechanics and the art of working efficiently. It teaches you how to focus both your attention and your efforts for maximum productivity. It teaches you to see, and what to look for: to feel—your own rhythms, the material, and the feedback from the tool—less smooth, smoother, smoothest, sharp, and sharper.

This is where woodworkers learn to make each motion pay off. You come to understand that the edge is not scrubbed back and forth across the stone but rather stroked with direct intention each time it is moved; that there is clear focus of effort, pressure, and attention at the cutting edge itself, not the bevel; and while the bevel does remain flat, not rocking on the stone, it is the edge of that bevel that's being sharpened and must be zeroed into with both the mind and the body.

Additionally, learning this and how to do it, and how to do it each time, makes it easier to understand other tasks: that each stroke of the plane is individual, dependent on the grain of the wood at that particular place, the angle of attack, your speed, your body position, the diminishing sharpness of the blade, and your increasing fatigue.

That sawing is not a tiring repetition of frantic arm motion but a series of individual strokes, each advancing the cut on the shoulder of the scribe line and to the maximum amount the wood and the cut of the saw will allow.

That clearing waste for a dovetail or mortise with a chisel is a series of distinct, clean, and precise cuts of exactly the same amount, to the line, so waste is cleanly excavated the first time to its final shape (though perhaps not its final size).

Understanding this—and eventually, with mindful practice, internalizing this—makes each stroke of the plane, the chisel, or the saw produce optimal results, and the work proceeds quickly.

Because of the importance of sharpening in teaching body mechanics and the art of working efficiently, I always strongly encourage woodworkers to sharpen without a jig. I also feel it is faster overall. Fortunately, the bevel on the thick cast steel plane blade is quite wide and it is relatively easy to feel this bevel when working and keep it flat on the stone. But this wide bevel will also teach you that pressure is not applied equally across the bevel. Because the edge steel is so much harder, if you apply equal pressure when honing, you will gradually wear away the softer backing steel quicker and the bevel will get thinner over time. It will also take you much longer to sharpen. You must apply greater pressure at the edge while keeping the bevel flat to the stone. But, you will find out, this is true of all blades, especially if you want to shorten the time it takes to hone an edge.

Jig drawbacks

Use a sharpening jig and your energy is dissipated, half of it going to the roller, half to the bevel, and very little going directly to the edge of the blade, which is where all of your energy should be going. The roller becomes a blindfold, obscuring your interaction with the edge you are sharpening. It keeps you from ever learning the feel of the bevel sitting flat on the stone as you stroke it; from learning to focus your attention at the edge, while keeping the bevel flat to the stone; from learning not to rock or lean, yet produce maximum results at that cutting edge where you want it.

Because the jig dissipates both your energy and your focus, effort is wasted and time is lost. It is slower, and it is disruptive. Add to that the problem of jigging the blade the exact position in the apparatus—because if it is not exact—not close but exact—you create a new bevel on the blade when you go to sharpen—and your time and tedium increase exponentially.

Learn to sharpen with the attention of the mind and body focused to your fingertips, because in the end, this will be how you will be doing woodworking. Yes, there is a learning curve, but really, woodworking is just one big learning curve. The challenge woodworking offers is one of its appeals. You can take a shortcut, but it will catch up to you later. Time invested here will serve you throughout your further woodworking endeavors.

BEVEL SHAPE

Three bevel configurations can be used on a sharpened blade:

- flat,
- hollow ground, and
- micro-bevel.

Traditional sources I have seen emphasize the bevel must be flat—for several reasons. First, it gives maximum support to the edge while allowing the thinnest possible bevel. A rounded bevel, usually a result of rocking the blade when sharpening, results in a much thicker bevel angle at the cutting edge, even though the average of the bevel overall may be the intended angle. This results in the blade ceasing to cut at the least bit of dulling, as the bevel behind the edge begins to rub and suspend the edge from the work. A hollow-ground blade undercuts the edge leaving little material to support it. It actually undercuts it more than you think because the actual angle is that of the tangent of the hollow just behind the edge. This is much smaller than the angle the blade was ground to and often results in a support angle behind the edge of much less than the 20° to 22° generally considered to be the absolute minimum practical bevel angle (see "Honing a Hollow-Ground Bevel" on page 55). This may or may not be a problem. Telltale indications the bevel is not working are chattering (even though properly bedded, the undercut metal leading to the edge is flexing under load); clogging at the mouth or throat of a properly adjusted plane (the blade—not sufficiently supported by the bevel—is flexing down under load, enlarging the mouth, causing it to cut a shaving larger than the opening can accommodate); or clogging between the blade and the chipbreaker, even though the chipbreaker is fitted properly (again, the blade's thin edge is flexing under load and opening a gap between it and the chipbreaker).

A flat bevel provides the thinnest possible edge with the greatest support behind that edge. If any of these problems show up with a flat bevel, it is because the bevel itself is ground at too small an angle, a geometry that is plain to see and easy to deal with. Additionally, with a cast steel blade, because the hard, brittle steel is too vulnerable without the support of the bevel behind it, it can actually chip; that is, it will dull really quickly and quite a lot.

Besides its potential functional problems, I have always believed the hollow grind presents maintenance problems as well. A grinding wheel leaves deep scratches, many of which seem to remain even after establishing a brightly honed bevel. Most grinding wheels are 60 or 80 grit; under a microscope the grooves left by the abrasive look like the Grand Canyon next to the pattern left by a 1200-grit sharpening stone. It is easy to hone what looks to the naked eye like a polished bevel and still have some of these deep grooves left. To ensure they no longer remain near the edge, I always give the bevel a few extra strokes on the first sharpening stone. However, waterstones cut so fast—much faster than the old oil or Arkansas stones—that this nearly eliminates the hollow. After two or three sharpenings, the hollow has been honed away. I could never understand the point of taking the time to regrind the hollow when the waterstones cut so fast. Now, Let's get back to working wood.

There are some occasions, however, when I purposely establish a hollow grind, even if an edge does not have to be reshaped (because of a nick, for instance). The primarily reason is to take the hump out of a rounded bevel. Sometimes, after a number of honings, I just lose it. The bevel is simply too rounded to easily flatten. In such a case I put it on a grinding wheel and hollow-grind the area between the edge and the heel of the bevel. I do not take it all the way out to the edge, both for expediency, and to avoid possibly overheating the edge. I grind away just enough that the blade sits flat on the sharpening stone and does not rock. I can then easily hone the blade to a flat, unrounded bevel. At the first honing, however, I do not necessarily take the time to fully remove the hollow left by the grinder. I just hone until the

Figure 5-1. Positions of Risk

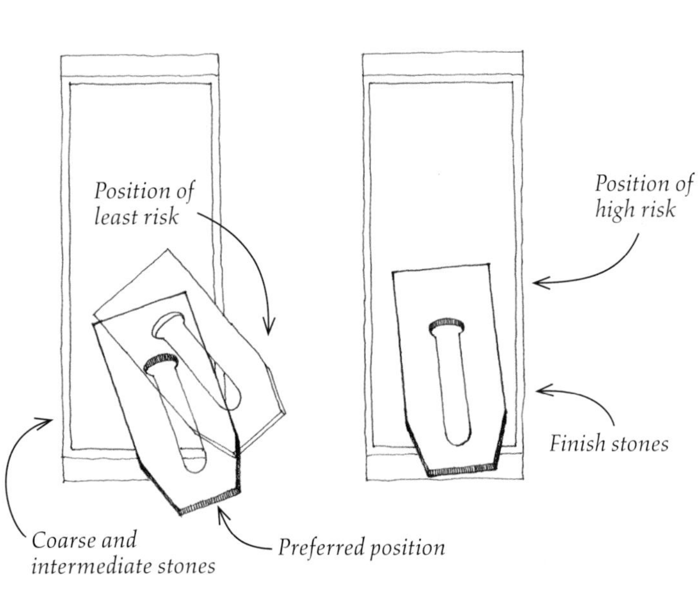

edge is sharpened. If a bit of the hollow remains, it is not enough to compromise the functioning of the blade, and it will be gone soon enough in the next honing or two, anyway.

A rounded bevel, usually a result of rocking the blade when sharpening, is also not desirable. It results in a much thicker bevel angle at the cutting edge, even though the average of the bevel overall may be the intended angle. A little bit of this (a very little) is acceptable and almost inevitable when sharpening by hand (I talk more about this a little further on). But too much results in the blade ceasing to cut at the least bit of dulling, as the bevel behind the edge begins to rub and suspend the edge from the work.

The micro bevel is, again, a maintenance issue with me. The micro bevel gives a good edge the first time. The next time you sharpen, you have two choices: (1) sharpen only the micro bevel, or (2) sharpen the whole bevel and the micro bevel. If you sharpen only the micro bevel, after two or three sharpenings, you will have a macro bevel. You will have lost all of the advantage of a micro bevel, and you have a main bevel that is rapidly developing a rounded profile. If you hone the main bevel to get the best edge, you must hone it all the way out to the edge, not just to the beginning of the micro bevel. Then, putting a micro bevel on the blade at this point is just redoing work

Anyway, if you hone without a guide (as I recommend), some slight variation in the bevel angle is unavoidable. In addition, with proper technique you can make this work for you. By rotating the blade edge to perpendicular to the length of the sharpening stone on your final stone (with the main length of the blade parallel to the length of the stone), rather than using the approximate 45° orientation that gives the most stability when sharpening, you assume a position of higher risk **(Figure 5-1)**. The slight increase in inaccuracy will ensure the edge itself is polished and slightly bolstered.

I believe many of these elaborate systems—hollow-grinding, microbevels, jigs—do not address one of the main issues of sharpening: its frequency. If you are using your planes to their maximum benefit, for periods, at least, you may have to resharpen several times a day—maybe every 15 or 20 minutes at some point in some projects. Fiddling with contraptions and a variety of angles each time consumes too much time and is distracting. Without all this stuff, but with a good set of stones and a properly established bevel angle, you can be back to woodworking after 3 or 4 minutes at the stones, which is sometimes less than the amount of time it would take to get a jig properly attached.

GRINDING

I was once told never to grind a Japanese blade, typically a high-carbon steel blade particularly sensitive to heat stress and degradation. Boy, getting out a nick in a blade without a grinder can be very Zen. I became enlightened, however, when a Japanese chisel maker told me that, yes, you can grind a Japanese blade on a grinding wheel—with the proper technique. The technique is simply to keep a finger directly behind the bevel, as close to the grinding wheel as possible. When the blade becomes too hot for your finger, it is too hot for the blade, and grinding pauses (**Figure 5-2**).

This brings up an important issue. Not just Japanese blades are sensitive to the stress of grinding. You need to treat any good blade in the same manner. While a grinding wheel can easily draw the temper of an edge, especially if the wheel is glazed, stopping short of changing the color of the edge is still too hot. Aggressively grinding, stopping just short of color change, quenching, and then regrinding, causes noticeable structural change in the edge. Especially when combined with quenching, which itself can cause microscopic cracking. All of this degrades the edge, reducing its cutting ability and life.

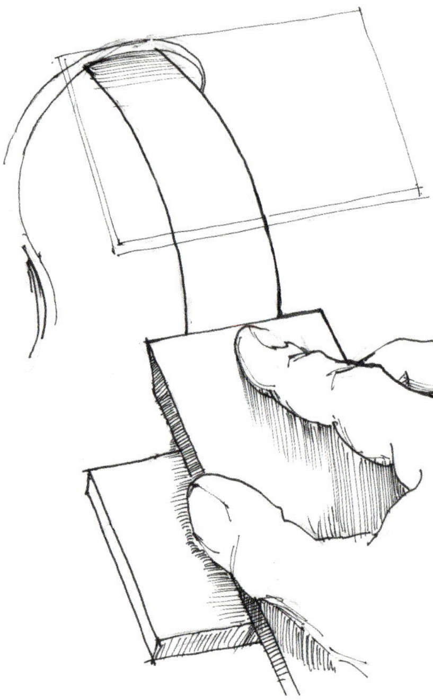

Figure 5-2. Keeping a finger at the edge directly behind the bevel will tell you when the blade is becoming too hot. If the blade is too hot for your finger, it is too hot for the edge.

GRINDING OUT A NICK

Do not remove a nick by grinding the bevel; grind perpendicular to the edge. After removing the nick, grind the bevel until it just reaches the edge. If you grind out the nick by grinding the bevel, you are always working at the thin edge. This thin edge has no mass to help dissipate the heat, and is therefore at greater risk for overheating.

Alloy steel blades are somewhat more forgiving of this treatment because the alloys usually added mitigate some of the effects of heat stress. However, a carbon steel blade will not tolerate the temperature extremes. Both for the time it takes and for the risk involved, it is a good idea to grind as little as possible.

At some point, you will have to reshape a blade edge. For this reason, some sort of grinding device is indispensable. The power-grinding wheel is the most common, and probably, all things considered, the most practical. Get the slow-speed version (1,750rpm or so) and 8" (20.3cm) wheels for less undercutting of the edge. Keep the wheels trued and clean. Keep your finger behind the bevel, and work patiently.

Alternatives

An alternative to the grinding wheel is the standing stationary belt sander, about 2" (5.1cm) wide. Knife makers and many metal workers prefer them. They cut aggressively but have less tendency to overheat because the sanding belt carries away much of the heat. (You still can be too aggressive and overheat the blade, but it is much harder to do than with a grinding wheel). This machine allows you several options for shaping the bevel. Besides the flat platen that produces a (nearly) flat bevel, usually you can work at one of the end wheels of the belt and achieve a hollow grind. The machine I have has an 8" (20.3cm) wheel that is usable. In addition, most machines have an arbor at the other side of the motor, which can be fitted with a grinding or buffing wheel.

Water grinding stones guarantee no heating of the edge. They tend to be slower (though not much) than power grinding or sanding, but they leave a great edge with little risk to the blade. They are, however, in some respects less versatile. You cannot do general reshaping tasks, such as grinding a new blade profile (as for a molding plane). On the other hand, the horizontal water grinder can sharpen power jointer and planer blades, something other grinders cannot easily do. Also, the horizontal wheel leaves a dead flat bevel, which no other grinding wheel does. It does need more maintenance than the others, though. The stones quickly wear and require frequent truing.

Vertical water grinding wheels have the same advantage as the horizontal water wheels. There is no risk of heat damage to the tool, but they leave a hollow grind. It is a matter of preference as to what shape you want behind your edge. Most of the wheels are much larger than most dry grinding wheels, so edges are undercut less. In addition, some of the systems seem quite elaborate—and expensive—and, considering you will probably have to get another system for the shop's other grinding/shaping tasks, the cost seems downright luxurious.

GRINDING ON A SANDING BELT

The natural tendency of a sanding belt is to round the pieces being sanded at both the approach to and exit from the piece. Reshaping the platen to give it a slight convexity compensates somewhat, reducing rounding at the approach and exit. Any remaining deviation from flat is little enough to easily remove when honing.

Alternatively, a partial hollow can be established within a few seconds by putting the blade on the end wheel (in which case you will need a tool rest there as well), just enough to establish good registration on the stones and speed honing to the edge.

SHARPENING STONES

It was not that long ago that Western woodworkers did not have many options for honing the edges on blades. Manmade oilstones or Arkansas stones were pretty much it. Oilstones were messy. They still clogged with debris, decreasing their effectiveness, despite all of the oil that was supposed to float away the debris. In addition, flattening them was impossible, and they did not cut very fast. Arkansas stones, a natural stone, were a step up, but the quality of the stones varied widely, and getting good quality stones was increasingly difficult as many of the best stone material had been mined out. And they shared many of the problems of the oilstones.

In the 1970s, manufactured Japanese waterstones became available, and they have revolutionized sharpening. Since

Figure 5-3. Besides using a straight edge to check the stones for flat (which I find difficult when the stones are wet), you can check by using your flattening stone, which in this case is a diamond stone. A few strokes with the flattening stone will reveal the hollow, stained with the iron removed in sharpening.

Figure 5-4. Here the stone is almost restored to flat.

Figure 5-5. Flat once again.

then, major strides have been made in the quality and type of product available. American manufacturers now make waterstones, and by reports, their product is equal to, if not better than, some Japanese stones. I cannot keep track of all of the different stones. I have settled on a number of stones that serve my needs, so I have not experimented widely with the different ones available. I suggest you consult the woodworking magazine reviews for comparisons of products and systems.

Nevertheless, you have to take some of the tests they do with a grain of salt. It is not simply a matter of which is the best sharpening stone, or the best sharpening system, but the best match, blade to stone. Though I have no verification for this, I suspect the technique used also is a factor in the effectiveness of different sharpening stones. I would not lose sleep at night over matching stone to blade, but some broad categories can be delineated. The clearest distinction can be made between the alloy steels and the carbon steels. Waterstones are much less effective on many of the alloy steels. On some alloys, waterstones do not really cut at all. If your waterstones seem ineffective on your alloy blades, you will have to use diamond stones, paper, and/or paste.

After that, determinations become much more subtle. The Japanese craftsman, intimately familiar with the character of his tools, will prefer different stones for different tools, because he knows that certain matches yield better results. For the rest of us, at least to start out, I would suggest a 1,200-grit stone to start followed by a 3,000 or 4,000-grit

USING AND MAINTAINING WATERSTONES

Before use, synthetic waterstones need to be soaked for at least 10 minutes, or until air bubbles stop coming out of the stone. If they do not have a wooden base, you can store them indefinitely in water. A large lidded plastic tub is good for this. If they have a wooden base, you can still store them in water, but eventually the base will fall off. Synthetic finish stones (#3000 and above) generally do not need to be soaked, but check with the manufacture and/or dealer.

Natural waterstones are never stored in water because doing so causes them to disintegrate. Coarser stones are soaked for five to 10 minutes before using and removed after sharpening. The natural finish stones generally do not need to be soaked, but again check with the seller. Natural stones will often crack, by the way, if they are allowed to freeze, whether dry or in water.

The stones will have to be trued before they are used the first time and frequently as they are used. There are a number of ways to do this. My favored approach now is to use a diamond stone rubbed against the waterstone. I have been using the same diamond stone now for more than eight years and it has not worn out yet, so it is cost effective. Alternatively, you can use sandpaper—220-grit wet/dry on a piece of ¼" (6mm) plate glass laid on a flat surface.

However, you will get only about two flattenings before the sandpaper wears out, so costs can add up. In addition, sandpaper tends to glaze some stones (such as the Bester), so it is not always an option. I have also flattened stones on a concrete block, which works fine until the concrete becomes polished and the block wears out of flat. Also, a special stone is sold just for flattening sharpening stones, which works fine, but eventually it too gets glazed and out of flat.

Some stones are harder than others, so the frequency of flattening will vary. Frequency also varies according to the task. A good procedure is to sharpen your finest smoothing plane blade first, right after flattening the stones. Then follow in order with blades of increasing edge curvature, right down to the jack. That way you can actually use the wear of the stones to help shape the blade edges. You can even set aside old badly worn stones to hone blades of significant curvature (like a scrub-plane blade).

In use, coarser stones are periodically washed clean and kept wet by adding a bit of water from the soaking container. The blade is abraded directly against the stone. The finish stones are kept barely wet, but not allowed to dry out; the slurry is allowed to build up, as this is what actually does the polishing, not direct contact with the stone. Using a *nagura* stone (a chalk stone available where waterstones are sold) raises the slurry more quickly.

intermediate stone, finishing up with a 6,000- to 8,000-grit stone, or finer.

A few other sharpening materials can be useful. I have mentioned diamond stones. These are particularly useful for flattening the back of blades, as you can hone on them almost indefinitely without wearing them out of flat. With a waterstone, if your blade back needs a lot of flattening, the waterstone soon wears out of flat and will have to be flattened again. If you wait too long to do it, the curve of the stone will be honed into the

STONE CHOICES

I use a #1200 Bester ceramic waterstone, an Aoto Mountain Blue Stone (about #3000), and a North Mountain Super Polish Stone (about #8000). I recently purchased a natural finish stone (#4 grade, all I could afford) for my best Japanese plane blades. If you are just starting out, I would suggest a #1000 or #1200 ceramic waterstone, such as the Bester, and a #4000 or possibly #6000 finish stone.

LISTENING

Learn to recognize the sound of the full bevel being stroked on the stone: whenever the blade is rocked or lifted, the pitch of this sound of the blade on the stone will change. It will sound different when just the heel of the bevel is stroked, and different again when just the edge is stroked. In fact, there is a slight bit of difference in sound when pressure is applied more toward the edge than the heel—even though the blade is sitting flat on the stone.

Responding to the feedback that sound gives you is an important lesson that will carry throughout all your work. It can tell you when you a nearing the end of the cut with a handsaw even though you can't see it, when a power tool needs to be turned off—immediately—and investigated for a dangerous problem, and when you have just lifted the blade off its bevel and are starting to cause problems for yourself.

back of the blade, so using a non-wearing "stone" is helpful here **(Figures 5-3, 5-4,** and **5-5** on page 100**).**

If your plane blade back is badly out of flat, it may be faster to use carborundum on an iron plate (*kanaban*) to flatten it. The iron grabs the carborundum and keeps it from grinding the plate (though it will wear out eventually and have to be replaced). (See "Flattening the Back of a Plane Blade" on page 122.)

TECHNIQUE

I learned to sharpen on the floor. It has a number of advantages: you do not need to build a special table and have it take up space in you shop, and sitting, kneeling, or squatting can actually be restful to legs that have been standing all day. However, I do not seriously believe I can convince many people reading this to even try it, though I do highly recommend it.

What I learned from using this position is that it is of little importance whether you are on the floor, sitting, or standing. What is important is the height of the stone relative to the body, and a solid, centered position that allows both movement and stability. The stone should be about 4" or 5" (10.2cm or 12.7cm) below the belly button. Lower than this and your will overextend your arms at the end of the stroke. Any higher and your elbows will be too bent and flailing about. Both positions will cause you to rock the blade on its bevel, rounding it over. Even if you use a jig, this is a good position, because it maximizes the energy of your movement.

Position yourself to maintain good solid balance even at the extremes of each stroke. If standing, have your feet apart, one slightly in front of the other. Feel the bevel lying flat on the stone and learn to recognize the feel and sound when the bevel loses full contact with the stone and rocks. Stop and feel the bevel's position again. Train your body to follow the bevel, to internalize the movement required to keep that bevel flat to the stone, and to maximize the expenditure of energy directly to the cutting edge itself. Have your mind focused on this cutting edge and this bevel in solid contact with the stone, with the body following in total attention and coordination. This is the beginning of skill.

NOTES ON SHARPNESS AND SHARPENING

You can get a polish on new blades and still have deep scratches from the manufacturing that you can't see. Likewise, after grinding a blade you can hone a bright polish on the edge and not have removed all the grooves from the grinding. As well, you can get a wire edge from honing and not have a fully sharp blade. And you're going to have to polish out the broken edge where the wire edge broke off.

Five strokes on a stone (as some would suggest) may turn a wire edge but the blade is not fully sharpened; you're feeling the high points of a dull blade rolled over by the stone; grooves from the previous stone or an uneven edge can remain.

Skipping grits in sharpening is like skipping grits in sanding: you're polishing the high spots between the deep grooves left from a coarser grit. It may work for razors, surgical and kitchen knives, but not so much for plane blades. While you can get an edge that works most of the time and makes nice shavings (in some woods), it won't eliminate tearout when the work becomes difficult; the remaining grooves will tear the wood on difficult grain.

While I don't really think you need more than three stones for most blades, and some can be done with two (I'm not sure most alloy blades benefit from the extra stoning), jumping from a 1,000- or 1,200-grit stone to a 8,000- or 10,000-grit stone is too much. Similarly, finishing with 600, 1,200, or even 3,000 grit on a good carbon steel blade is not going to give you an edge that will stay sharp very long and be able to give tearout-free results.

Listen to the shaving; you can get an idea how sharp the blade is by the sound. The sharper the blade, the quieter the cut; a softwood, cut with a well-sharpened blade, makes very little sound.

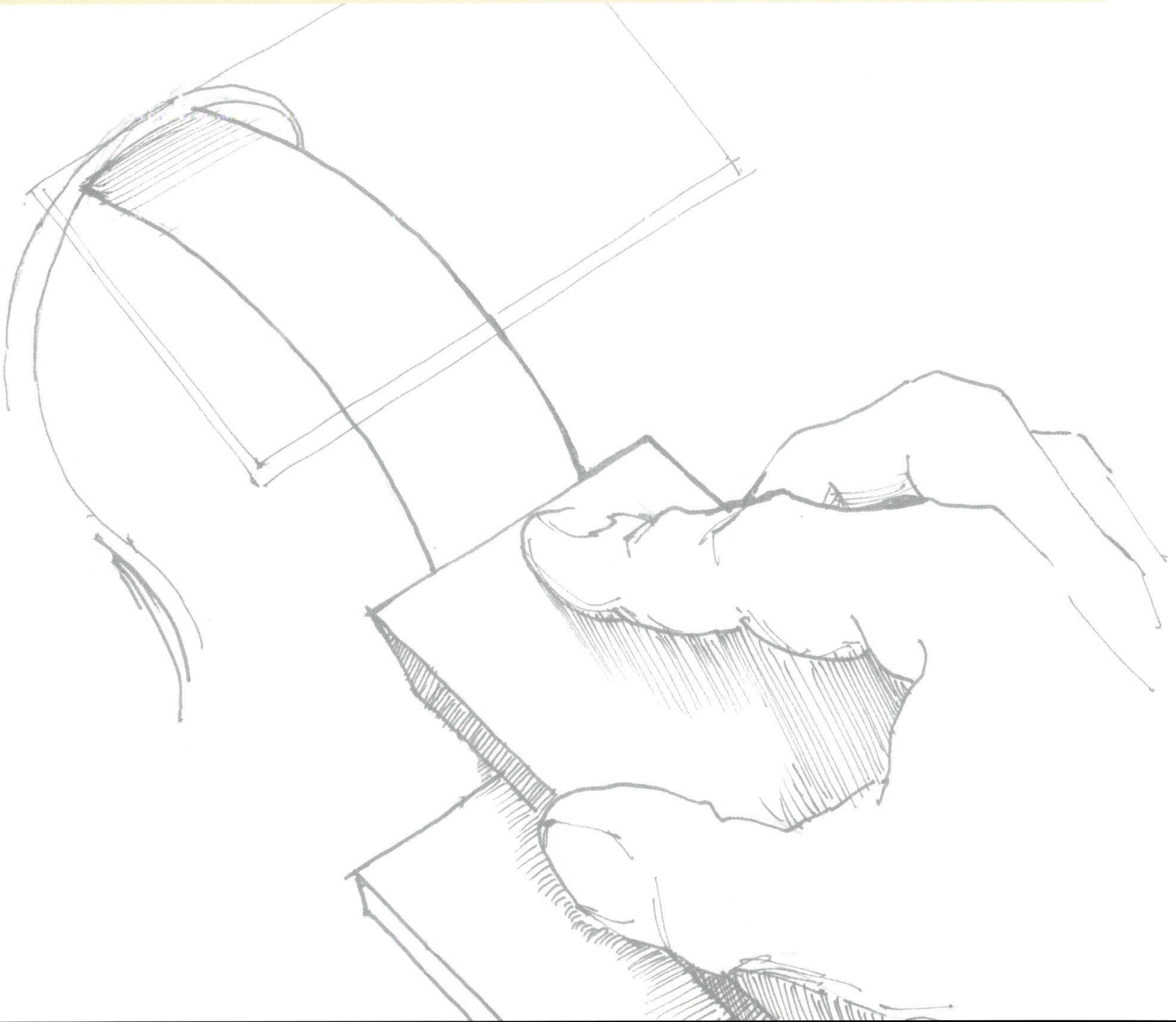

SHARPENING

Years ago, a young man apprenticed to a furniture maker in Japan showed me this sharpening technique. It has served me well. I suspect it will do likewise for you.

Figure 1. Before beginning to sharpen, first find the bevel. You do this by putting one or two fingers down on top of the blade directly opposite the bevel, while simultaneously tilting the blade up with a single finger of the other hand underneath. Tilt the blade up and down with this finger while keeping pressure down on the bevel with the other hand until you can feel the blade rest securely on the flat of the bevel. Do this exercise every time before you start sharpening, and several times during.

Figure 2. Similar to the exercise, when sharpening, the first one or two fingers of the off hand—the left if you're right handed—finds and maintains a steady pressure down on the bevel. At the same time, the right hand lightly grips the blade with the thumb and second finger, maintaining the angle, with the first finger applying downward pressure on the bevel (along with those of the left hand). The third and fourth fingers are lightly wrapped underneath. The number of fingers in each position may vary as sharpening proceeds, but the basic positions of the first fingers of each hand putting pressure on the bevel with the rest of the fingers of the right hand maintaining angle of the blade remain the same. With the longer Western blade, the hand must wrap over the top of the blade. This makes the correct height of the sharpening stones especially important, as a too-high position will result in an awkward turning of the wrist when sharpening. These blades are also trickier as they are thinner and the bevel gives less of a support base, and the long blade makes it easy to lever it out of the correct angle.

When moving the blade back and forth over the stone, the finger(s) of the left hand maintain a constant pressure down on the bevel to make sure it stays in constant contact with the stone. The right hand generally does the moving, assisted by the left hand though neither hand does only one task: they each assist the other.

Listen to and feel the bevel: when you sense you are no longer holding the bevel in constant contact with the stone—stop, relax your hands, do the exercise of finding the bevel, and start again.

Special Note: *Do not* attempt to steady the blade by putting fingers on the stone and dragging them along as you sharpen. This will soon cut through your fingertips, though you will not feel it until after it has happened, resulting in a painful, slow-to-heal wound.

Figure 3. The back of the blade is lapped with a similar grip and pressure distribution as when doing the bevel: the right hands grips the blade with the thumb and second finger, with the first finger putting pressure on the very edge of the blade. The fingers of the left hand also put pressure just at the blade's edge. While the blade is never, ever lifted, the right hand does contribute an upward pressure at the off end of the blade while simultaneously focusing pressure down at the edge. The blade, of course, stays in solid contact with the stone the whole time.

Once you have had some practice sharpening and have gotten a better feel for keeping the bevel, you can begin working on an advanced technique. This is to actually put the focus of the sharpening effort right at the edge while still keeping the bevel flat on the stone when sharpening. It took me a while to discover this: after I got proficient at keeping the bevel flat, I noticed that over time the bevel angle on my laminated blades was getting smaller. I finally figured out that because the edge steel is harder than the backing steel, equal pressure across the bevel will wear away the softer steel quicker, eventually making the bevel angle smaller.

To compensate, I concentrated my pressure when sharpening on the edge itself, while still keeping the bevel flat to the stones. Blades suddenly became sharper a lot faster. To do this, the right hand that supports the blade gives a little bit of pressure—focus—on the cutting edge itself by increasing the support it gives underneath the end of the blade while simultaneously concentrating the front fingers on the edge. I could say something like "the right hand lifts the end of the blade imperceptibly" instead to describe this, but this would give the wrong impression: it is an upward pressure there coupled with focused pressure at the blade's edge (rather than just the bevel). The blade is never actually lifted because this would round the bevel.

The required bit of curvature can be put on a smoothing plane blade by alternately putting pressure on each corner of the blade with the fingers that reside above the bevel. This is done three or four strokes at a time, on each stone. Similarly, pay attention to the distribution of pressure with the fingers. Unequal pressure may result in an unexpected and unwanted blade shape.

CHAPTER

6

HOLDING THE WORK

OF SLAVES, DOGS, AND DEADMEN

Over many generations, European cabinetmakers developed a very sophisticated bench for holding work that was to be planed and joined. This bench, especially when used along with its various accessories, will hold pieces of almost any shape in virtually any of the positions that might be required to effectively work them: shaping, dimensioning, smoothing, joining, whatever. If you work in a variety of styles, especially in the traditional styles, you will eventually have to invest in this classic bench, or one like it.

This large board is held in the front vise and supported on pegs set into the face of the bench's legs while its edge is planed. The ability to hold work securely, and position it quickly, greatly increases productivity.

While there are numerous variations of the European bench, they all have at least one distinguishing feature: a row of dog holes—traditionally square, sometimes round in contemporary versions—into which adjustable height pegs, or *dogs*, are put. Used with a *tail vise* on the end of the bench, the dogs run the length of the bench at regular intervals near the front edge. The tail vise also has one or more dog holes, allowing the user to clamp a length of board between a dog in the bench and a dog in the end vise when the vise is tightened. This innovation allows a variety of shapes and sizes of boards and panels to be fastened securely while they are being planed or otherwise worked, a very helpful feature, especially if the boards don't sit well or if you have to plane across the board.

The bench also typically has a vise on the front (at the opposite end of the bench from the tail vise) that is used to hold work for almost everything else that must be done, as well as being used for holding smaller pieces when planing. This front vise has a number of variations depending largely on the type of furniture being made and the bench's region of origin, and each has its advantages and drawbacks. The leg vise, one of the oldest forms of a vise, can hold a variety of sizes and a limited amount of shapes, but in its traditional form is cumbersome to readjust while working, usually requiring the readjustment of a lower stop to accommodate pieces of different thicknesses, though some new versions have an improved mechanism that makes it as fast as any vice.

The shoulder vise, which is built as part of the end frame of the bench and has the clamping face mounted to the screw with a swivel fitting, can clamp a variety of straight and tapered pieces, but can get in the way when working edges on long pieces, which actually is not that big a problem unless you do large work. The classic woodworking vise we're all familiar with, like the Record, can have a quick-adjustment mechanism, either a lever-operated or a reverse-turn nut-release, making it easy to go back and forth between large and small pieces quickly. But it cannot easily hold tapered or odd-shaped pieces, and eventually the parallel stabilizing rods gets worn enough that the grip becomes unreliable. An Emmert-style vise, designed for use by patternmakers, can hold just about anything, in a lot of different positions; though it can require some jigging if, for instance, you want to shoot the edge of a long piece. Unfortunately it is no longer made and if you can find one, it is expensive.

However, just for planing, the form of the front vise is less important, as any one of the types will hold the work sufficiently.

The main problem I find with the classic European bench is it can be a bit cumbersome or slow when you have to plane regularly shaped pieces, especially when you have many of them to do. On medium-to-small size pieces, the time it takes to dog and undog a work piece is roughly equal to the time it takes to plane a side. Thus, using the bench can double your work time.

Our predecessors noticed the problem. Specialty trades, for instance, often used much simpler benches and holding devises where work could be rapidly repositioned, with fresh pieces quickly replacing the finished ones. Craftsmen often worked by the piece, so speed was of the essence. If you did not have to take the time to turn a crank or vise handle to hold a piece and then turn it again to release it, you were saving time and energy, and making more money. Many of the tradesmen were compensated barely above subsistence as it was.

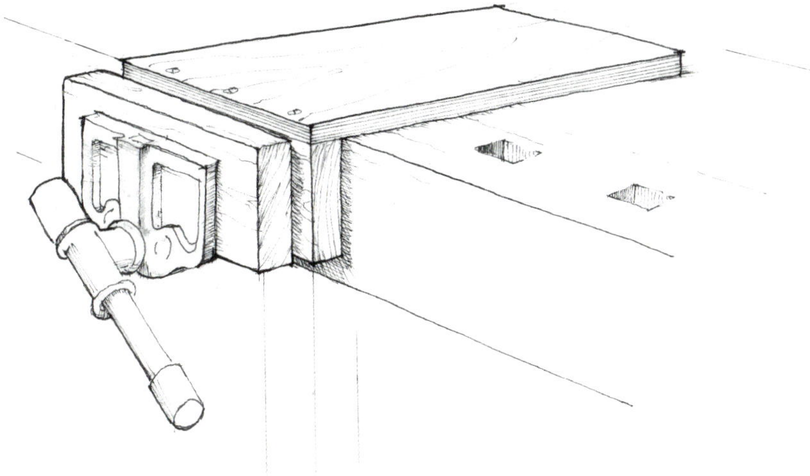

Figure 6-1. For push planes, this simple planing stop clamps in the front vise. The top piece is ½" (1.3cm) thick or less. The block clamped in the vise is preferably solid wood ¾" (1.9cm) thick or thicker.

Simple stop

The vast majority of pieces the woodworker will want to smooth with his plane can be worked against a simple stop fixed to the bench. Although bench dogs and vises of the European bench are useful for holding work pieces while chiseling or shaping as well as planing, it is often not necessary to clamp regular-shaped pieces down to the bench with dogs or other clamping devices just to plane them. A work piece can have its first side smoothed (if it is small, a side can be smoothed in a pass or two), flipped end for end (to maintain the best grain orientation), planed, then turned onto its side and planed, and then flipped again end for end—all without having to reach for a vise handle. You can smooth a stack of parts quickly this way.

For planing, and even for much basic woodwork, you really do not need an elaborate bench. A stout plank with a stop fixed to it often will be the fastest and most effective way to hold the work. This stop should be as wide as possible, not a single iron or wood peg, in order to handle boards of various widths without the push of the plane causing the board to pivot away from you. The stop should preferably be a strip of wood fitted near the end of the planing board in a tapered dado or sliding dovetail so it can be removed or replaced. Or, like I've often seen in Japanese benches, a pressure fit stop, or a pair of them about 3" to 4" (7.6cm to 10.2cm) wide and ⅜" (1cm) thick, that can be tapped up and down, or completely out of the way, depending on the thickness of the work being planed.

A simple planing board, used with a holdfast and a few vise-type accessories, will be quite serviceable, and portable, and will probably serve the woodworker's planing and hand tool work quite well. If you have a

A SIMPLE BENCH

Years ago, in the basement of a house I was renting, I came across a 4x10 (10.2cm x 25.4cm) beam in amongst some scrap lumber, abandoned by the previous tenant. It was 8' (2.44m) long, had a series of pairs of 5⁄16" (8mm)-diameter holes drilled through the broad face down its length, and a ledger screwed along the whole length of one edge. Obviously, someone had intended this to be a workbench, perhaps in the Japanese style. However, as it was, it did not appear that usable to me. Nevertheless, the wood was a nice piece of fir, dry and straight. I used it for years as a portable bench on the worksite supporting it on a pair of workhorses, and gradually became aware of its potential **(Figure 1).**

I have since installed two removable stops of different heights at each end that slide in on tapered dovetails. They can be removed or moved to opposite ends as needed, with just a tap of the hammer. I need stops at either end because I use both push and pull planes **(Figure 2).**

I installed a wooden hook near one end above the ledger similar to the hook on the Roubo bench in Scott Landis' *The Workbench Book* (Taunton Press, 1987). This allows me to set a board on edge on the ledger and push the end of the board into the hook (again, without having to clamp or use a vise) to stabilize it while shooting the edge **(Figure 3).** The ledger along one side can also be used for shooting edges by setting the plane on the ledger with the board flat on the surface of the bench and using the bench as one large shooting board.

Into the holes, I inserted 5⁄16" (8mm)-diameter dowels about an inch longer than the thickness of the bench. As it turned out, most fit snuggly, allowing me to adjust their height by tapping them up or down with a hammer. I generally do not use these as stops because they are rather small, but more for positioning alongside work to keep it from shifting to the side, because of either an irregular end or diagonal planing. If I had to do over again I probably would make the holes ¾" (1.9cm) in diameter so dowels in them would be stout enough to use as stops, and then the holdfast could be used as well in the holes.

When I use the bench in the field, if I need to hold a piece for shaping or cutting, I clamp a large hand-screw clamp to the top at the end. This works quite well and, unlike many vises, will hold tapered pieces **(Figure 4).** If I really wanted a vise, I would probably fix it to the end rather than the face, so as to not interfere with the ledge on the front. In addition, for holding pieces to be shaped, a chairmaker's vise (sometimes called a carver's vise) could be clamped to the top through one of the holes drilled through it, allowing a variety of positions along the bench **(Figure 5).**

For some complex pieces and operations I still have to resort to my European bench, but for most planing operations I find this simple bench very versatile and much faster.

Figure 1. The planing bench in its simplest incarnation, sitting on a pair of workhorses (Japanese-style, in this case).

Figure 2. Full-width stops are fitted into dovetailed grooves near either end, so that they can be easily tapped out and removed or exchanged. Holes have been drilled for holdfasts.

Figure 3. This hook captures pieces for edge-planing when set on the ledger.

Figure 4. Clamp a handscrew to the bench for use as a versatile vise.

Figure 5. A chairmaker's vise can be clamped to the top.

Figure 6. The bench has seen adjustments and additions as I worked with it over time. I placed a couple of stout dowels in the bottom of the bench to fit into holes drilled into the workhorses to keep the bench from scooting around under heavy planing.

Figure 7. I added a tool shelf behind the work surface and added a slotted stop against which I can work. In order to keep the horses from rocking from heavy planing, I pressure-fit a lower shelf on the stretchers of the horses to lock in their placement, pressure-fit the tool shelf, and added diagonal braces. Half-lapped and notched at either end to tightly fit to the top rail and stretchers of the horses, these help make the whole assembly rigid. Moreover, everything disassembles without tools.

Figure 8. The planing bench at its home in the shop. When not being used in the field, the bench rests here atop my tool chests.

European-style bench, however, there are a number of things you can do to speed planing operations.

Adding versatility

To avoid having to repeatedly dog and undog boards you want to surface-plane, or having to install a fixed stop to work against on your bench, you can simply clamp a short board in the tail vise so it projects above the bench top and plane against it. This works best, of course, for short pieces. A device can be made for the front vise of only two pieces of wood to plane longer pieces (**Figure 6-1** on page 109).

For planing the edges of long, narrow pieces that will flex if not fully supported, I put a 4" (10.2cm) handscrew clamp in the tail vise (**Figure 6-2**). On the side of one of the jaws of the clamp, I have glued a strip of veneer (**Figure 6-3**). The veneer allows the other jaw to be adjusted freely when the clamp is held in the vise. When using the clamp, I first adjust it so the jaw opening matches the work it is holding. I position the clamp in the vise at a height that works with the piece I am planing (so it extends above the bench surface less than the height of the board being planed), tighten the tail vise to hold the clamp, and then the clamp to hold the piece.

Figure 6-2. A handscrew clamp in the tail vise is a versatile clamp for holding work to be planed.

Deadmen and helper boys

For planing the edges of long, wide pieces, you can use the front vise to hold pieces up to around 5' (1.5m) long if they are not so narrow that they flex when planed. Longer pieces will have to be supported. There are a number of ways to do this. The first is to build a way into the bench. This assumes you are building your own bench or are willing to do some major modifications to an existing bench.

One way to increase the versatility of the European bench is to build the legs flush to the front edge of the bench and drill a series of ¾" (1.9cm) holes in the front right leg. This allows work up to about 3' (91.4cm) wide (such as a door or tabletop) to be supported on edge, on a dowel or holdfast inserted into one of the holes. The left end clamps into the front vise and the right end sets on the dowel or holdfast. You can drill holes in the left leg as well, as shown here, to aid in positioning large heavy work before fixing it in the vise, but it is not necessary. This works for pieces long enough to span from leg to leg.

For shorter pieces, some sort of helper (often known as a *deadman, slave,* or *helper boy*) is needed. If you are building your own bench, you can build two stretchers in the front, one low and one high, with runners on them to accommodate a traveling helper, similar to those found on Shaker benches. This is a board 6" to 8" (15.2cm–20.3cm) wide with a series of staggered holes that slides back and forth on the stretchers (**Figure 6-4**). Some of the holes match the height of those you drilled into the legs. If you do not have the option (or energy) to build or rebuild the legs on your bench, a portable helper can be made, several designs for which exist (**Figure 6-5** on page 114).

Figure 6-3. Glue a piece of veneer to the side of one jaw to provide clearance that enables the other jaw to be moved while the clamp is in the vise.

Bench dogs

I have several recommendations for bench dogs. First, get rid of the metal ones that came with the bench. Sooner or later—and probably sooner—your plane blade will find them, often at high speed. Not only does this take enormous chunks out of the edge, but it damages the plane bottom as well. In addition, this assumes you do not simply set the plane down on one, nicking the blade or dinging the sole. In fact, remove all metal objects from the bench, including other tools, especially when planing, because they tend to knock into one another. Make new dogs out of wood; you can make lots of them and keep one in every hole to save time.

In general, when planing, I would avoid any of the metal dogs and the variety of metal stops and holding devices available, because even aluminum or

Figure 6-4. Bench Slave

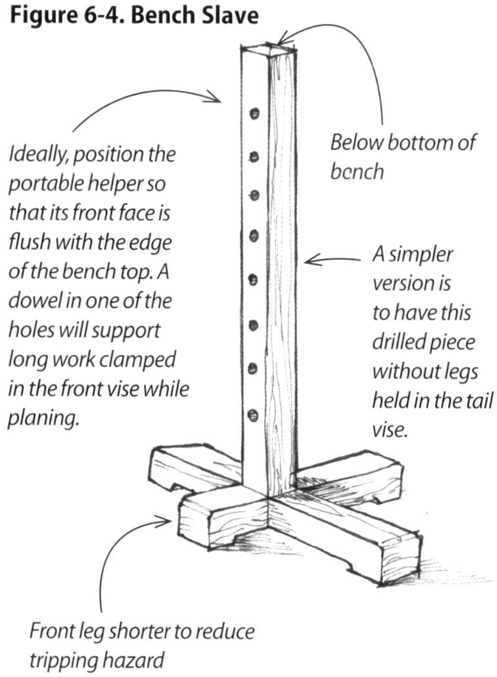

brass is going to at least ruin a good edge, though you might get away without having to regrind. With the Roubo toothed stop, you will definitely have to regrind, or maybe throw the plane away. There's a reason why the tail vise and dogs were invented and this stop pretty much disappeared. Even with its toothed grip (which damages the end of the board), pieces can rotate unexpectedly, especially if you're prepping a rough board that's not sitting flat on the bench. If you're using a holdfast to keep it from rotating, then that's a nuisance that's slowing you down.

Figure 6-5. This European-style bench has peg holes in the legs and a traveling helper that rides on the top and bottom stretchers to help support long and wide pieces when edge-planing.

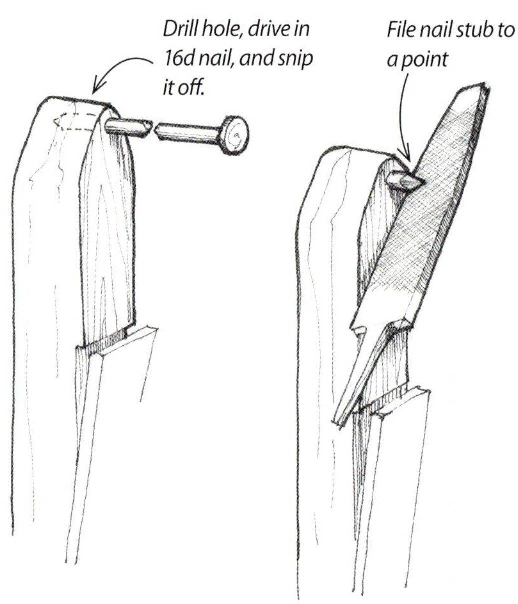

Figure 6-6. Bench Dog with Tapered Head

If you have an opportunity to build a bench, you can put a second row of holes towards the far side of the bench, in line with the first. This is useful for putting extra dogs in to resist the tendency of the board to work free when planing cross-grain, as well as sometimes helpful for holding awkwardly shaped pieces, and for use of a holdfast.

A worthy variation on the bench dog is one that tapers and has a metal point fixed in its face (**Figure 6-6**). This is particularly useful for shaping or planing stock that must be rotated as it is worked. The safest variation has a 10d (or bigger) nail bedded in the face of it. Cut the nail off about ¼" (6mm) or so above the surface and file it to a point. If used frequently, the top of the dog will receive wear from the plane. With the metal point bedded only in the face, your plane does not find metal.

A faster way to make this dog is to drive a screw through the back until the point protrudes from the face. If the pieces you are planing are large and you use the dogs infrequently, these will probably serve as well, especially if you use a trim-head screw and countersink the head. I say probably, because, if you end up using the dogs a lot, you can end up planing the top of the dog down over time and eventually knick your blade on the screw head.

Bailey Pattern Plane

Japanese Plane

Chinese Plane

European Horned Plane

Wood Block Plane

CHAPTER 7

SETTING UP THE PLANES

AND TUNING THEM TO WORK TO THEIR FULLEST

Basic procedures for setting a plane up are performed in a specific order, followed by tweaking of the various tactics—throat opening, blade shape, bevel angle, etc.—which will determine the plane's function. The same basic procedures are followed in the same order:

1. Inspect the plane for condition issues
2. Prepare the blade
3. Prepare and fit the chipbreaker (if there is one)
4. Bed the blade properly
5. Configure the sole
6. Adjust the mouth
7. Attend to the details of the body and sole
8. Attend to the details related to the grip and finish

Refurbishing the sole of an old coffin smoother.

SETTING UP A TRADITIONAL WOODEN PLANE

There are specific things to look for with these planes and some slight differences between the antique planes and the new ones.

1. Inspect the plane: old planes

Inspect the body of the plane. Look for rot, or worse, and more common, beetle holes or wormholes. Avoid these. I once bought a transitional Bailey plane with a few beetle holes—the inside was nearly hollow. Beetle holes appear as tiny pinholes. However, do not mistake holes made from brads used to hold temporary fences nailed on by a previous owner for beetle holes. Holes from brads are acceptable, though sometimes hard to distinguish from the beetle holes.

Often a body will shrink over time, especially if the plane was made on the East Coast or Europe and was moved to the West or Southwest, or was made in China or Southeast Asia and was imported to anywhere in the United States. The body will dry out and shrink around the blade causing the body to crack, or at the very least, warp badly around the blade. If this is not too severe, the opening for the blade in the body can be carefully pared to give the blade more room (once you get the blade out). If it is too severe, you may have to remove too much wood, weakening the body, especially if it is a traditional Western plane, which leaves very little material on either side of the blade.

In this case, the blade may have to be ground down a bit to make it narrower. If the body is cracked at the cheek that holds the wedge, the plane is probably useless, as this area is under a lot of stress, and regluing may not hold (**Figure 7-1**). Minor checks can often be tolerated; cracks around the throat, if not bad, can be injected with glue and clamped, or fitted with wood wedges that are then glued in. Handles can of course be refitted. Twists can be planed out, but if the distortion is too severe, squaring up the body to the flattened sole may remove too much wood at the wedge area on either side of the blade, weakening the plane and leaving it unstable.

Usually the mouth wears open on an old plane. If the plane is to be used for smoothing, a piece can be inlaid into the bottom to close it up. In some cases, install an adjustable throat. This gives the plane some added versatility, plus the throat piece is removable for maintenance or replacement.

Check the condition of the blade and its chipbreaker. Also, check the amount of useable steel left in the blade (**Figure 7-2**). Most old blades are laminated cast steel. With careful examination, the lamination lines can be discerned. Oftentimes, the steel will have been sharpened away, or nearly so, leaving little usable steel edge in front of the slot. Finally, check the hard, brittle-edged steel for cracks and other signs of abuse. Check to see that the chipbreaker does actually work with the blade; sometimes these have been switched.

1A. Inspect the plane: new planes

Manufacturers are producing few new traditional wood-block style planes. Those produced tend to be high-end well-made planes. The new horned-style planes I have seen are also of excellent quality. Both style planes should require only tuning up of the sole rather than the major makeover that is often required of an old, used plane.

With a new wood plane, it is always a good idea to pull the blade/chipbreaker assembly out and let the plane sit for a few months and allow it to acclimate to your shop. If your shop is drier than where the plane was made, this will save you the agony of trying to withdraw a blade seized by a shrunken body and the coincident possible damage to the plane. Waiting for the plane to acclimate before fine-tuning it will save you time in the end. After the plane has acclimated, check the body for twist and check that the blade has enough room on either side for lateral adjustment. If the plane body has twisted, then the blade bed may have some twist as well. Inspect the fit of the wedge to the body and chipbreaker and the mouth opening. Accept no checking or cracking (unless it is cracked around the blade because you failed to remove the blade). While checking or cracking might be tolerated on an old plane, there is no need to have to deal with this on a new plane—it will only get worse.

After you have inspected your plane, either old or new, and have assessed the issues that have to be dealt with, you can begin to set up the plane.

Figure 7-1. This cheek crack (on the left) is precarious, but so far has held.

Figure 7-2. I thought this blade was thoroughly exhausted. If it had been a modern blade, it would have been: modern blades are sheet steel blanks tempered for only the bottom inch or so of their length, after which the blade gets softer and softer and is pretty much unusable the last ¾" (1.9cm) before the cutout. In this case, however, this is from a Stanley #9, production of which stopped during World War II; so it turns out the blade is laminated, and after close inspection there is still a little more than a ⅟16" (2mm) of hard blade steel left. If you used this blade and sharpened two or three times a week, you might still be able to get another couple of years' use out of it.

2. Prepare the blade

A new blade, or an old blade that needs to be rejuvenated, is always prepared by flattening the back first. If there are serious nicks in the blade, the bevel may be ground first to remove them, and then the back prepared. After the back has been flattened to a mirror polish, then the bevel is honed.

THE BACK OF THE BLADE

You don't need to flatten the entire back of a plane blade (as you do a chisel), only the last 1⁄16" (2mm) or so. A big enough area to land the chipbreaker securely and gapless. This area must have the mill or sanding marks, coarser grits, and (on an old blade) all minute pitting totally polished out. Putting a 1° micro bevel here without properly polishing out these marks will leave the blade dull (and yes, you can get a wire edge on a dull blade).

The point of flattening the back of the blade is not so much to flatten the entirety of it, but to guarantee that there is an area at the cutting edge, big enough to support the chipbreaker, that is dead straight and flat, corner to corner, and highly polished. The rest is preparation to ease maintenance in the future, and the low areas behind the edge are somewhat like the hollow ground into the back of a Japanese blade.

In flattening the back, you present the entire back of the blade to the stone, keeping it flat, but you put pressure right at the cutting edge so that there will be a long flat reference plane (probably with some low spots) behind the edge and up to it. The edge itself is flawlessly flat.

Unless the back is badly rolled—the result of sanding in the manufacture of a new blade, or someone's misinformed sharpening job on an old blade—flattening the back overall is not that big a deal. If you can't do it (with proper technique) in less than seven or eight minutes, return a new blade, or debate whether an old blade is worth another seven or eight minutes. And with a new blade that's rolled by sanding, don't bother even starting; take it back.

Listen to the shaving; you can get an idea how sharp the blade is by the sound. The sharper the blade, the quieter the cut; a softwood, cut with a well-sharpened blade, makes very little sound.

Once the back has been polished, sharpening involves only touching up the back on the final polishing stone and not reworking it with all the stones used in first flattening it.

Ideally, the entire back should be flat, in a flat plane the length and width of the usable edge steel. Practically, however, low spots can be allowed in this area as long as the area at the edge itself is at least 1⁄16" wide (2mm) and the full width of the blade. Low areas behind that will eventually get polished out as the blade is sharpened back with use. In the rare case this doesn't happen over time, the back can then be reflattened until the flat area at the blade edge is again continuous.

Before starting, remove the chipbreaker, if attached, and inspect the edge of the blade for damage and the back for rust severe enough to cause pitting that is too deep to be honed out (**Figure 7-3**). Such pits, when the edge is sharpened down to them, will leave a track in the finish work. If the blade is to be used on a relatively rough plane, a jack plane for instance, some minor pitting might be allowed, as the planes to follow will erase any tracks left behind. However, the blade will overheat in the area of these pits, rapidly dulling the blade and necessitating frequent re-sharpening or even regrinding. After inspecting the blade, grind the bevel if necessary to remove any nicks and/or to shape the edge. Flatten the back down to a mirror polish, then go back and sharpen the edge. (See Chapter 5, "Sharpening Plane Blades," on page 92)

3. Prepare the chipbreaker

Inspect the chipbreaker for a damaged or badly formed edge. If the problem is severe, see if you will have enough metal left after removing the damage to have a functioning chipbreaker; if not, replace it. Refine the shape of the top contour so there is a micro bevel that meets the blade at an angle of about 50°, or such an angle that the combination of blade angle and chipbreaker angle totals 90° to 100°. If the particular configuration allows enough material to remain, put a large second bevel of about 25° behind the micro bevel. The second bevel improves chip clearance and helps eliminate throat clogging.

Next, hold the chipbreaker and the blade together in their final position, and then up to a light **(Figure 7-4)**. No light should appear between the edge of the chipbreaker and the back of the blade. Correct the edge of the chipbreaker if necessary, maintaining its geometry, by stoning the underside on a perfectly flat stone **(Figure 7-5)**. If the edge is badly off, careful work with a smooth file may speed this step, followed by careful stoning. Back-bevel the underside of the chipbreaker slightly so that it meets the blade at a knife's edge **(Figure 7-6** on page 124**)**.

Both the underside and the top micro bevel closest the edge should be stoned down to a polish **(Figure 7-7** on page 124**)**. Finish the last strokes of the stoning on the top to ensure that the edge will meet

Figure 7-3. This blade has surface rust with only one bad spot at the corner, which can be worked around.

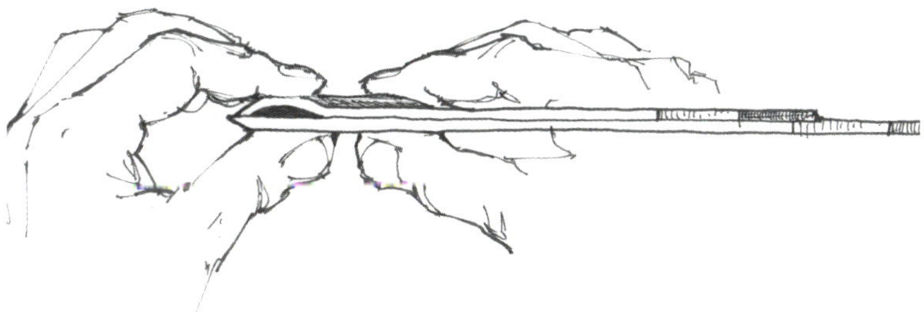

Figure 7-4. Hold the chipbreaker and the blade together in their final position, and inspect the fit.

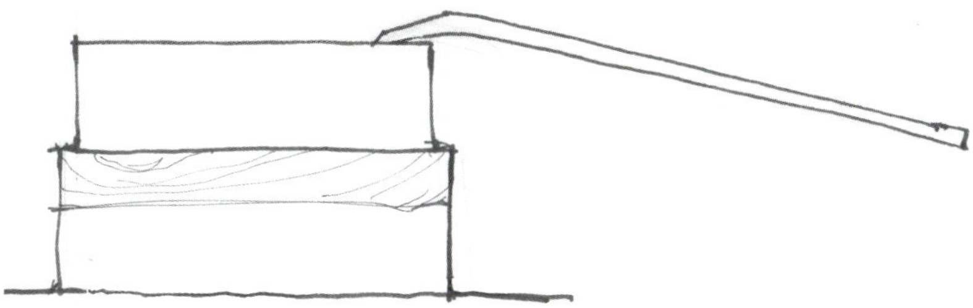

Figure 7-5. Position the chipbreaker on the stone slightly below horizontal to ensure the edge is slightly back-beveled.

FLATTENING THE BACK OF A PLANE BLADE

There are a number of techniques that can be used to flatten the back of a plane blade. Which technique to best choose in flattening a particular blade is dependent upon how much work must be done to get it flat.

No matter which technique you use, you will have to finish with your sharpening stones, and these must be flat, so start by flattening your sharpening stones. (See "Using and Maintaining Waterstones" on page 101.)

Before starting work on the blade, appraise the flatness of the back. Hold the blade up to a large light source, sighting along the blade so that you can catch a reflection that goes all the way across the back. Tilt the length of the blade up and down and study the reflection. If the entire back lights up down to the edge, you have a dead flat blade and you will only have to hone it through your usual series of stones. If, however, only a portion of the length of the blade lights up and this moves up and down the blade as you tilt it, then the blade has a curve to it; the shorter the reflection, the more the curve.

In this case, do not try to flatten the entire length of the blade. Only the lower portion—about ½" (1.3cm) minimum to maybe 1" (2.5cm)—needs to be flattened, depending on your blade's curve. Flattening more is incredibly tedious, requiring the removal of a lot of steel. More importantly, it is not necessary to get a functioning blade.

Finally, look at the back edge. Tilt the blade until the reflection rolls down to the edge. If you have to tilt the blade more than a little to catch a reflection there, or if you can continue tilting the blade and continue getting a reflection, indicating a rounded edge, then a different strategy is called for. In this case, before starting to flatten the back, you should grind the main blade bevel back until the rounding or back-bevel is eliminated.

After you have appraised the condition of the back of your blade, developed a strategy, and made sure your stones are flat, begin flattening by stroking the blade's back on your coarsest stone. Hold the blade perpendicular to the length of the stone, use the entire length of the stone, and as much of the full width as possible, back and forth, keeping at least 1" (2.5cm) or more of the blade on the stone at all times.

Figure 1. To flatten a severely out-of-flat blade on a kanaban (iron plate), put about ¼ teaspoon of carborundum in the center of the plate. Add 3 or 4 drops of water to the carborundum. In the background is a stick that can be used when holding the blade.

Figure 2. Rub the back of the blade back and forth using the whole length of the plate. Use of a stick allows you to increase the pressure on the blade at its edge while reducing finger fatigue. The blade and stick are held with the right hand, with the left hand keeping a constant downward pressure. Do not be tempted to rock the blade. The blade must remain flat on the stone at all times. If you lift the right hand even one stroke you will round the edge enough to require 15 or 10 strokes to remove the damage.

Make sure the blade stays flat on the stone—no lifting or rocking. Keep pressure on the blade right behind the edge to keep from gouging the back. After about 30 seconds to a minute, clean and look at the back of the blade. If the new flat is within about 1⁄32" (0.8mm) of the edge at all places (check the reflection as before), you can probably continue using the waterstones for the whole process, moving to each individual stone as the polish pattern of each becomes continuous across and down to the entire edge.

If you have to spend more than about four or five minutes of continuous work on a waterstone, you will have to re-flatten it before continuing. Therefore, if a minute of vigorous work on the coarse stone leaves more than about 1⁄32" (0.8mm) of edge undone, you are probably better off going instead to a coarse diamond stone to flatten the blade. If not, you can wear your waterstones out of flat, necessitating re-flattening the stones (and most probably the back) several times before you are done. (If you have ceramic or Arkansas stones you can probably do the whole flattening process on either of those. Just make sure they're flat before you start and remain flat as you work as they do wear, albeit much more slowly). After the flat on the back reaches the edge, you can go back and do your normal sharpening sequence on your (flat) stones to polish the back.

If after about a minute on your coarse stone you show the new flat at 1⁄16" (2mm) or more away, consider measures that are more drastic (though you can continue to work away on the diamond stone if you prefer). The cheapest, fastest, and most effective way to flatten a badly out-of-flat plane-blade back is to use the Japanese method of carborundum (silicon-carbide) on an iron plate (*kanaban*). The carborundum particles grip the softer *kanaban* (though it does wear it out—eventually), and abrade the tool steel. The iron flattening plate, at Japanese tool suppliers, is about $14. An ounce of carborundum is about $3, though if you can find a lapidary supply house you can get a lifetime supply for about $5.

The beauty of this method is the grit breaks down as you use it, so you can start with 60 or 90 grit, which is very coarse (for a blade in particularly bad condition), or 120 grit (if you think the blade is not too bad). Either gradually breaks down to about 6,000 grit, while increasingly refining the surface. In one step (and about 5 to 10 minutes of vigorous rubbing), you can go from a nasty old blade to a mirror-polished jewel.

To use the flattening plate, put about ¼ teaspoon of carborundum in the center of the plate and add 3 or 4 drops of water to it **(Figure 1).** Begin rubbing the back of the blade back and forth using the whole length of the plate. Periodically bring the excess carborundum back into the center of the plate so all the carborundum is broken down at the same rate **(Figure 2).** Stray coarse pieces of carborundum will scratch the blade, so make sure it is all used. Continue rubbing as the carborundum breaks down into a smooth paste, occasionally adding a drop or two of water if the paste gets too dry to rub. As the paste gets extremely fine, check your progress; you should see a consistent flat at the edge.

Figure 3. The carborundum has broken down into a paste and is rubbed until dry.

Continue rubbing until the back shows a high polish and the paste is transparently fine and rubbed dry **(Figure 3).** Then add 1 (or maybe 2) drops of water and vigorously rub until the paste is dry again. This will bring up a very high polish. Inspect the blade. Hopefully, the mirror polish of your newly flat back now extends all the way to the edge. If not, you will have to do it again, though you can probably start with 120 or 220 grit now. With the final polish, you do not have to follow up with any work on the stones; you can go right to the bevel.

Make sure to keep the carborundum separate from your stones, because it can embed itself and continue to scratch a blade for a long time. Wash the blade and everything else in separate water and rinse thoroughly.

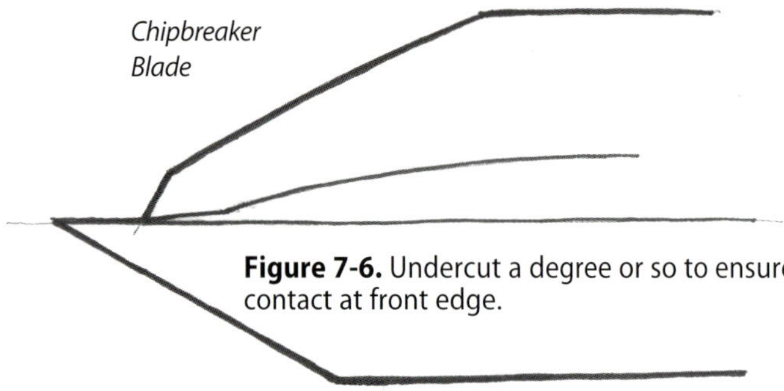

Figure 7-6. Undercut a degree or so to ensure contact at front edge.

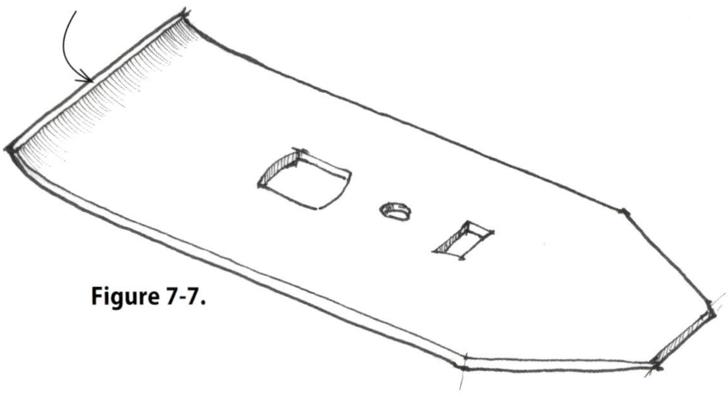

Figure 7-7.

Figure 7-8. Finish the last strokes stoning the chipbreaker on the top edge.

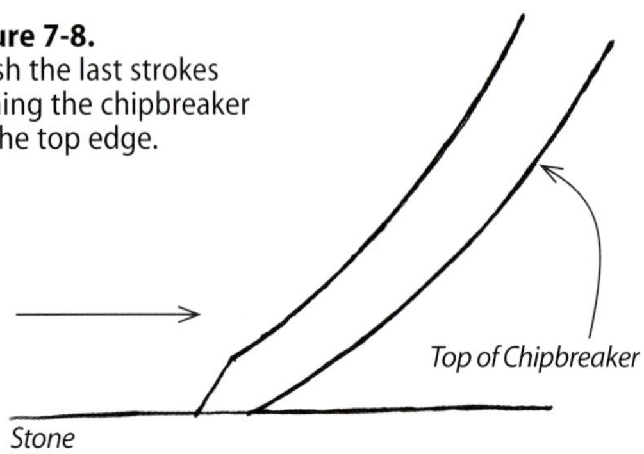

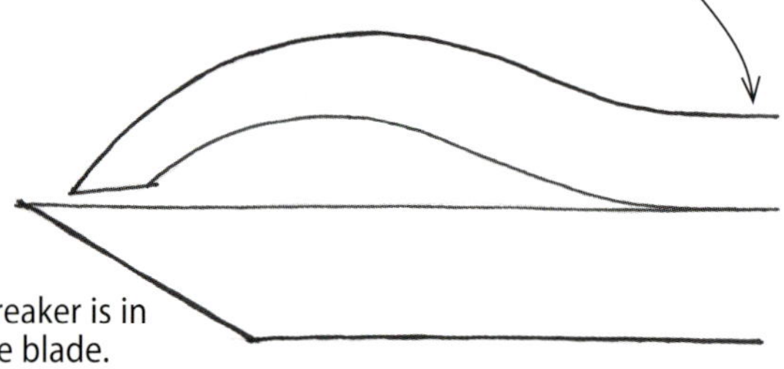

Figure 7-9. Make sure the chipbreaker is in tight contact with the blade.

tightly to the blade (**Figure 7-8**). Make sure there is no wire edge (this may be difficult as the steel is often pretty soft). Hold the chipbreaker and blade up to the light again (**Figure 7-4** on page 121) and check the fit. If the edge appears straight, but is high on one corner and squeezing them together does not close the gap, twist the chipbreaker in a vice until the edge fully contacts the blade and no light shows. Make sure that the chipbreaker is sprung slightly so that tightening its screw attachment brings the edge of the chipbreaker down tight to the blade (**Figure 7-9**). In some cases, the chipbreaker may have to be bent slightly to achieve this.

Attach the chipbreaker to the blade (**Figure 7-10**), adjust its position according to the work to be done, check again, finally, that no light comes through the meeting of the two at the edge, and tighten the screw down.

4. Bed the blade properly

If your plane block has shrunk, you may first have to widen the escapement where the blade and chipbreaker fit. You will also need a little additional room (± 1⁄32", or 0.8mm) to allow for lateral adjustment. If you have to remove a lot of wood here, and you are afraid it might weaken the plane, you may have to grind the width of the blade and chipbreaker down. (Remember, if the plane is twisted as well, you will be removing some material later from both sides.)

Determine that the notch for the chipbreaker screw is big enough, correcting as necessary by careful paring with a sharp chisel.

Check the blade seat for flatness and lack of twist by sighting down the ramp or blade bed (**Figure 7-11**). Carefully pare this with a chisel (or you can use a float if you have one) to take out the twist. Once you have the twist out, as best as can be visually determined, begin seating the blade. Screw the blade and chipbreaker together with the chipbreaker in its final position. If you have a tapered blade, check to see that its back (underside) is arched along its length. If it is, you will have to pay particular attention to the bed down near the sole and at the top of the plane, as that is where the blade will contact it. If your blade is parallel and not arched (some will arch with the chipbreaker attached), you will have to make sure the blade is contacting the bed at least at the bottom and top, similar to the tapered blade, and that it is not sitting on a high spot in between.

With both blades, you can check the flatness of the bed top to bottom with a small straightedge, and correct as necessary. After that, you will have to use one or a combination of techniques to finalize the fit. First, set the blade/chipbreaker assembly onto its bed in its approximate final position and hold it down in the

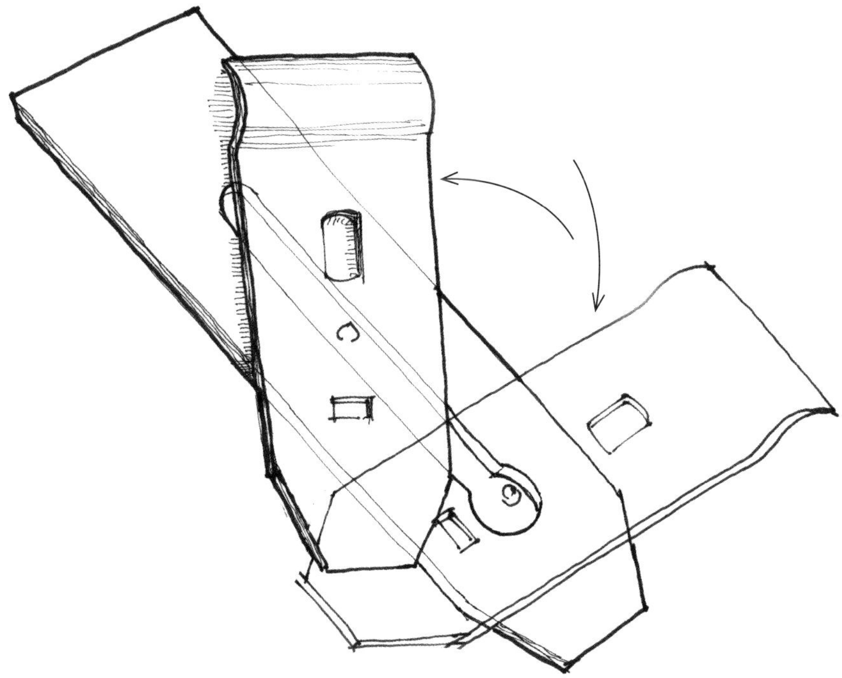

Figure 7-10. To avoid damaging the edge of the blade, always install the chipbreaker at the top of the blade (no matter which end of the blade the hole for the screw is located) rotating the chipbreaker over the blade and down into position.

Figure 7-11. Blade Bed

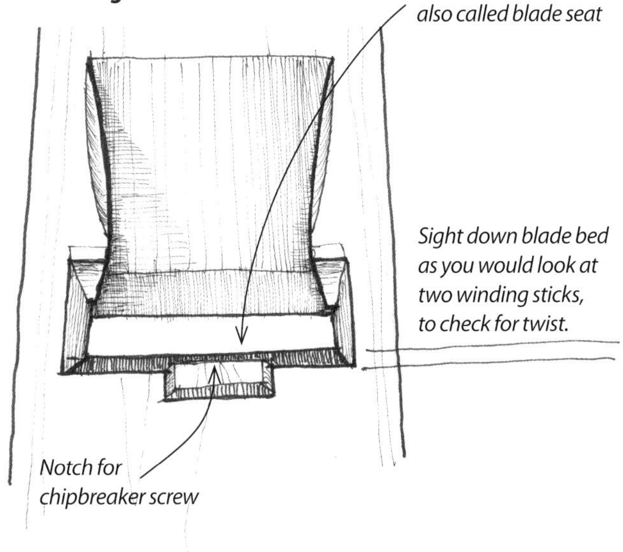

CHECKING FOR A CUSTOM FIT

In some rare cases, the wedge or blade seat, or both, may have been custom-fitted to the hand-wrought blade assembly and will appear to be twisted or out of parallel. Check the blade assembly for matching eccentricities, and then put the blade into position and operating tightness.

Inspect the fit, checking especially that the blade beds solidly, especially at the heel, and the wedge is tight all around. Check visually, tapping and pushing, looking (and listening) for deflection. If it appears contact is good, and the blade does not chatter in use, then you are all set. If it chatters, see "Troubleshooting" on page 146.

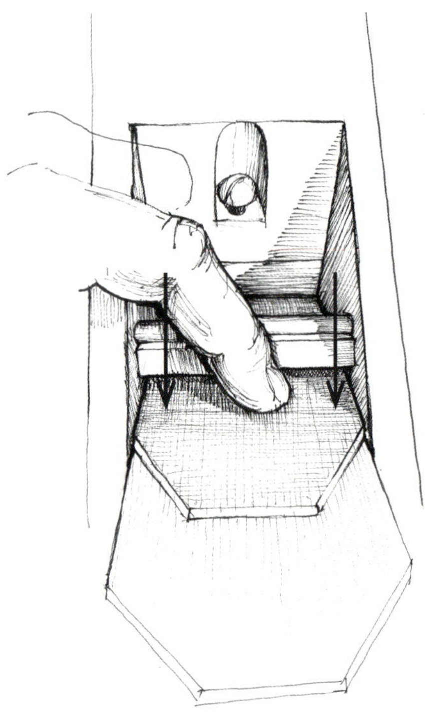

Figure 7-12.
Check the fit of the blade by tapping it on each of its corners.

center with one finger. With a finger of the other hand tap the four corners one by one (**Figure 7-12**). They should make little or no noise when tapped: if you hear a clicking or tapping sound on one or opposite corners, that (those) corners are low.

Pare the high corners until all the corners are silent when repeating the test. In addition, you can use the Japanese technique of rubbing pencil lead on the back of the blade and then rubbing the blade assembly in its position on its bed. Where the lead has rubbed off are the high spots. Pare these away with a chisel, and repeat the process until you get solid bearing across the bed at least at the bottom and the top. This last technique is particularly good for fine-tuning the fit.

Once you are confident the blade/chipbreaker assembly is well bedded, check the fit of the wedge to the assembly: chipbreakers often have a singular curve and the wedge must fit well. (They can sometimes be carelessly switched). Adjust the fit as necessary. The wedge must also fit its abutment on the body. The angle must be correct so it is in continuous contact with its abutment, and both sides must be equally tight. You can check for equal tightness by tapping the wedge lightly into position (with the blade in) and pulling from side to side: both sides should have equal resistance to withdrawal. If one side pulls free easier than the other, that side is not as tight. Remove a very thin shaving off the top of the tighter of the wedge until, when tested, the resistance is equal. Check the fit one shaving at a time; and do not distort the angle of the taper.

5. Configure the sole

This is the basic concept for flattening and configuring the sole of a plane that I use: instead of trying to make the entire sole of the plane flat within a very close tolerance, only a minimum of three narrow parallel areas, ± ¼" (6mm) wide across the width of the sole, need be in line with one another and contacting the work. Areas in between these are relieved slightly (± 0.002", or 0.05mm) to reduce maintenance. There are always at least two areas in front of the cutting edge, one at the front and one at the mouth of the plane, that form the basic reference area for moving the plane over the work. And there is always at least one behind the blade, its location dependent on the task the plane is expected to do—dimension, true, or smooth. And on longer planes, especially truing planes, there are more than three contact planes.

Based on practical experience and the traditional practice of Japanese woodworkers, I suggest a further refinement: you can relieve the reference area(s) behind the blade a small amount instead of keeping it in the same plane as the two (or more) areas in front of the blade. The actual amount depends on the task the plane is expected to do. My suggestion is, planes used for truing a surface, such as jointers, have their reference surfaces all in the same line. Smoothing planes should have the reference area behind the blade relieved ever so slightly to facilitate the plane reaching into any very slight low areas of the work that might remain from previous preparation.

MARKING

Because the surface of the blade bed on an old wooden plane may be darkened with age and dirt, pencil lead may not read very well marking high spots for shaving. Try a China marker (wax pencil); crayon in red, blue, or white; machinist's bluing; or, surprisingly, Vaseline, which will leave a glossy mark in contrast to the dull, darkened surface. Because the bearing area may be rather small, sometimes you may have to recoat and reinsert the blade several times to get a reading.

Jack planes could, at your discretion, have the reference area behind the blade relieved slightly more than what the smoothing plane is relieved to make it easier to attack areas when initially dimensioning a piece. Configuring the sole like this, besides facilitating maintenance and the task the plane is expected to do, also helps deal with the continued distortion of the sole that results from the blade-fixing action of the wedge or lever cap tending to push the sole down. This stress is dynamic and changes easily. In order to deal with this variable, I do not have any reference areas right there in my planes, but further back beyond the blade bed area (**Figure 7-13** on page 128).

Doing the work

A wood plane bottom flattens differently than a metal plane bottom. First, it is never sanded. I know this goes counter to most of what you will read, but there are good reasons for it. Sanding embeds grit into the bottom of the plane and is released gradually during use of the plane. (For the same reason, you should never plane a surface that has been previously sanded,

WHAT REALLY HAPPENS

If you examined what happens when a plane cuts, it might appear the area behind the blade should be exactly in line with the blade edge and project more than the two areas in front—much like how the outfeed table of a power jointer is set up—nearly even with the cutters.

In practice, however, it is often helpful to slightly relieve the third working surface, not only from the blade edge, but often from the other two leading surfaces as well. This is because as the blade edge wears, it withdraws—gets shorter (see "How an Edge Dulls" on page 55)—and a plane bottom that was fixed even with the sharpened edge would soon hold the worn edge off the work.

Figure 7-13. Contact Areas

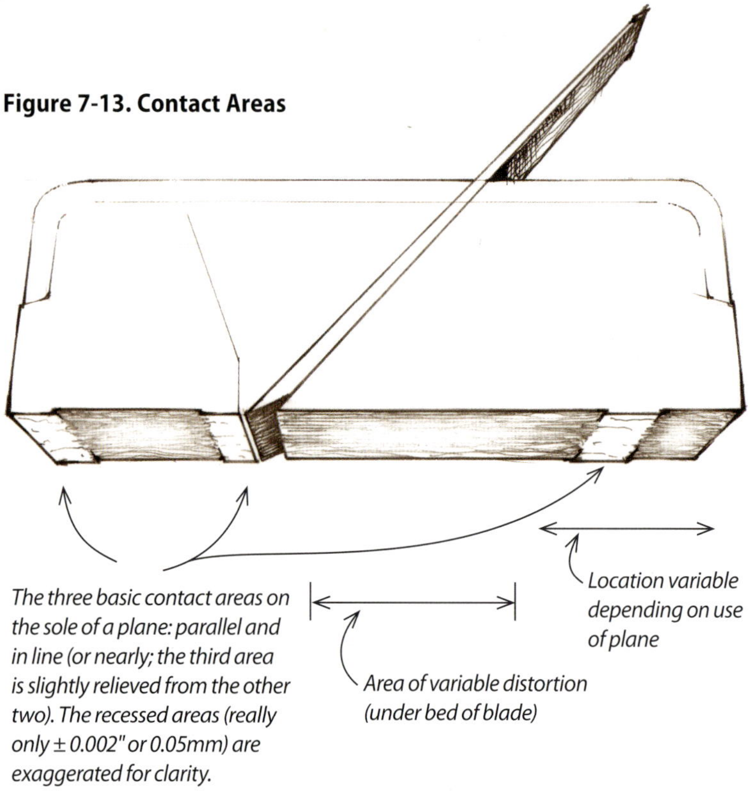

as the grit left in the surface will also rapidly dull a plane blade.) Anyway, sanding is too slow and tedious if any amount has to be taken off, and too indefinite in its results.

If you are setting up a large antique or used plane for the first time, it may require a fair amount of work. With the blade wedged down to working pressure (this is important!), but retracted from the bottom about 1⁄16" (2mm), put a straightedge across the area immediately in front of the mouth and check to see if this is straight (**Figure 7-14** on page 131). On an old plane, chances are you will find a worn hollow; the whole of the plane's sole will have to be brought down to this level until this area is straight and crisp at the mouth. Check the body for twist with winding sticks, and then check along its length.

If the plane must be corrected 1⁄16" (2mm) or more, then you will want to run it over the power jointer, or plane it carefully with another plane (**Figure 7-15** on page 131). (When running a plane over the power jointer, always remove the blade assembly! There is too much danger that the blade will loosen under the vibration of the cut or more material will be removed than anticipated, and the blade will contact the power jointer's cutters, an extremely dangerous occurrence. After the work with the power jointer, the blade assembly can be reinstalled to finish preparing the bottom.) With either the power jointer or another plane, remove as little material as possible. The first cut with either should remove just a whisper of a shaving. Better to remove too little than misjudge and remove too much. The best technique will be a series of light passes, each cut being as productive and removing as little material as possible.

GENERAL TECHNIQUES FOR ADJUSTING THE PLANE BLADE

Adjust the blade by turning the plane over and sighting down the sole from the front of the plane **(Figure 1).** Hold the plane so that the background or lighting provides contrast between the black line of the blade protruding and the light reflecting off the sole. Using the plane's adjustment mechanism, advance the blade until you can just see it begin to protrude below the sole as a thin black line. Adjust the blade laterally until this line is parallel to the sole. Advance or retreat according to your best guess of the depth of shaving you want. Make a trial and readjust as necessary.

Needless to say, sometimes the blade can be hard to see, especially if it is set fine, you are a beginner, or you have aging eyes—or all three. Sometimes you find the black line you thought was the blade was actually the bed of the blade—and you wondered why the blade stubbornly refused to cut. Sometimes on a steeply pitched blade, there is too little contrast between the blade and the sole of the plane. In this case, you are better off sighting down the sole from the back where the light will shine off the bevel of the blade and contrast with the mouth opening **(Figure 2).**

Another technique some woodworkers recommend, and one I use to supplement the others, is lightly feeling the protrusion of the corners of the blade with your thumbs. This would seem to risk cutting your thumbs, but the technique is quite common, and I have seen both Westerners and Japanese craftsmen use it. It is a good way to tell if the corners of the blade are protruding evenly, though I have yet to get the hang of using this technique to the exclusion of the others **(Figure 3).**

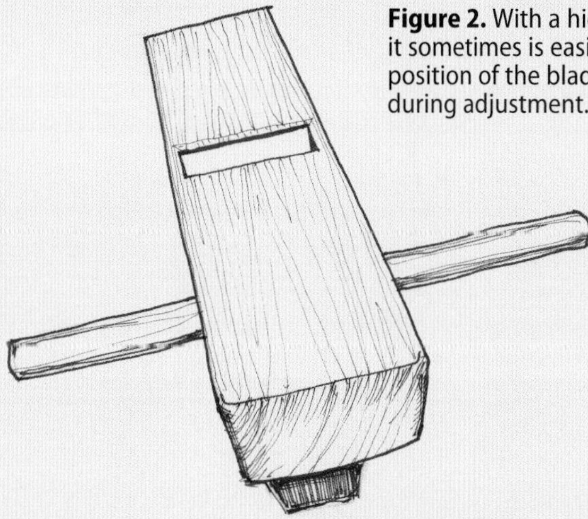

Figure 2. With a high-pitch blade, it sometimes is easier to see the position of the blade from the back during adjustment.

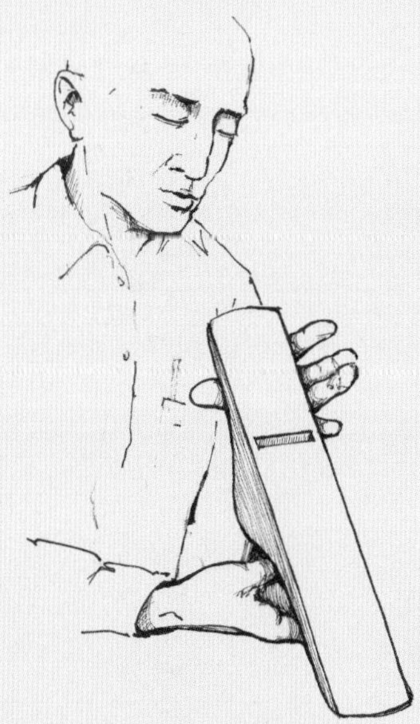

Figure 1. Sight down the sole of the plane to see the depth the blade is set at.

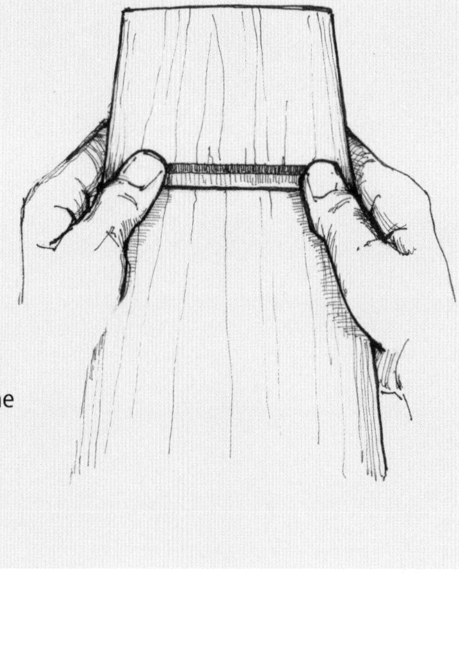

Figure 3. Use your thumbs to check that the corners of the blade are set equally.

ADJUSTING A WEDGED, TAPERED BLADE

Set the plane down on a clean wooden bench and carefully insert the blade until it just touches the bench. Hold the blade down tight to the bed with a finger and insert the wedge without moving the blade's position **(Figure 1A).** Push the wedge tight with your hand so the blade will not move (or fall out). Tap it gently with the mallet to lightly set it. Turn the plane over and sight down the sole to see how deeply the blade is set.

Holding the plane upside-down with one hand with a finger (or fingers) and putting pressure on the blade to keep it from falling out (just in case), lock the elbow of your other arm to your side (to increase accuracy) and tap the top of the blade to set it deeper. Tap the back top of the plane body (or the striking knob) to back the blade off. Tap the side of the blade to adjust it laterally.

Each time you move the blade with a tap, tap the wedge to snug it up (do not over tighten, however): since the blade is wedge shaped, every time you set it deeper it loosens. Remove the blade by tapping it deeper (to loosen it), then tapping to back it off to loosen the wedge. Keep a grip on the blade with your non-striking hand at all times **(Figure 2A).**

Adjust a wedged parallel blade similarly, except the blade will not loosen as it adjusts down. It may loosen however, when adjusting the blade back and forth, so it is a good idea to give the wedge a light (I emphasize light) tap with every two or three adjustment taps of the blade, to keep the wedge from loosening unexpectedly.

On planes with a tension rod holding the blade assembly, such as the Primus, adjusting the blade down will tighten the tension rod. If you are not careful, you can overtighten the rod and damage the plane. Usually you have to adjust the tension as you go if you are making significant blade adjustments.

Always store the plane, even if overnight, with the wedge and blade loose—with only enough pressure to keep the blade from falling out when the plane is picked up. If storing the plane for a long time, remove the blade and wrap it in a lightly oiled cloth.

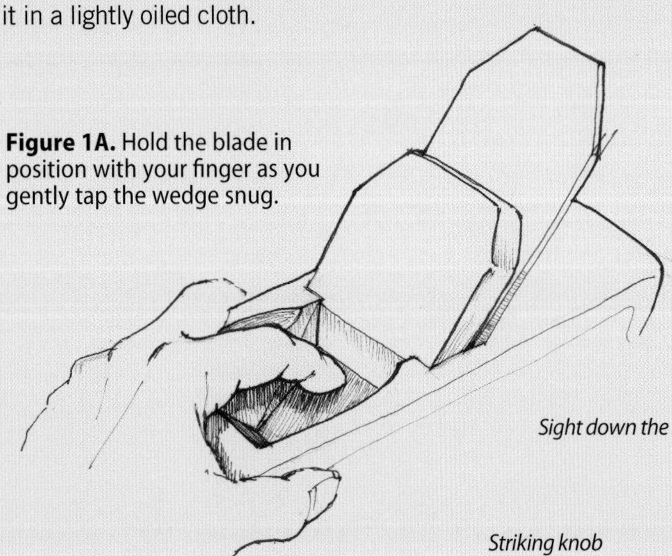

Figure 1A. Hold the blade in position with your finger as you gently tap the wedge snug.

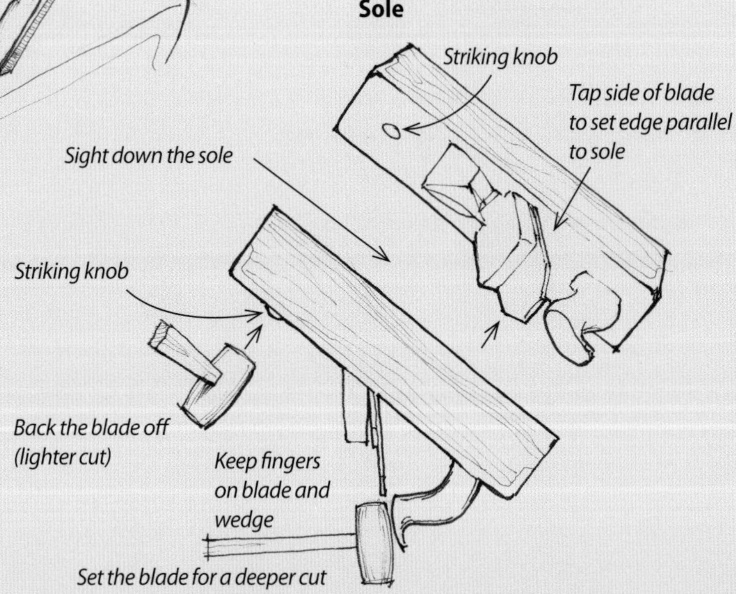

Figure 2A. Sight Down the Sole

Once the planing has flattened the sole (there generally will be no areas of the color of the old wood left where the critical reference areas will be), check to see that the sides of the plane are square to the sole. Make corrections by setting the newly corrected sole against the power jointer's fence or by using a jointer plane. With either method, check your progress frequently with a square. Also, carefully watch the areas at either side of the blade. You do not want these to get too thin. In some cases, the best you may be able to do is to establish a basic reference area that is square to the sole, and you will have to stop short of surfacing the whole side.

Reinstall the blade assembly (again with the edge withdrawn from the sole about 1⁄16", or 2mm) and check the sole with a straightedge. There should be only a couple hundredths of an inch variance. If more, carefully plane the high spots with a finely set plane or a handled cabinet scraper, just until the three critical areas of the sole contact, or nearly contact, the straightedge. Refine the sole further, if necessary, with judicious scraping.

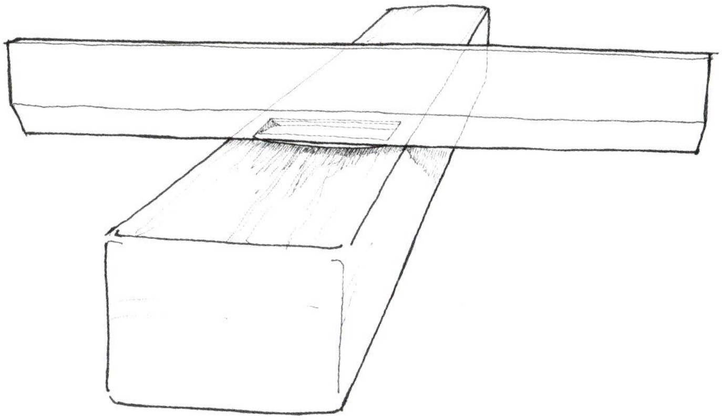

Figure 7-14. Check with a straightedge to see if the mouth is worn.

Figure 7-15. This jointer plane is badly twisted, so areas are being hand-planed first to give good registry on the power jointer.

I do not recommend the Stanley #80 for the task because the blade-adjustment mechanism flexes the scraper blade into an arc, resulting in a concave cut. You want a flat cut, so a handled scraper with a flat bottom, and a straight blade is the best tool. A Japanese scraper plane, made for tuning up the soles of wooden planes, is a good choice, though it is made for work across the grain and the commonly available smaller ones are a little less efficient in truing up large areas. Many Japanese craftsmen make their own scraper planes in larger sizes, often with 70mm (2¾") blades, in order to more effectively flatten the soles of their larger planes.

Once the sole is flat within a couple of hundredths of an inch, you can begin refining it. If the plane is for rough work, this might actually be flat enough, but for any other type of plane, it must be further refined. Check with a straightedge again that the area in front of the mouth was flattened by your

A TWISTED PLANE

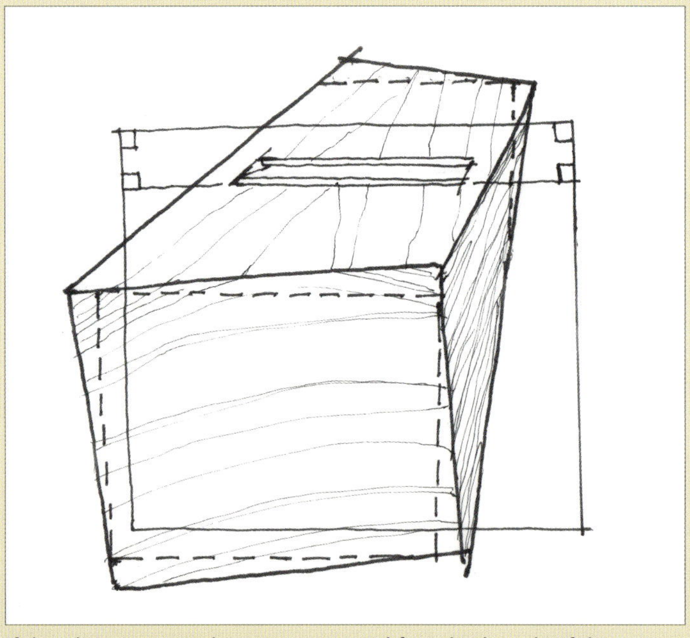

If the plane is twisted, remove material from both ends of the plane equally to bring these areas into line with the throat. This will preserve your best chance of keeping the blade seat square to the length of the plane.

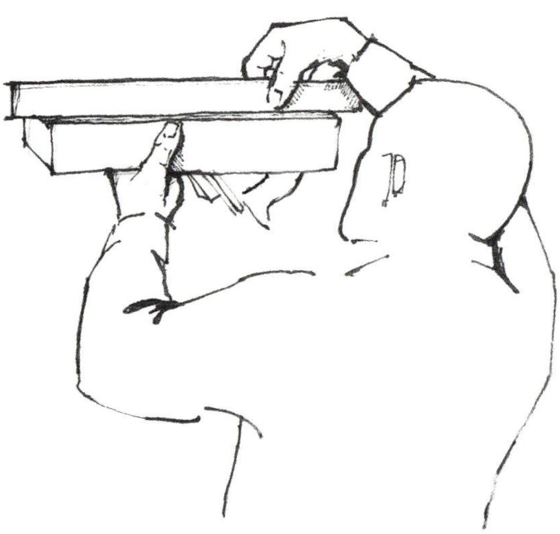

Figure 7-16. Check the configuration of the sole by putting a straightedge against it and holding it to the light. Light will shine through where the straightedge does not contact the sole.

work so far and is not still worn hollow; straighten this out if it is, re-leveling as required (hopefully your earlier work removed all of this). I usually use a Japanese scraper plane. Using a card scraper is another option, but it is a bit more difficult. Check the length for high spots and the three critical areas with winding sticks again for twist. With a scraper or scraper plane, lower the areas between the critical areas until there is the barest bit of light showing against the straightedge **(Figure 7-16)** then bring the critical areas into line **(Figure 7-17)**. This may require the non-critical areas be lowered again, and going back and forth until the critical areas are all in a plane, and the areas in between are slightly lower. The relieved areas are only several thousandths of an inch lower than the contact areas, perhaps slightly more so on a roughing plane, less on a fine smoother. I usually smooth the roughness left by the Japanese scraper with a card scraper, being careful to enhance and not destroy the geometry I have carefully constructed. The whole strategy of relieving non-critical areas simplifies maintenance of the sole as you are only maintaining the relatively small contact areas in a plane, rather than the entire sole.

6. Adjust the Mouth

On an old plane, the mouth most likely will be worn open and will have to be closed down by inlaying a new piece into the sole in front of the blade (new wooden planes will have a mouth sized for its intended use, or will have an adjustable mouthpiece). Use the same wood, if you can, as the body, or build a 3-layer sandwich with the center made of the same wood as the plane, and the surface material of very hard wood, such as ironwood (ipé) or lignum vitae. The inlaid piece should be about ⅜" (1cm) thick or thicker, depending on the throat configuration, but the surfacing material only has to be about ⅛" (3mm) thick. Making the core material of the inlaid piece out of the same wood as the body of the plane will help reduce the chance that it will shrink at a different rate and separate from or crack the body (see "Fitting a Sole Plate at the Mouth of a Plane" on page 136). If you expect the plane to perform a lot of fine smoothing work for which it will depend heavily on the condition of the mouth, you might want to inlay a ¼" (6mm) thick piece of brass (**Figure 7-18**). It will wear better than wood and it need not be so big that the amount of friction noticeably increases and it becomes difficult to work or install.

You might want to consider inlaying a movable mouth, similar to those on the Reform planes. The process is very similar to inlaying a fixed sole plate, but it adds versatility, allowing the plane to be used for a coarser or finer work, as desired. In some respects, it is easier to do, in that a tight-fitting mouth is accomplished by loosening a screw and moving the piece closer to the blade, rather than by delicate paring. Also, it can be longer lasting because as the sole wears and is repeatedly flattened, gradually opening the mouth over time, the movable sole plate can be moved

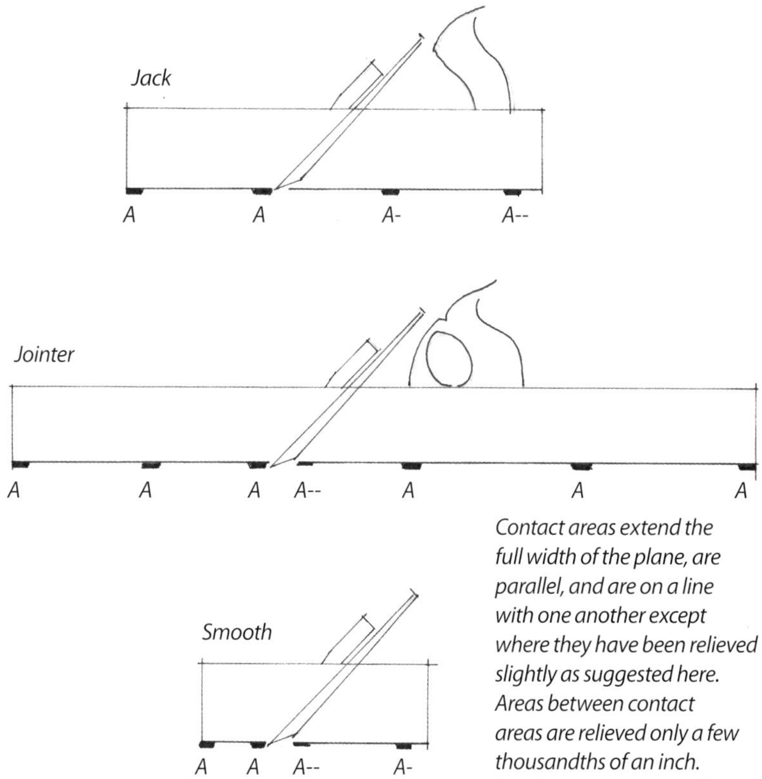

Contact areas extend the full width of the plane, are parallel, and are on a line with one another except where they have been relieved slightly as suggested here. Areas between contact areas are relieved only a few thousandths of an inch. A to A-: 1 or 2 passes with a card scraper; A to A--: 2 to 4 passes with a scraper.

Figure 7-17. Schematic of Contact Areas of the Sole of the Western-Style Wood Plane

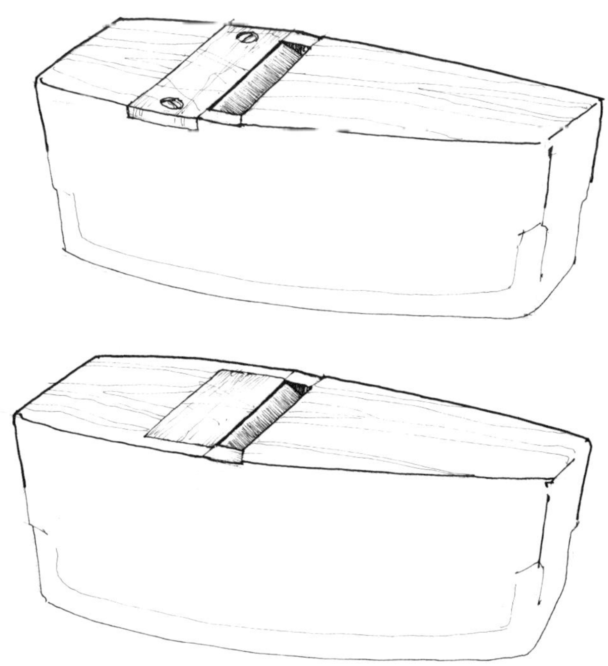

Figure 7-18. Tighten the mouth of an old plane by installing a brass plate, as shown in the drawing at top. I have also seen iron plates used in old repairs. Another option is inlaying a hardwood piece, as shown at the bottom.

THE OILER

For all styles of planes and planing, it is helpful to have a large oiler sitting on the bench. Drag the sole of the plane over it (backward) periodically while working, to keep the sole of the plane—and the blade edge as well—lubricated while working. This allows planing rhythm to be virtually uninterrupted.

The oiler should be around 3" (7.6cm) in diameter: a lidded canister, a drilled out block of wood, even a low wide tin can, or, traditionally, a large bamboo knuckle. Rip rags to about 3" or 4" (7.6cm or 10.2cm) wide. It will take most or all of a bed sheet. Wrap the rags continuously in a coil until you reach the desired diameter—usually slightly larger than the hole it is to go into. Wrap the end to be inserted with heavy plastic such as a plastic drop cloth or Visqueen, and work the whole roll into the hole. About ½" (1.3cm) or more of the cloth should protrude from the container; cut the plastic off even with the container. Saturate the cloth with camellia oil (available at Japanese tools suppliers), which provides light, contaminate-free lubrication.

Two oilers, both made from a section of bamboo. The larger one is about 3" (7.6cm) in diameter and sits on the bench when used. Take the plane to the oiler and stroke its sole over it during planing as part of the rhythm of work. The smaller one is about 1½" (3.8cm) in diameter and is picked up to be used.

closer to the blade to compensate, rather than having to replace a fixed piece.

After you have finished fitting the sole plate, you will have to go back and touch up the level of the plate to make sure it is in the plane of the other contact areas. Have a contact area about ¼" (6mm) long by the width of the sole right at the mouth and relieve the rest of the sole plate to make sure the leading edge of the plate does not catch the work.

Test what you have done: tap the blade out to a working position, to take a light cut, and make a trial shaving. Because the blade is sharp, if it will not cut, the sole is not flat—and make sure the board you are planing is flat. Back the blade off just enough to clear the bottom, and check for flat. A wood body is more flexible than an iron body, and the dynamics of the sole configuration may change slightly when the blade is finally adjusted to its working depth. Touch up the bottom, and try another cut; the degree of flatness will determine how fine a cut you can make. Continue this process until the plane makes the cut you want.

7. Attend to the details of the body and sole

After flattening the sole, I like to relieve the long edges on either side of the sole with a chamfer of just a few degrees just to the edge of the blade opening. This reduces the area of the sole that must be maintained, simplifying future maintenance. I also like to make a relief cut on either side of the blade opening to make sure this area is not high (it's easy

GETTING RID OF THOSE BURNISHING MARKS

#1

#2

#3

If you've ever had trouble with remnants of shavings bunching up at the corners of your blade, causing burnishing marks or the plane to ride up and not cut, try modifying your sole with this refinement. This cut is common on Japanese planes (called a "mimi"), but I have occasionally found something similar on old wooden Western planes. The cut seems to allow the dregs of the shaving to escape out the side.

Figure 1. Make a vertical cut at the edge of the bed of the blade, angled back slightly, perhaps 1⁄32" (0.8mm).

Figure 2. Make a shallow cut starting at the line of the mouth opening (careful not to cut into the edge of the mouth) back until you meet the first cut at about 1⁄32" (0.8mm), and then rotate the chisel to meet the angle of the first cut, freeing the chip.

Figure 3. On most planes (except the jointer, usually) I cut a slight chamfer down both sides of the sole from the side of the plane to the mouth opening, angling off about 1⁄32" (0.8mm). This reduces the area of the sole that I need to maintain flat.

to miss when conditioning the sole), and to help eject chips that tend to collect at the corners of the blade. The leading edge of the sole should be crisp to prevent shavings from sliding under the plane while working, so do not round this edge.

8. Attend to the details of the grip and finish

If flattening and straightening removed some of the plane's original chamfers, you can reinstate them if you want, or make new ones to suit your hands. Totes can be repaired, remade,

Figure 7-19. Round off the back of a horned plane and relieve the little ridge alongside the horn to fit more comfortably in your hands.

FITTING A SOLE PLATE AT THE MOUTH OF A PLANE

Every plane should have a mouth opening sized to the task it is to perform, Or, said another way, the mouth opening should not be much larger than the thickest shaving the plane is expected to make. The performance of every plane in general—and a smoothing plane in particular—will improve if it has a sharp, properly sized mouth opening.

Fitting a sole plate at the mouth of a plane is a good way to restore an old wood plane whose mouth has worn and become too open to give the best performance. Many old wood planes are quite affordable, have good quality cast-steel blades, decent chipbreakers, and many years of service left in the bodies. Repairing the mouth opening with a sole plate will rejuvenate such planes, giving exceptional value for the effort.

Rather than chiseling an opening for the plate by hand, this technique uses a router and a custom-made template. Though time is spent making the template, I believe this is offset by the speed, and in particular, the accuracy of the router in cutting the flat bottom recess, which is difficult to do accurately by hand. Reuse the template for sole plates on planes with the same blade width.

The sole plate, the piece used to repair the mouth, should be the same species of wood as the body of the plane, with the grain oriented the same way—traditionally, flat-cut with the bark side down. It should be ½" to ⅝" (1.3cm to 1.6cm) thick, about as wide as the plane body, and long enough for several repair pieces. Do not rip it to final width yet.

1

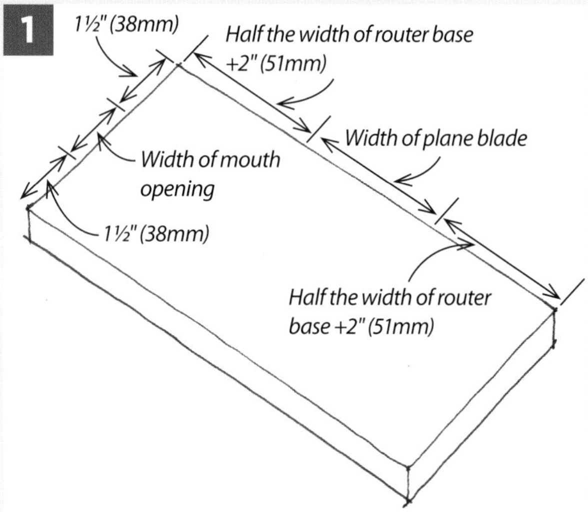

2

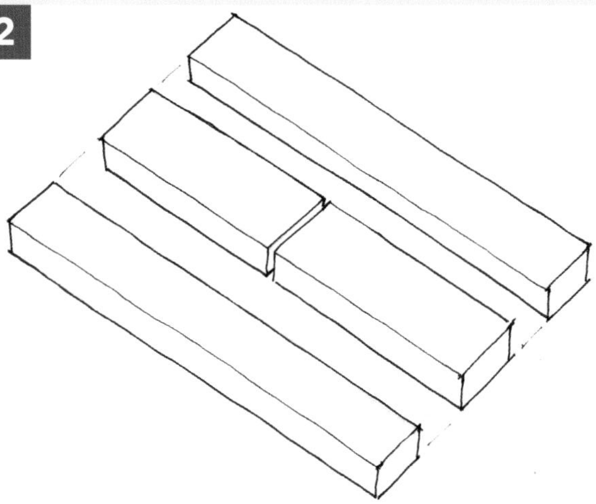

3

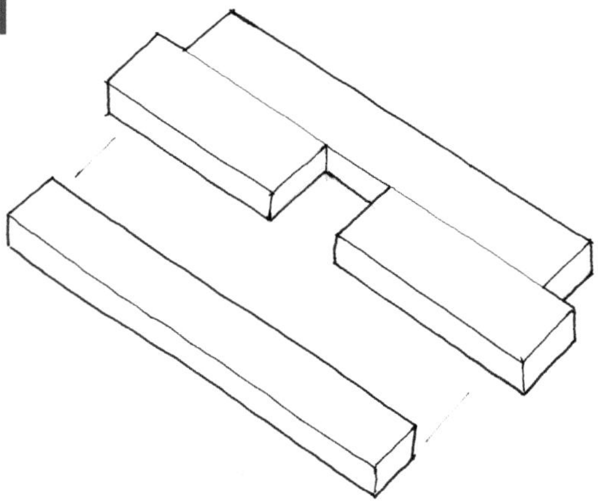

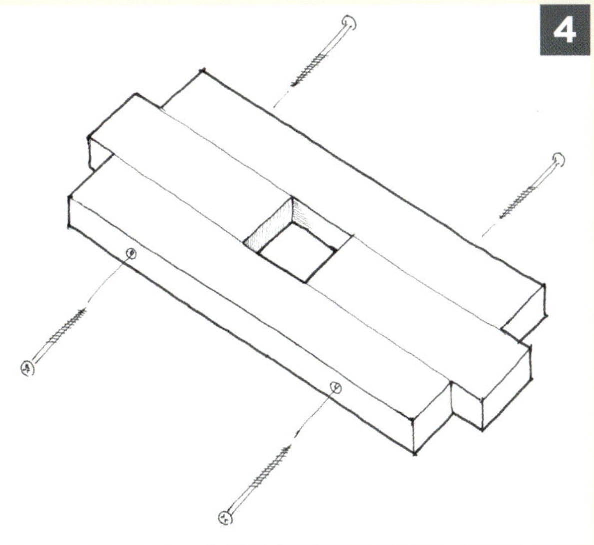
4

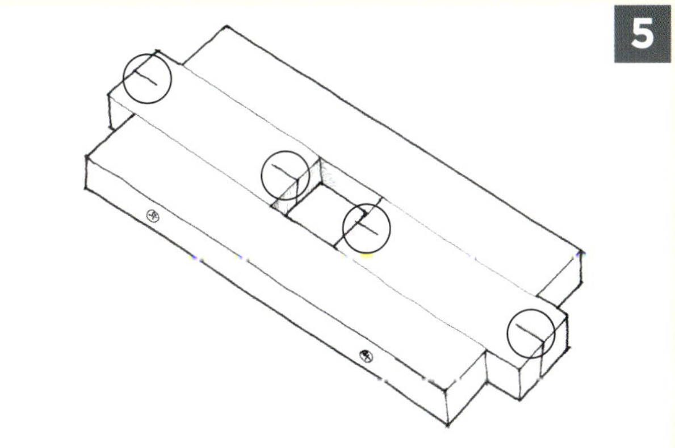
5

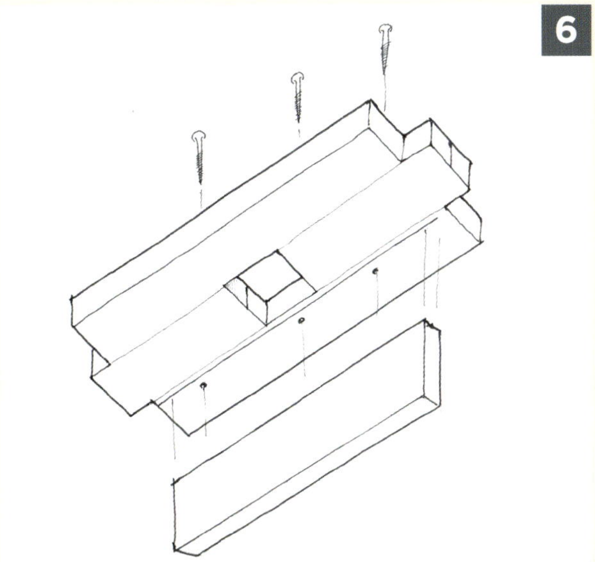
6

1. Prepare some ¾" (1.9cm) MDF to make a jig for routing the sole-plate recess.
2. Rip 1½" (3.8cm) off one side, then rip a piece the width of the mouth opening. With the saw still set at this width, rip the sole-plate blank to width. Having the jig and the blank exactly the same width simplifies fitting the repair. Next, cut the center piece in half
3. Mark a distance equal to or less than the blade width (this dimension is less critical—the sole plate is roughly square) at about the center of both of the sidepieces. Using 5-minute epoxy (to allow hand alignment to set the pieces and reduce clamp time), glue the two centerpieces to the side-piece at the mark. Work on a clean, flat surface to help align the faces.
4. Glue the second side to the centerpieces, reinforcing the glue with screws or dowels. Pre-drill the screws to prevent splitting. You can trim the ends of the centerpiece flush, if you want.
5. Mark centerlines on vertical faces of the centerpieces.
6. If your plane is too short to have the jig clamped without interfering with the router, clamp the jig in position and screw a fence to the jig at the side of the plane. Use the fence to clamp the jig when routing.
7. Mark a centerline down the sole of the plane. Adjust the plane blade so it just barely cuts, and mark the position of the blade edge with pencil on the sole and down the sides. Then remove the blade.

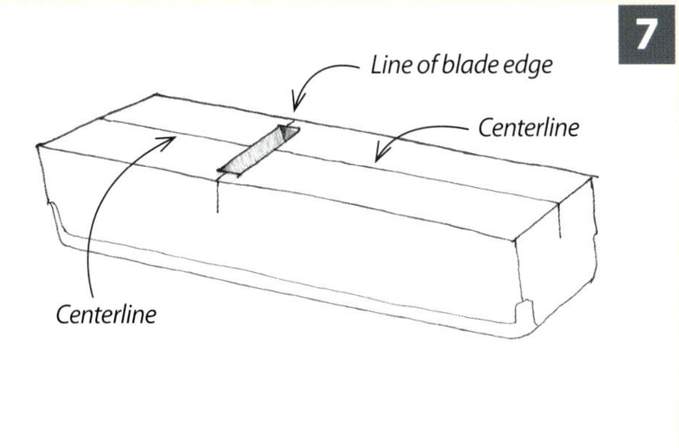

7

FITTING A SOLE PLATE AT THE MOUTH OF A PLANE (CONTINUED)

8

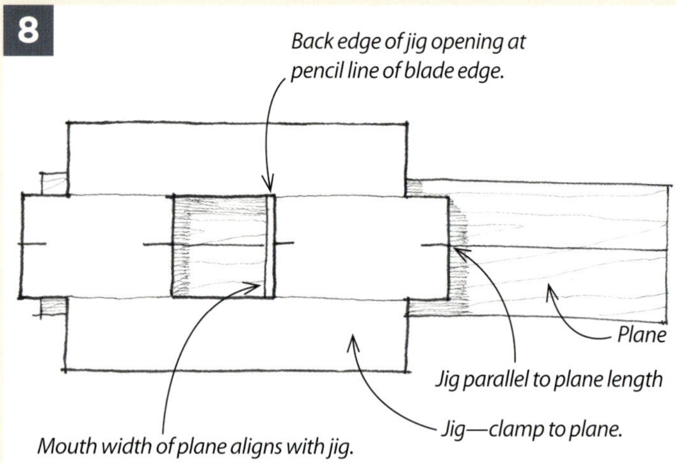

9

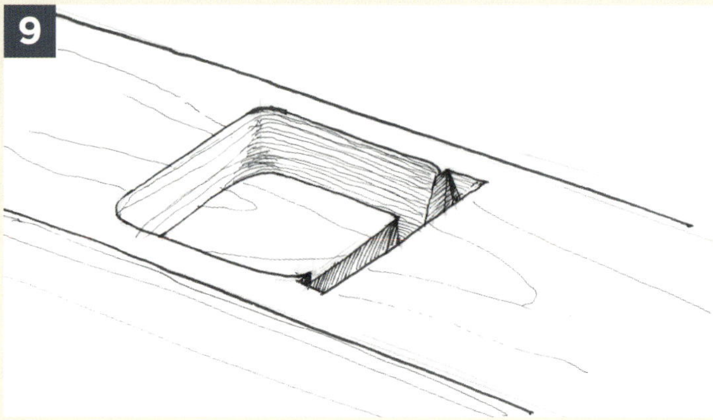

10

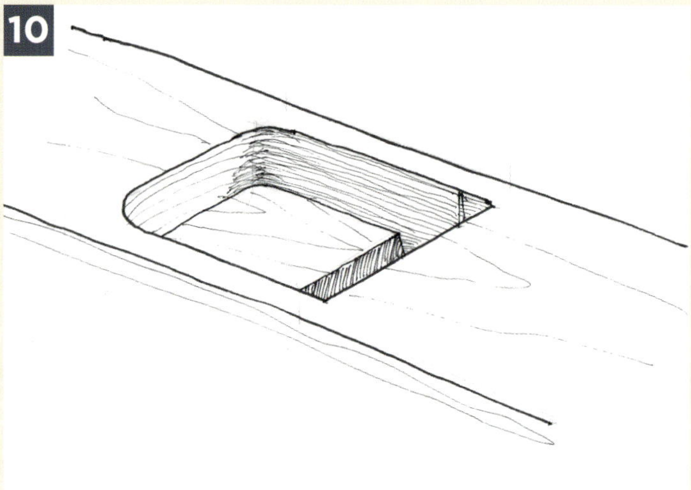

8. Align the jig with the centerlines of the plane, the back of the jig opening (the plane-blade end) slightly behind the pencil line indicating the blade edge. Verify that the jig opening aligns with the width of the mouth opening; this position takes precedent over alignment with centerline markings. Use the centerline markings to make the jig parallel with the length of the plane. Clamp the jig to the plane.

9. Use a ½" (13mm)-diameter by ¾" (19mm)-long pattern-routing bit with a top-mounted bearing. Set the depth and begin the cut by plunging to the full, or nearly full, depth in the center of the jig (so you do not damage it). Finish routing in the recess.

10. Square the rounded corners at the blade edge, carefully preserving the wedge abutments if they intersect. You can square up the other corners of the recess, or round the corners of the sole plate, your choice.

Cut the length of the sole plate to match the blade edge line. Fit the sole plate into the recess and insert the blade into its position. The sole plate might be slightly larger than will allow the blade to be set to its cutting position. If not, move the sole plate to its final position in relation to the mouth opening you want and glue it in place.

If the sole plate is too long, remove it and trim it on the shooting board until it just fits, establishing the mouth opening you want. If you want a throat-clearance angle less than 90° (70° or 80° is common for a plane other than a fine smoother), or, alternatively, if you want to increase the chip clearance angle for a fine smoother, plane the mouth end with the piece shimmed up on the shooting board to achieve the angle you want. This will, of course, shorten the sole plate, so be careful you have enough left. Be aware, the angle may complicate fitting at the wedge abutments. Lastly, glue the sole plate in.

SETTING UP A FLEA MARKET FIND

1. What's wrong with this picture? This is how it was found at the flea market: everything in backwards. $15. Moulson Brothers blade, J.R. Tolman body (Tolman died in 1864). Couple minor cracks in the body, but serviceable. The body had shrunk around the blade and it took some work to get it out. I both ground the blade and chipbreaker's width down a little and pared out the blade opening.

2. The chipbreaker was undamaged. The blade had a significant double bevel, which I've seen before on old blades; obviously an attempt to reduce the amount of bevel one had to sharpen.

3. The blade had some rather deep pitting though.

4. One minute on a diamond stone revealed how much had to be done. I decided that carborundum on a steel plate (kanaban) would be the fastest. This is two minutes on the kanaban starting with 90-grit carborundum. The pits are deep on the right side of the blade.

5. Fresh carborundum and four minutes.

6. Fresh carborundum and five more minutes. Got it! Some low spots at the corners, but they will be ground out when I grind the bevel. Total of about 12 minutes to get the back flat—and the pits were deep enough I debated whether or not to attempt it.

SETTING UP A FLEA MARKET FIND (CONTINUED)

7. I ground the bevel back square, then ground it at 30°. The large secondary bevel that was on there when I started is probably about 25°. Careful grinding took about 10 minutes.

8. I straightened and honed the edge on the chipbreaker, but when I screwed it to the blade it didn't fully tighten.

9. So I filed the nut on the chipbreaker thinner so the screw would pull the blade up tight.

10. The sole before flattening.

11. I used a Stanley #60½ block plane to initially level the sole.

12. As usual the sole is badly worn at the mouth. The front edge had been beat up as well, but that is of less concern.

13. I checked for twist with winding strips, and the sole was twisted—and it was not square to the sides. I corrected both of these with a plane.

15. The body had shrunk around the plane over the years so I had to pare the sides of the opening for the blade. Luckily, there was extra material on the side that was interfering with the lateral adjustment of the blade.

16. Trial run. Put a nice polish on a piece of poplar. The blade shape could still be finessed, as well as the bevel angle on the chipbreaker, though.

14. I started to define my contact areas with the Japanese scraper, but the sole is so small I just went right to the card scraper.

17. The mouth, however, is over a quarter of an inch in width. I estimate that this plane has lost a good ¼" (6mm) or more in height over the years (153 years+ at this writing). This wide mouth causes two irritating things to happen: #1, it catches when coming onto the board unless you make very positive contact with the sole as you start the stroke. The second irritating thing that happens is that the shavings fall out on nearly every stroke, getting between the plane and the work. This requires you stop and remove a shaving almost every stroke, or else the plane won't cut. Though this plane will give good service like this, with the chipbreaker doing the yeoman's share of reducing tearout, and I kind of hate to mess with the patina of this old tool, fitting a sole plate will give the tool new life and perhaps it will be able to take part in building many fine pieces, keeping both it and many poorly manufactured pieces of furniture out of the landfill.

SETTING UP A FLEA MARKET FIND (CONTINUED)

18. So I decided to fit a movable sole plate. Using the jig described in "Fitting a Movable Sole Plate," page 184, I cut a recess for the fixing screw with a router and drilled a hole for the screw's shaft.

19. On the sole, before I started, I marked the position of the blade's edge when set deep enough to just begin to cut. You can see faint pencil lines either side of the mouth. I will use those to determine the length of the throat piece after I have cut the recess for it. I routed a recess for the plate using the jig described on page 184 and elongated the screw hole so the plate could be moved forward and backward after it is installed.

20. I had a sandwich left (at the top) from some other throat plates I had made for other planes. It has a core of about 5⁄16" (8mm)-thick beech and facings of 3⁄16" (5mm) pau ferro, all parallel. I measured the length of the recess to my pencil lines I made at the blade's edge and cut the plate. Then I rounded the front of the plate to match the recess. In front is a completed sole plate made for a 2½" (6.3cm) blade, and the screw that will be used to fix the plate.

21. The sole plate fitted, fixed with the screw, and planed flush. The plate will move about ⅛" (3mm), starting with a maximum mouth opening of about 1⁄16" (2mm). This means that if a 1⁄16" (2mm) mouth opening is acceptable, another ⅛" (3mm) could be taken off the sole of the plane for maintenance before the sole plate would have to be replaced.

22. The fixing screw. The aesthetics of screws: I chose a slot drive round head stainless steel screw, but it could easily be brass.

23. Working pretty well now. To get the finest shaving the blade needs a little less curve and the bottom could be flatter still.

or reshaped as per your requirements. You can take this opportunity to remake a broken tote to fit your hand. Note that if you go to remove a closed tote, it will often have a dovetail-shaped cut at the back of its tenon (as can be seen in **Figure 8-34** on page 182) to help keep it from rising out of its mortise in use. This cut likewise makes it more difficult for you to remove the handle.

If you have a horned plane, it is often helpful to round off the back of the plane to engage the hollow of your hand, and to relieve the little ridge alongside the horn so it doesn't cut into your hand (**Figure 7-19** on page 135).

If an old plane is particularly dirty it can be cleaned and finished with a little boiled linseed oil well thinned with mineral spirits or limonene, applied with 0000 steel wool to remove the dirt. One light coat is enough; you don't want a sticky build up. Many times collectors have ended up putting on many coats of linseed oil so they look good on the mantle, but linseed oil can get very dark with age and tends to collect dirt as it takes a long time to dry—so that may be why your plane looked dirty to begin with. Don't apply any finish to the bottom!

SETTING UP CHINESE PLANES

I'm including Chinese-style planes because they are available off-the-shelf with blade angles of 60°+, which I find useful for not only tropical hardwoods, and many Australian hardwoods, but also some northern hemisphere woods such as oak. The blade-holding mechanism on a Chinese-style plane is similar to the old

Figure 7-20. Chinese planes rely on a small, crisp mouth opening to help break the chip. The narrow brass piece dovetailed into the sole at the mouth of this Chinese plane is typical.

European wood planes, so much of what was said about setting up a wooden plane applies here to the Chinese plane.

1. Inspect the plane

The Chinese planes are wooden bodied planes, and as such are susceptible to the same problems discussed in "Setting Up a Traditional Wood Plane"—so you can use that as a guide when inspecting your plane. However, there are a few extra things to note. The traditional high-pitch Chinese smoothing plane depends almost entirely on a restricted mouth opening to reduce tearout.

For this reason there is usually a narrow piece of brass dovetailed across the width of the mouth to reduce wear (**Figure 7-20**). Inspect this carefully to see that the plane block has not shrunk across its width causing it to split around the brass piece. If it has, and is only a hairline crack, you may be able to tap the sides of the plane with a small hammer gently at the area of the sharp point of the dovetail and cut a few wood fibers, reducing the stress on the block. Any more than the slightest crack and you will have to tap the brass piece down and out from the top and carefully remove the slightest bit of wood to make the inlaid piece fit. Then tap the mouthpiece back in place, flush with the bottom of the plane.

As with any wooden plane, it is best to remove the blade when you first get it and set the plane aside for a few months to acclimate before setting it up. After that period check the fit of the brass insert again and, if need be, adjust the lateral clearance of the blade.

CHECK THE BRASS MOUTHPIECE

When first putting the plane up to acclimate, check the brass insert at the mouth. If it shows signs of cracking, drive it out and store it along with the blade. Refit it after the plane has acclimated. If it initially seems okay, you can leave it in, but check it frequently.

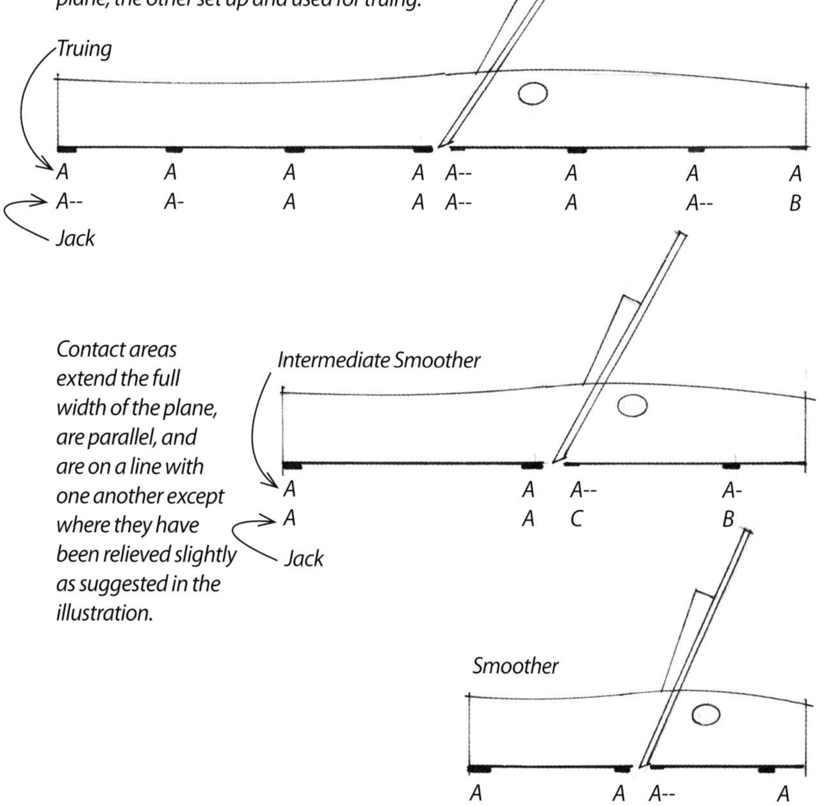

Figure 7-21. Schematic of Contact Areas of the Sole of Chinese-Style Plane
Traditionally, a woodworker could have two jointer-length planes: one set up and used as a jack plane, the other set up and used for truing.

5. Configure the sole

After performing all of the setup procedures presented earlier in general terms, follow the same procedures used for configuring the sole of a wooden bodied plane. See pages 120–126 for Steps 2–4. But, if your plane has a piece of brass inlaid at the mouth—not all of them do—you will not be able to use a power jointer (probably not necessary here anyway), or a handplane to level the sole. However, the piece of brass set at the mouth is soft enough to be worked with many woodworking tools and can be leveled with a good quality cabinet scraper, including a handled scraper (**Figure 7-21**).

6. Adjust the mouth

The mouth opening on all the planes should be very tight, just large enough to let a fine shaving through. With tropical hardwood, you are not going to be removing a very thick shaving anyway. But a smoothing plane should show only the very slightest bit of light when the blade is positioned to cut and the plane is held up to the light (**Figure 7-22**). If the gap is too large, the blade can be shimmed with a piece of paper, moving it forward and closing the gap, but be careful: if the gap is small to begin with, a common sheet of typing paper may be too thick.

7. Attend to the details of the body and sole

After the sole has been flattened, I often like to relieve the long edges, as I do on my other wood planes, on either side of the sole with a chamfer of just a few degrees, just to the edge of the blade opening. Doing so reduces the area of the sole that must be maintained, simplifying future maintenance. I also like to make a relief cut on either side of the blade opening to make sure this area is not high—it's easy to miss when conditioning the sole—and to help eject chips that tend to collect at the corners of the blade. The leading edge of the sole should be crisp, to prevent shavings from sliding under the plane while working, so do not round or chamfer this edge (**Figure 7-13** on page 128).

8. Attend to the details of the grip and finish

Most planes available now come with the body of the plane shaped, smoothed, and ready to go, with the possible exception of the cross handle, which may need some shaping and smoothing to fit through the hole in the body. This cross handle is meant to be pressure-fitted and is left unglued so it can be tapped out of its oval hole for storage. Another form of cross handle is permanently attached to the top in a similar position right behind the blade. In China, this is often shaped to an ox-bow curve to accommodate the hands.

Sometimes you can get unfinished planes from China or Southeast Asia. I got several once—a jointer, jack, and small block plane—through a friend of a friend from Thailand (**Figure 7-23**). These had the profile band sawn and the escapement cut for the blade and wedge, though the

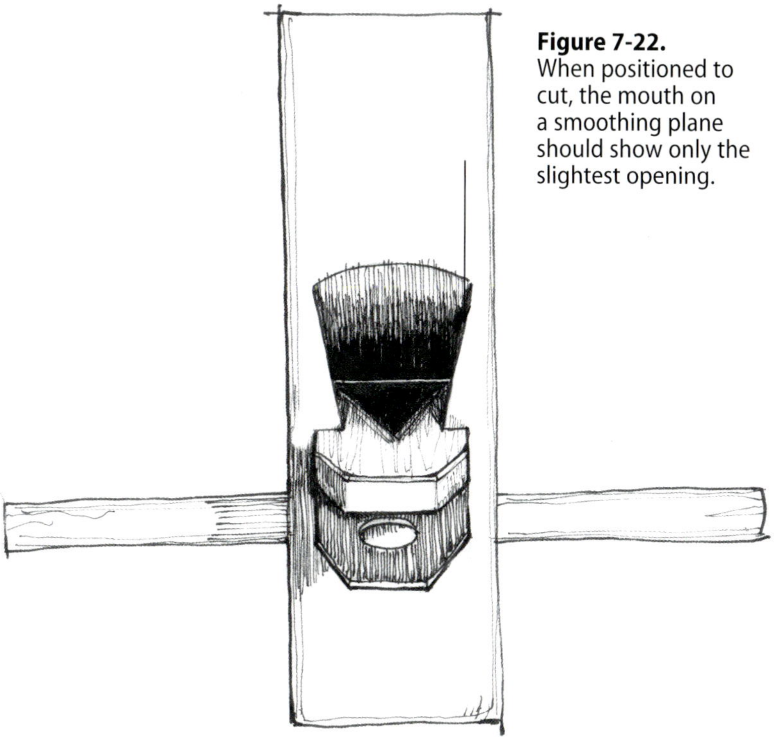

Figure 7-22. When positioned to cut, the mouth on a smoothing plane should show only the slightest opening.

Figure 7-23. Both these planes came unfinished with only the shape band sawn, the chipwell and abutments cut, but not fit, and the hole drilled for the cross handle. The plane at top is in its original state, with its accompanying (unfinished and unfitted) parts. The plane at bottom has been completed, tuned, shaped, and smoothed.

wedge was unfitted, as was the blade. On some of them, the chipbreaker was drilled but not sharpened, badly shaped, and of such mild steel, that I do not believe it was usable. However, the blade, a little roughly finished, was laminated steel (not immediately apparent until I sharpened it—I almost threw it away). It has turned out to be a decent blade. On the jack plane, I threw away the useless chipbreaker and set a brass piece in the mouth to close down the opening. I also had to finish fitting the cross handle and smooth off the shape from the rough band sawing. It has turned out to be a dependable performer. A few years earlier, I had picked up a very nice smoothing plane, which was set up and ready to go, and this gave me the model to finish setting up these others.

TROUBLESHOOTING

Using a handplane can be immensely rewarding, but it is not without its frustrations. Sometimes it seems you have done everything right but your results are still disappointing—or inconsistent. I cannot begin to answer all the questions you will ask yourself while you work, but a review of the information contained in this book should answer most of them. I will try to answer some basic questions here I hope will tie information together and send you in the right direction when analyzing a problem.

1. Problem: The blade leaves a series of repeated parallel marks on the work, perpendicular to the stroke of the plane.

This is called blade chatter and happens because the blade or blade edge is flexing under pressure of the cut. The edge digs deeper into the wood until the blade's resistance to bending exceeds the resistance of the wood, and the blade springs back up. At that the blade re-engages the wood, begins to flex, and the process happens all over again. Blade chatter happens primarily because the blade is not fully supported at the heel of the bevel, or because the bevel angle is too small (and thus the metal leading to the edge is too thin). There are a number of things to check, in the following order:

A. Check that the blade is bedded properly. The things to look for here depend somewhat on the type of blade you have: parallel or tapered.

Wood-body planes with parallel blades: Check that the blade bed is both flat, or maybe even ever so slightly concave, and that it is not twisted. Use a straightedge to check the bed for flat, and sight down the blade bed to check that the top and bottom edges are parallel and the bed is not twisted. If the chipbreaker is screwed on, make sure that the slot for the screw head is deep enough and that it is not riding up on a slot that is

EFFICIENT PLANING

If you use a too finely set plane to level the work, you must make many more cuts to bring the surface down to sufficient flatness. Each cut makes the blade a little duller. The use of intermediate planes reduces the number or strokes needed to level the work, thus reducing the amount of time, effort, and dulling cuts; and saves the edge on your finish plane for final smoothing.

too shallow. Check that the wedge fits the chipbreaker—the chipbreaker is not necessarily flat, and the wedge should closely match its contour. Go through the bedding procedure described in the next section.

Planes with tapered blades: Go back to the section on setting up old wooden planes and recheck your setup of the blade, chipbreaker, and blade bed. If everything checks out there, check further, using a technique similar to fitting a Japanese blade. Rub soft pencil lead over the back of the blade, put it into working position, and secure it with the wedge. Adjust it up and down about ¼" (6mm) a few times and then remove the blade. Inspect the blade bed: You should have graphite marking at the bottom of the bed where the heel of the bevel would be and at the top of the bed (other areas are ok also, but these areas must be contacted). If you don't have satisfactory contact across the width of the blade bed, pare away the areas marked with graphite (these will be the high spots), and recheck with the same method until the marking indicates full-width contact in the critical area of the heel of the bevel, and full-width contact at the top of the blade bearing.

Also, check the fit of the wedge to the contour of the chipbreaker again. Check also that both sides are wedging up tight and not just one. Usually if only one side is wedging down, you can tell by pulling the tightened wedge sideways: the wedge should give equal resistance in each direction. Also, check that the wedge is bearing over its entire length, especially down near the blade. Check for gaps visually, as well as by pressing down on the blade and wedge in different areas, trying to detect some motion or flex. Verify any suspicions with feeler gauges and using the graphite marking technique. You should not be able to put a feeler gauge of any thickness anywhere along the wedge. Correct the fit as required.

B. The second most probable cause of blade chatter, and probably the primary suspect on a well setup plane, is the bevel angle.

If the bevel angle is too small, the bevel itself will flex and cause chatter. "Too small," however, is relative. The bevel angle must be appropriate for the depth of cut, the blade (cutting) angle, and the type of wood. For instance, a bevel angle may be just barely sufficient for a certain depth of cut, but may begin to chatter if set deeper, or if used to plane a harder wood.

Another important factor related to the bevel angle is sharpness: When a blade dulls, it encounters greater resistance to the cut, causing the edge to flex down and begin to chatter. You may notice this in the midst of working—the same plane that has been cutting well on the same piece of wood starts chattering and the only thing that has changed is the sharpness of your edge. This means your bevel angle on this blade is at the limit of its performance. You will have to keep this blade very sharp, or increase the bevel angle. If you suspect that the bevel angle is incorrect, or too small for the work you are doing, reconsider and adjust your bevel angles (see "Bevel Angle" on page 54 and "The Correct Bevel Angle" on page 54).

KEEP YOUR EYES ON THE PRIZE

The goal here is to get a beautiful surface suitable for the chosen finish and position of the piece in the work, in the most efficient manner possible. This is not an academic exercise. On the other hand, when you are learning about planes and trying to improve your skills, a little extra effort trying to figure out what is going on before turning to scrapers and sandpaper will be rewarded in the end. Ultimately, you have to decide when handplaning is no longer the most productive solution. Learning to make that decision is also part of the acquisition of skills.

2. Problem: I cannot cut as fine a shaving as I want. The plane goes from a cut slightly too deep to no cut at all.

Either your plane or the work is not flat enough. Check the plane first—you probably have missed some area on the sole when you tuned-up the plane. This is easy to do. Go back and check it again.

The other factor is the work. If the work is not sufficiently well prepared, (not flat enough), you may have to set the blade deeper than you want to get the plane to cut even intermittent areas of the surface. If your plane does cut a fine shaving here and there, or maybe even at only one small place, then the problem probably is in the preparation of the work. You should go back and prepare it better.

3. Problem: I get tearout.

Using the information in this book, you should be able to see markedly improved results in the performance of your planes; with practice, I hope you will find yourself planing woods and getting results you hadn't previously thought possible—and also knowing when to put down the plane and head for the scrapers and sandpaper.

The setup of the plane is critical: a large portion of the skill required for effective planning resides here. Technique adds to this effectiveness, but does not compensate for it.

To reduce tearout, first, sharpen the blade. Match the blade steel to the work and make it sharp. Use an appropriate blade pitch (if you can), adjust the chipbreaker and mouth opening to restrain the shaving, and use as light a cut as you can for the stage of the work.

If your plane and the surface of the work are well prepared, you can usually get good, reliable, tearout-free results on the final surfacing in most woods, though there will be those pieces that defy your best efforts. It is much easier to get tearout-free results when the plane is set for a fine cut, but in order for this to work, the surface must be ready for a fine cut, that is, properly prepared.

Avoiding tear-out is a much bigger problem when preparing stock because preparing stock means removing a lot of wood, which necessitates a deeper cut, with the chipbreaker and mouth opening set back accordingly. This setup, of course, diminishes the effectiveness of these two major tactics in eliminating tearout. As preparation proceeds, you can gradually adjust the chipbreaker and mouth openings down to restrict the shaving, also taking a lighter cut. This is also a good opportunity to re-sharpen the blade. At each stage of the preparation you want to see tearout improve, aiming for its total elimination by the final smoothing.

Avoiding tearout also entails reading the wood and changing directions as you move across the surface accordingly. You learn the character of your wood as you plane, and you respond. Curly areas that change direction in the middle of the board may necessitate rotating the plane as you approach that area, to change the angle of attack, and then rotating it back again. Planing adjacent boards where the grain direction changes at the glue line often requires that you plane along the glue line in each direction without bridging the joint. Holding the plane at a bit of a diagonal localizes the cut a bit more and sometimes helps to be able to skirt along the joint.

Tearout hot spots notwithstanding, you should plane the entire surface in overlapping strokes across the width and length of the piece and back again. If you finish with scraping and sanding, do not be tempted to give trouble areas extra strokes, as this will distort the surface and be readily visible after the finish goes on.

A technique both Westerners and Japanese use is to dampen the surface of the wood with a wet rag to soften the wood fibers. This supposedly allows the fibers to be sheared cleanly. I have had indifferent results trying this, and I suspect that it is not going to work in all woods, particularly those that prefer a higher cutting angle. I think it is worth further experimentation, however.

4. Problem: The mouth of the plane jams with chips.

First, take the blade out of the plane and check to see if the chips are jamming in the mouth itself, or at or under the chipbreaker. The chips may appear to be jamming at the mouth when in reality they are jamming at the chipbreaker and backing up to fill the mouth. This is the more likely occurrence.

If the chips are jamming between the chipbreaker and the blade, and not actually at the mouth, the chipbreaker's fit to the blade must be tuned so that it fits tight. The underside edge of the chipbreaker where it meets the blade must be straight, and slightly undercut (**Figure 7-6**). The chipbreaker also must be formed so it puts sufficient pressure at the interface between it and the blade to keep chips from forcing their way in.

If all of these are tuned up and chips still find their way in between the blade and chipbreaker, then possibly the edge of the blade is flexing under the pressure of the cut and opening up a gap between it and the chipbreaker. The bevel is flexing because it is too small (and thus the metal leading to the edge is too thin); or the blade is flexing because it is not properly supported. Sometimes the chipbreaker is rigid enough—and not tight enough—to allow a badly supported blade or too thin edge to flex independently of it. Check the bevel angle of the blade and consider regrinding it to a larger one if it appears questionable. As well, check the blade seat and make sure the blade is fully supported. Correct these and verify that the chipbreaker has enough pressure on the edge to maintain contact under working conditions (**Figure 7-9** on page 124).

Chips will also jam at the mouth of the plane itself because someplace there is insufficient clearance. Check that the blade is not set deeper than slightly less than the width of the mouth opening. Also, check the throat opening and the upper surface of the chipbreaker to be sure there is sufficient clearance between it and all points of the chipbreaker. Sometimes if tolerances are very close, a blade will flex down into the wood in use and take a deeper chip than it was set for—deeper than what the mouth or throat opening will accept. This is actually blade chatter, but since it happens only once and jams instead of leaving chatter marks, it is hard to diagnose this as the blade or blade edge flexing. If all the tolerances look sufficient, then check the bevel angle and blade support.

5. Problem: The plane leaves tracks or ridges in the work.

Rotate the work so the light source shines parallel to the work surface. Look closely and see if it is a ridge or a step. If it is a ridge, then you have a nick in the blade. You will have to go back and re-sharpen.

If the track is a step, then one or both corners of the blade are set too deep for the shape of the blade. You need to back the blade off or adjust the lateral adjuster until the blade no longer leaves steps. If it no longer cuts, then you need to either flatten the bottom of the plane some more or prepare the work better as described above. Check the different sections for the appropriate blade shape for the plane you are using.

6. Problem: The plane seems to leave shiny streaks on the work.

These are usually burnishing marks from some slightly higher spot on the sole of the plane. The most likely culprit is the area just to either side of the blade opening, since these are easy to neglect. This is why I relieve these areas on my planes; however, another missed spot on the sole can do this as well. Also, sometimes shavings can collect at the mouth (especially at the corners), pack tightly, and cause burnishing.

KEEP THE SURFACE FLAT

Do not get distracted with localized problems. You must plane the entire surface the same amount—difficult areas as well as straightforward—in order to maintain flat. Otherwise, not only will the surface appear irregular but also the plane will begin to bridge the troubled areas by riding on the adjacent, less planed surfaces. These higher areas will then have to be planed down in line with the low areas before you can go any further.

CHAPTER

8

MAKING & MODIFYING PLANES

EXPANDING YOUR OPTIONS

A little more than a hundred years ago—and still today in some places—woodworkers were expected to make their own handplanes. For a woodworker today, making your own planes allows you to customize your tools to specific criteria and not be limited by what is available commercially. Your planes can be larger or smaller than what is commercially available, with blade angles, widths, and lengths more appropriate to the work you are doing.

Some of the planes made in this chapter. From the left: a fore plane, a jointer plane, a panel plane, a 50° coffin-sided smoothing plane, and a 55° coffin-sided smoothing plane.

This chapter gives you instructions for a full set of wooden-body planes in the Western tradition, planes ideally suited for work on the hardwoods we most often encounter. In addition, while I do not describe making a Krenov-style plane here, I have included what I think is a useful modification to it. I also have included some modifications you can make to planes you may already have that will improve their performance (see "Fitting a Movable Sole Plate When Making a Krenov-Style Plane" on page 188).

MAKING TRADITIONAL WOODEN-BODY PLANES

Based on traditional wooden planes still found in Europe and North America, the planes in this set are familiar to many. The lengths, blade angles, and blade widths are intended for use on moderately sized work in hardwoods. I have chosen to do a set of planes in this style not only because it has evolved to be ideally suited to working in hardwoods and is familiar to the majority of readers, but also because it easily allows the maker to adjust the relationship of blade angle, width, and shape to the length and function of the plane. It also allows the use of full-length blades—avoiding what I consider a shortcoming in the Krenov-style plane, giving you the option of using antique tapered or parallel blades as well as modern blades. While an entire set of planes is shown here, giving you some economy of manufacture, you do not have to make the whole set. You can make whichever ones you feel are useful to the type of work you do, and, of course, you can modify them as you see fit.

The planes are made using a hollow-chisel mortiser to cut the blade bed and chipwell—either an attachment mounted in a drill press (which is quite affordable, assuming you have a drill press) or a large floor-model mortiser, which not too long ago was an uncommon tool, but recently has become readily available. A table-mounted mortiser, unfortunately, will probably not have the capacity under the chisel. Larger planes require more clearance, so check the capacity of your machines. A drill-press attachment actually has more vertical capacity, because you can lower the table. The jigs used for the mortising cuts are the same for either machine.

This design uses a cross pin with a bearing plate and wedge, rather than tapered abutments and a wedge, for fixing the blade. The former is a little easier to fit than the latter, and though the chip well is more constricted, it is sufficient. All varieties of chipbreakers—except the Bailey-style chipbreaker—can be used with this system. The Bailey-style's *hump* interferes with the wedge. All planes are fitted with a movable sole plate to simplify long-term maintenance and get a tight mouth when needed.

The planes

The set I am building here consists of a **jack plane**, **fore plane**, **jointer plane**, **panel plane**, and two **smoothers**.

Jack Plane: The jack plane's blade is bedded at 43°, length 14" (35.6cm). It is in the Razee style to reduce weight.

Fore Plane: Inclusion of a fore plane, an unusual plane today, makes it easier to prepare large boards (boards too large to fit into your power jointer are the only ones you would probably consider doing by hand). Its length, 18" (45.7cm), and blade curvature, about 1⁄32" (0.8mm), bridges the gap between the jack and jointer planes, and, as well, allows the curvature of the jointer's blade to be reduced to about 1⁄64" (0.4mm) or less for use to better prepare a surface for the smoothing planes and to prepare edge joints. The fore plane is in the Razee style to reduce weight. The fore plane's blade is bedded at 45°.

Jointer Plane: The jointer has a full block for better feedback as to its angle on the edge of a board when edge-jointing. It Is 24" (61cm) long with the blade bedded at 47½°.

Panel Plane: In the Razee style for control and weight, the 12" (30.5cm) panel plane is included to more speedily prepare and smooth a surface after the 24" (61cm) jointer and before one of the two 8" (20.3cm) smooth planes. On most jobs, the surface it leaves will be all the planing you will have to do. It may be your most used plane. Its blade is bedded at 47½°.

Smooth Planes: The two smooth planes, in the coffin-shape for comfort, roughly 8" (20.3cm) long with blades bedded at 50° and 55°, will handle a range of hardwoods.

Materials

BLADES

Have your blades in hand before you start, as some antique blades come in sizes not made currently. For instance, I had both a 2¼" (5.7cm)-wide blade for the panel plane, and 2½" (6.4cm)-wide blade for the fore plane available. You can also find 2¾" (7cm)-wide antique blades for your jointer plane if you want.

For a set of full size planes as shown here, your choices for blade width could range as follows:

- **Jack:** 1¾" (4.4cm) (commonly available) or 1⅞" (4.8cm) (German blade size);
- **Fore:** 2⅜" (6cm) (modern) or 2½" (6.4cm) wide (antique);
- **Jointer:** 2⅝" (6.7cm) (modern) or 2¾" (7cm) (antique), though 2⅜" (6cm) is also a possibility;
- **Panel:** 2" (5.1cm) (modern) or 2¼" (5.7cm) (antique); and
- **Smoothing:** 2" (5.1cm).

In this set, I used, for the:

- **Jack plane:** a 1¾" (4.4cm) wide Hock A2 cryo blade with a Lie-Nielsen chipbreaker;

- **Fore plane:** a 2½" (6.4cm)-wide antique cast-steel blade with chipbreaker;
- **Jointer:** a 2⅝" (6.7cm)-wide Clifton forged blade with a Lie-Nielsen chipbreaker;
- **Panel plane** and the two **smoothers**, antique blades and chipbreakers: 2¼" (5.7cm) wide, and 2" (5.1cm) wide, respectively.

As a general recommendation, you could use good quality antique blades on all the planes. Alternatively, use:

- tungsten-vanadium, chrome vanadium, PM-V11, or A2 blade on the jack;
- A2 PM-V11 blades on the fore plane and jointer; and
- a good carbon-steel forged blade on the panel and smoothers. (Chapter 2 discusses blade steel at length).

BLOCK

Beech has been the preferred wood for this style of plane. Birch was also commonly used in the United States. Thick stock in beech is difficult to find. Birch is far more available. Oak, ash, walnut, cherry, and mahogany are also possibilities. Oak, a tougher wood than the other choices, grips the blade well but is often subject to severe internal cracking from the drying process. I do not recommend maple. Maple is hard and dense but does not grip the blade well.

Making the planes

1. ROUGH MILL THE BLOCKS AND GLUE-UP THE SOLE PLATES

Select the pieces so you can get a true quartersawn blank 2¾" (7cm) thick by the width of the blade, plus 13⁄16" (2.1cm). Do a cut list from the drawings for the planes you are making (**Figures 8-1 to 8-11** on pages 157 to 172), rough-mill your blanks, and let them settle (stickered) for at least a week, though six months is better (**Figure 8-12**). Also at this time, mill and glue up the sole plate blank (see "Fitting a Movable Sole Plate" on page 184) so the glue will be thoroughly dry by the time you want to use it (three or four days at least). After the blanks have settled for as long as you can let them, mill them down to within 1⁄16" (2mm) of their final dimension and let them rest again. Finally, square up the blanks one last time and bring them to 1⁄32" (0.8mm) or so of their final dimension (**Figure 8-13** on page 173).

2. LAY OUT AND DRILL

Begin by selecting your stock. Lay out the blade and chipwell per the drawings on pages 173 to 176 (**Figures 8-14 to 8-19**). Before excavating the chipwell, drill the hole for the cross pin in from both sides (to reduce errors, should the bit drift) until they meet. Drilling before excavating eliminates split-out in the chipwell.

3. MAKE JIGS

Then make up the jigs. The **sole-plate jig** and the **jig for the sole plate-screw** recess are described in "Fitting a Movable Sole Plate" (page 184). You will need **a jig for double sole plate screws** on the wider planes, but the method is the same as for the single-screw jig.

In addition to these jigs, you will need **mounting blocks** for mortising the plane blocks. Glue four layers of ¾" (1.9cm) MDF into a block about 9" (22.9cm) wide

Figure 8-1. Jack Plane

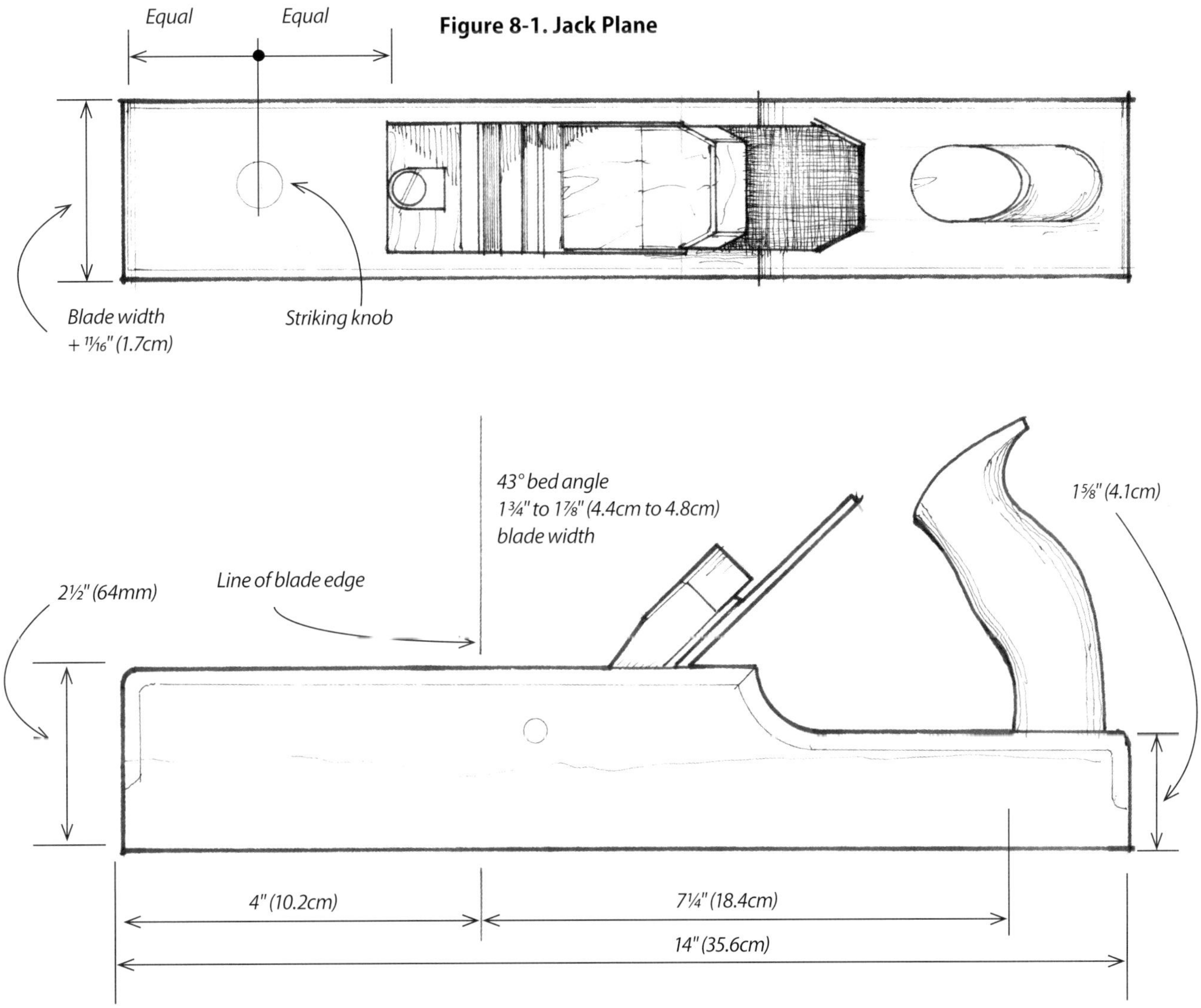

Figure 8-1A. Jack Plane—Details

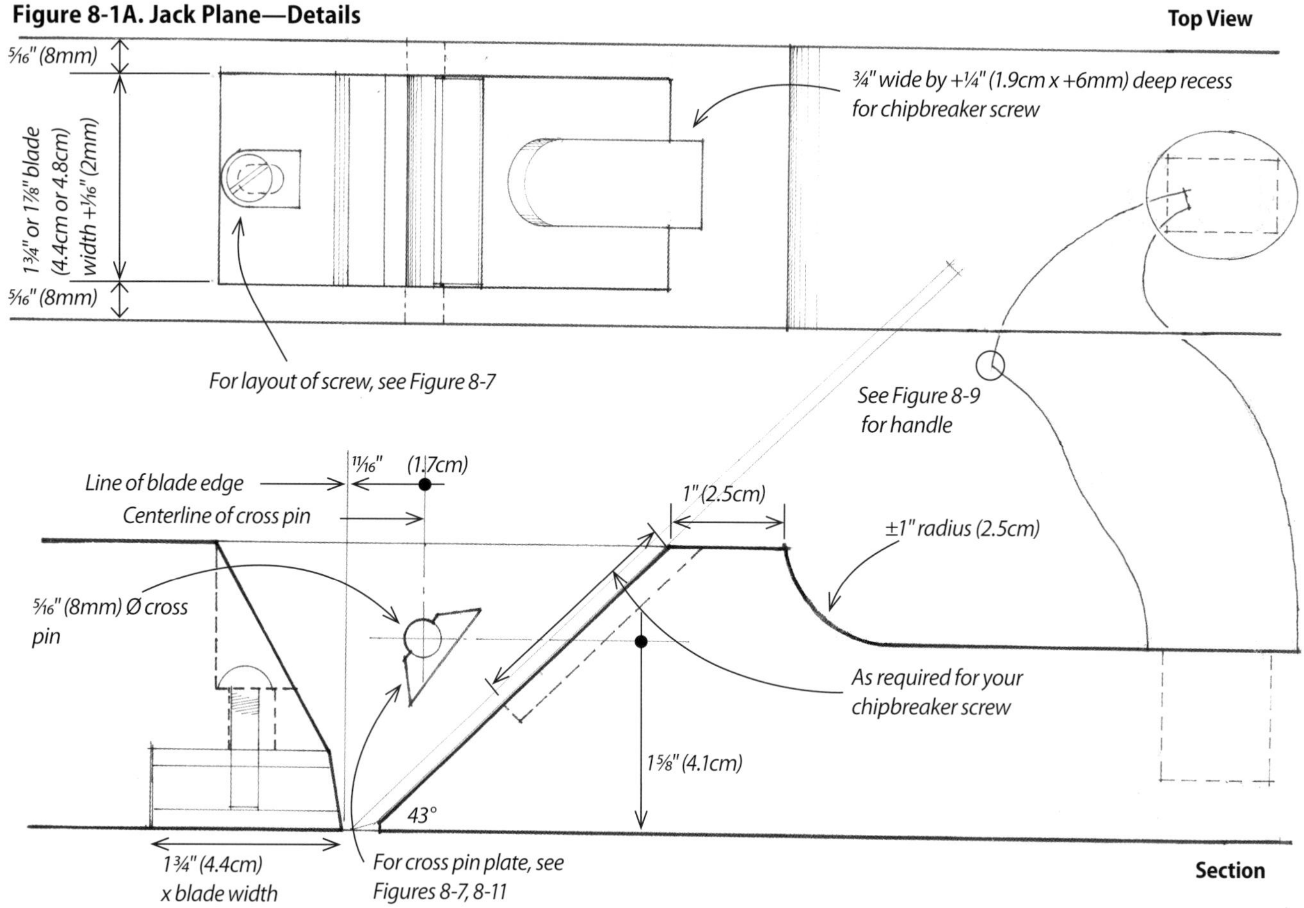

Figure 8-2. Fore Plane

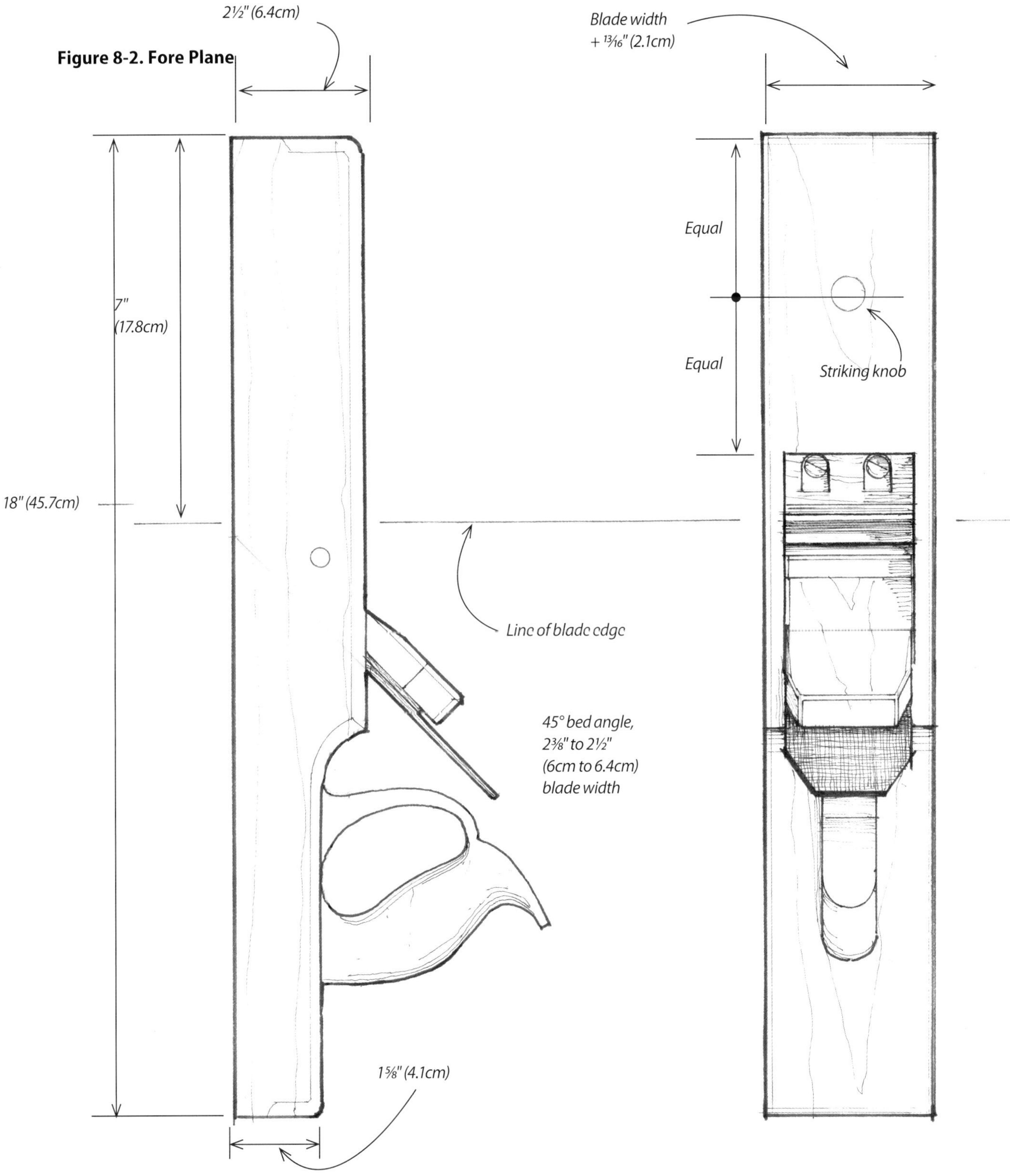

Figure 8-2A. Fore Plane—Details

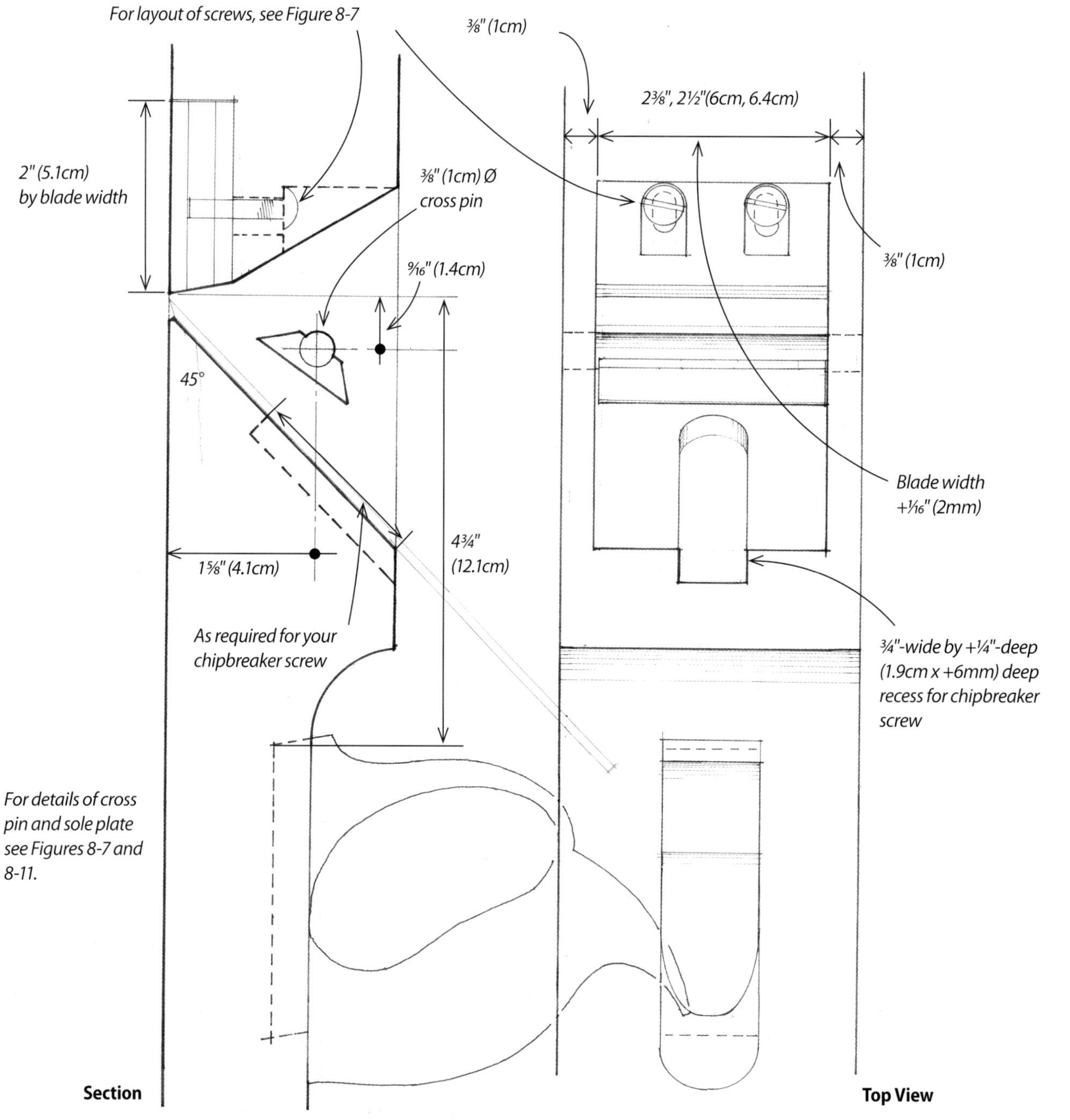

Figure 8-3. Jointer Plane

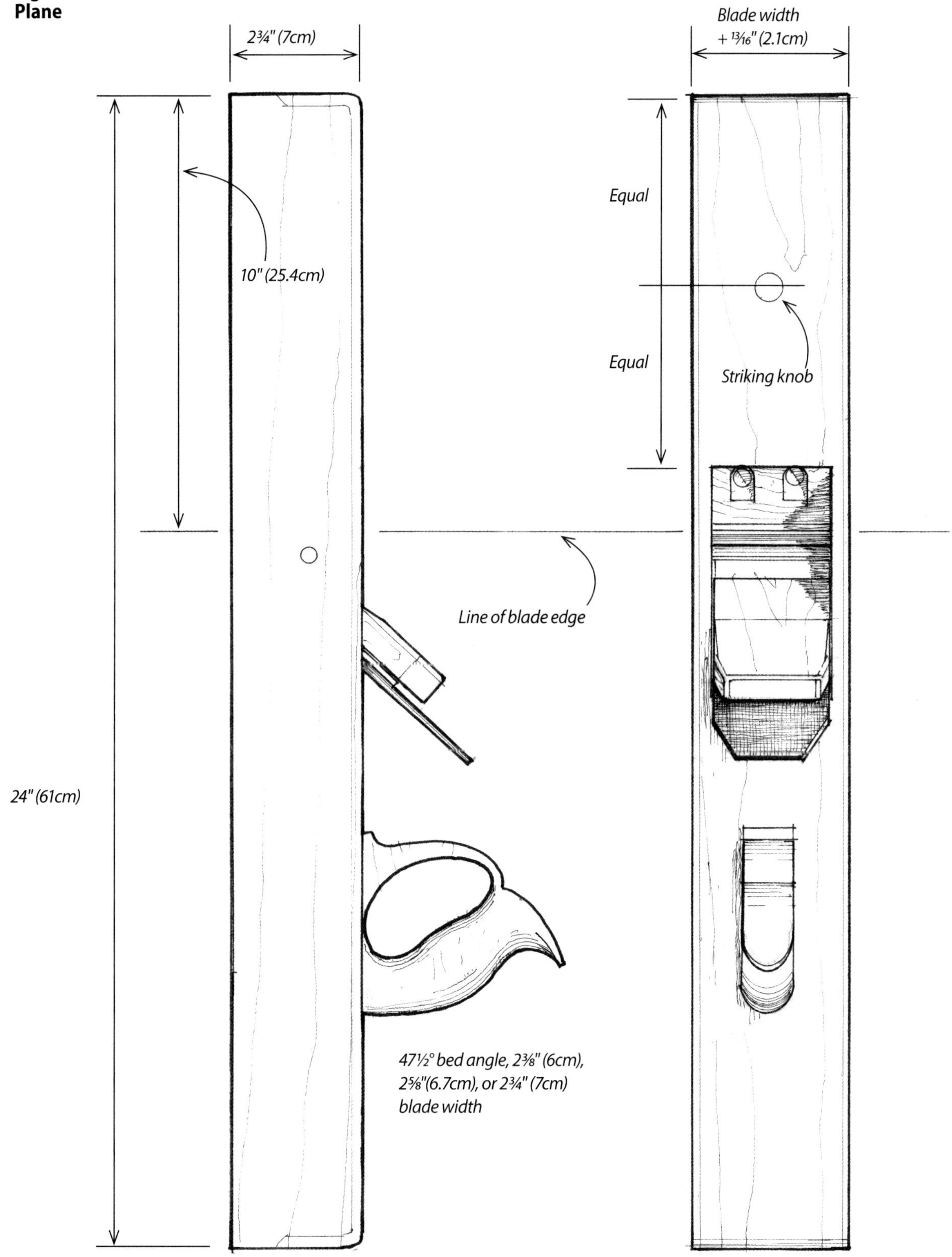

Figure 8-3A. Jointer Plane—Details

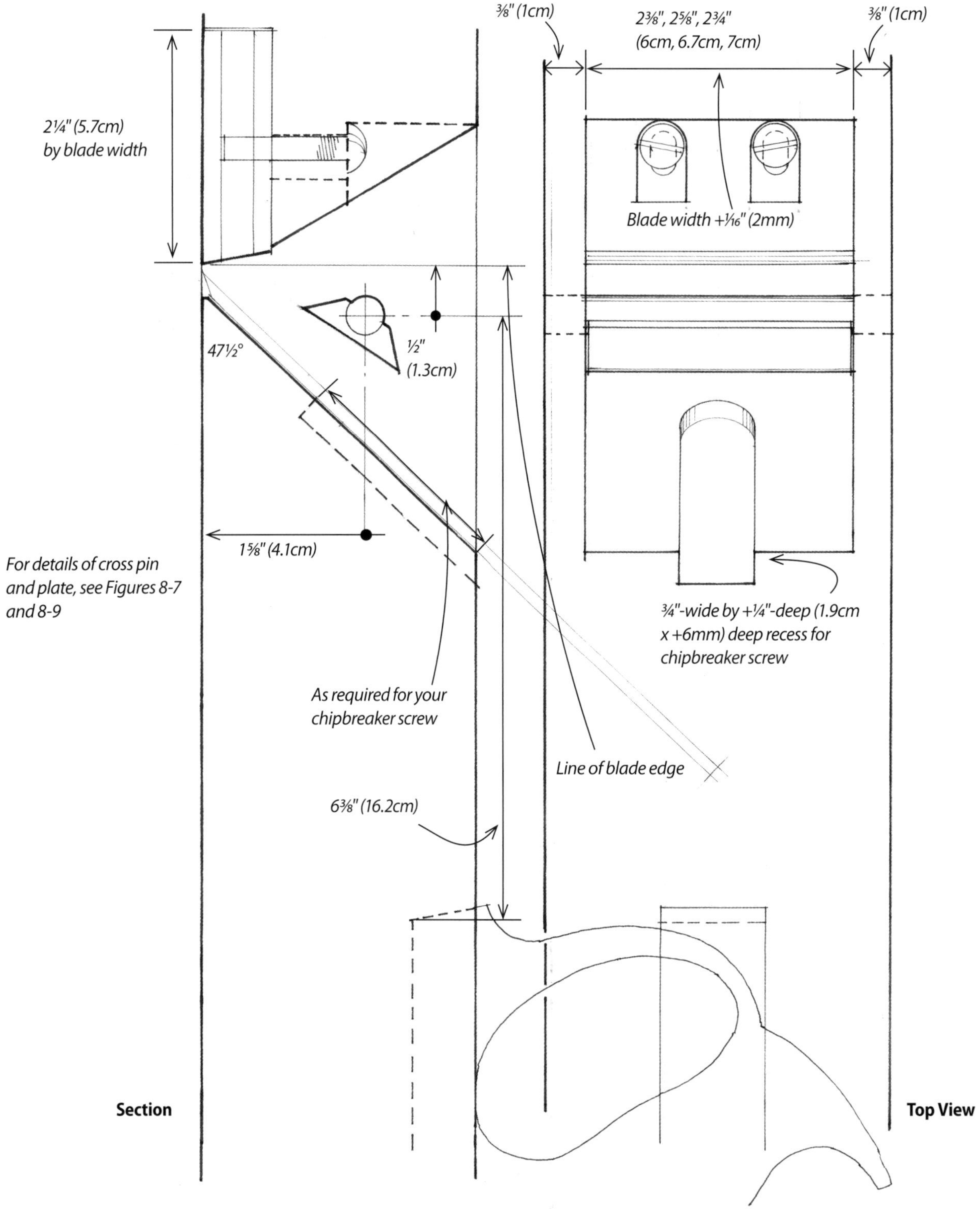

Figure 8-4. Panel Plane

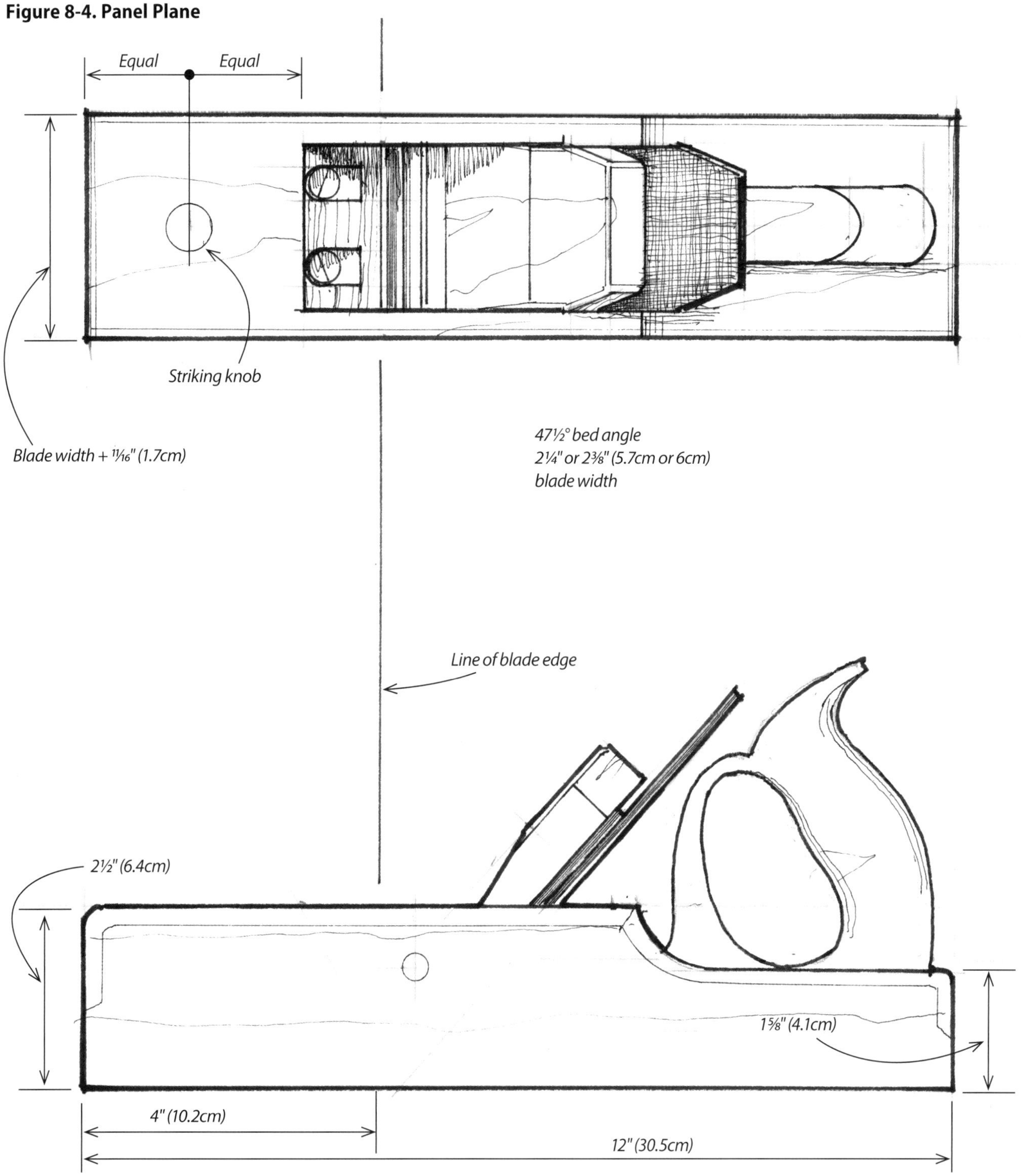

Figure 8-4A. Panel Plane—Details

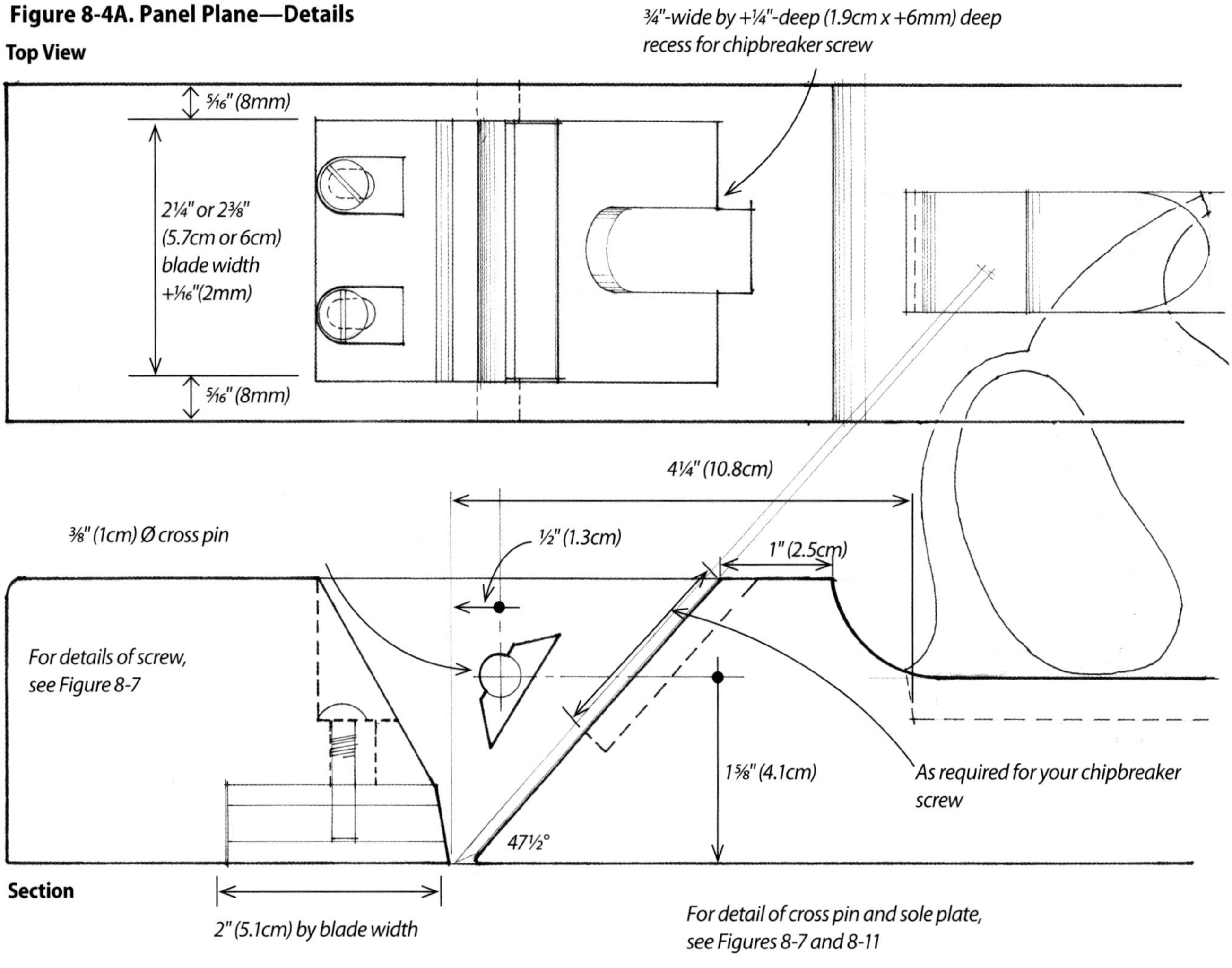

Figure 8-5. 50° Smoothing Plane

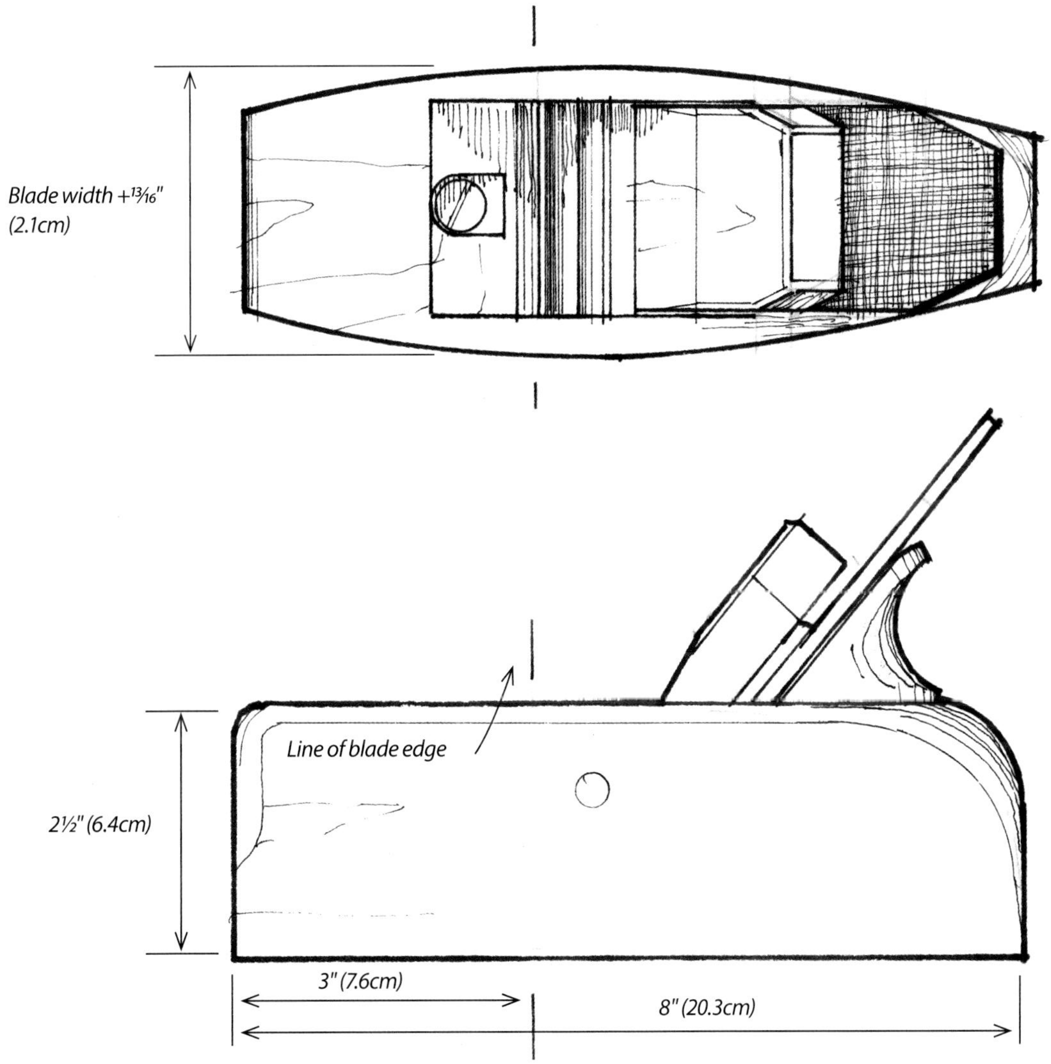

Figure 8-5A.
50° Smoothing Plane—Details

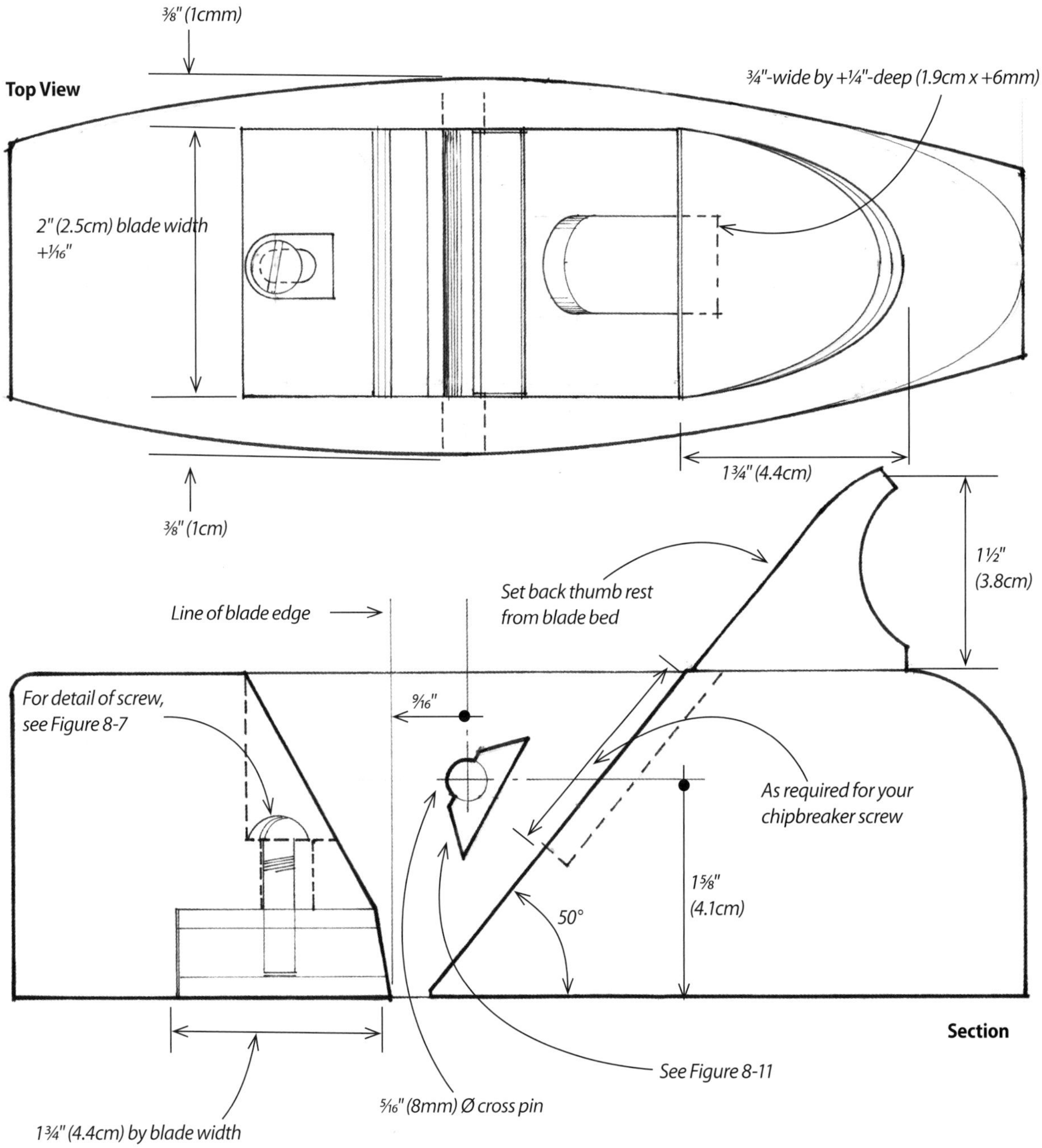

Figure 8-6. 55° Smoothing Plane

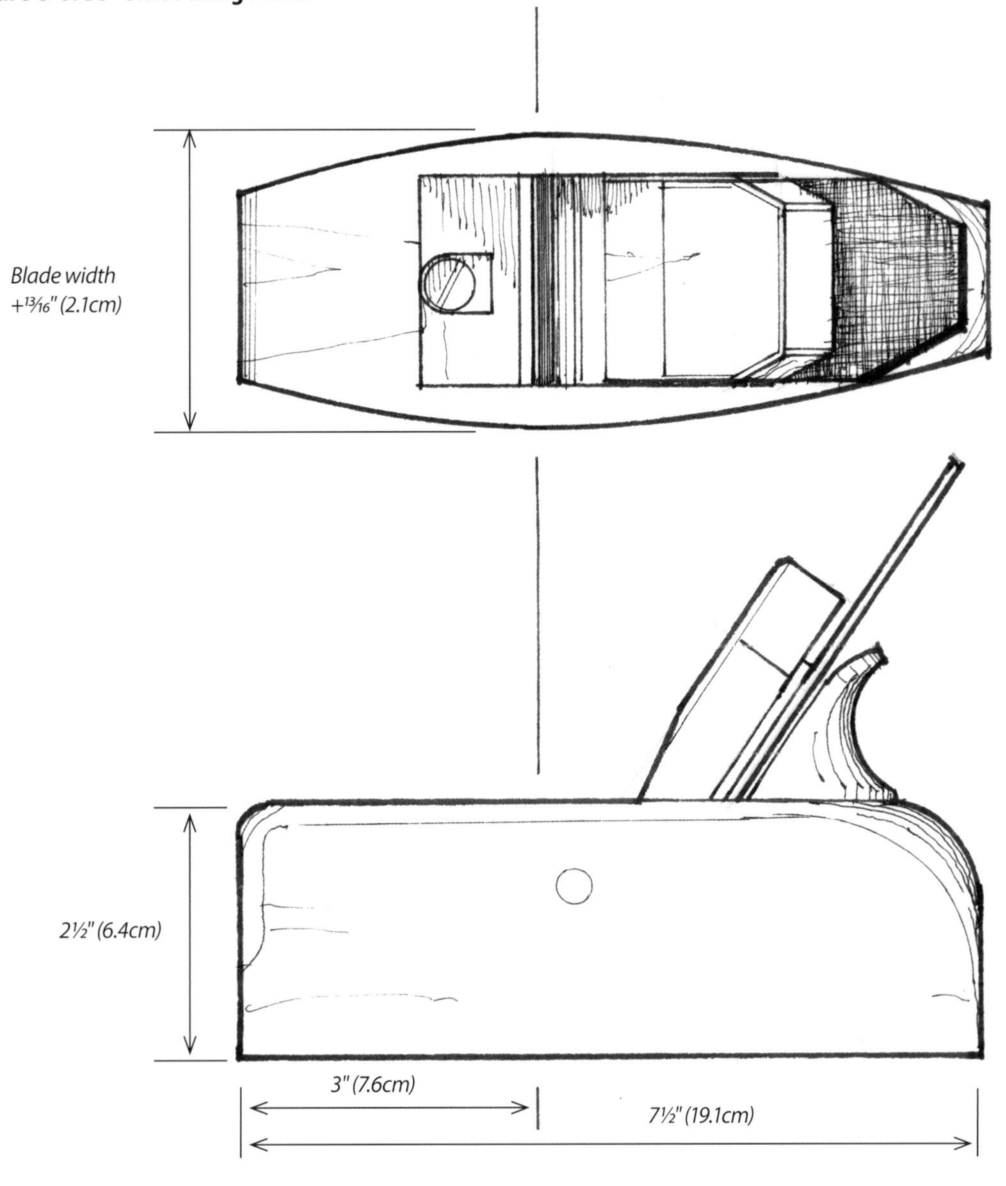

Figure 8-6A. 55° Smoothing Plan—Details

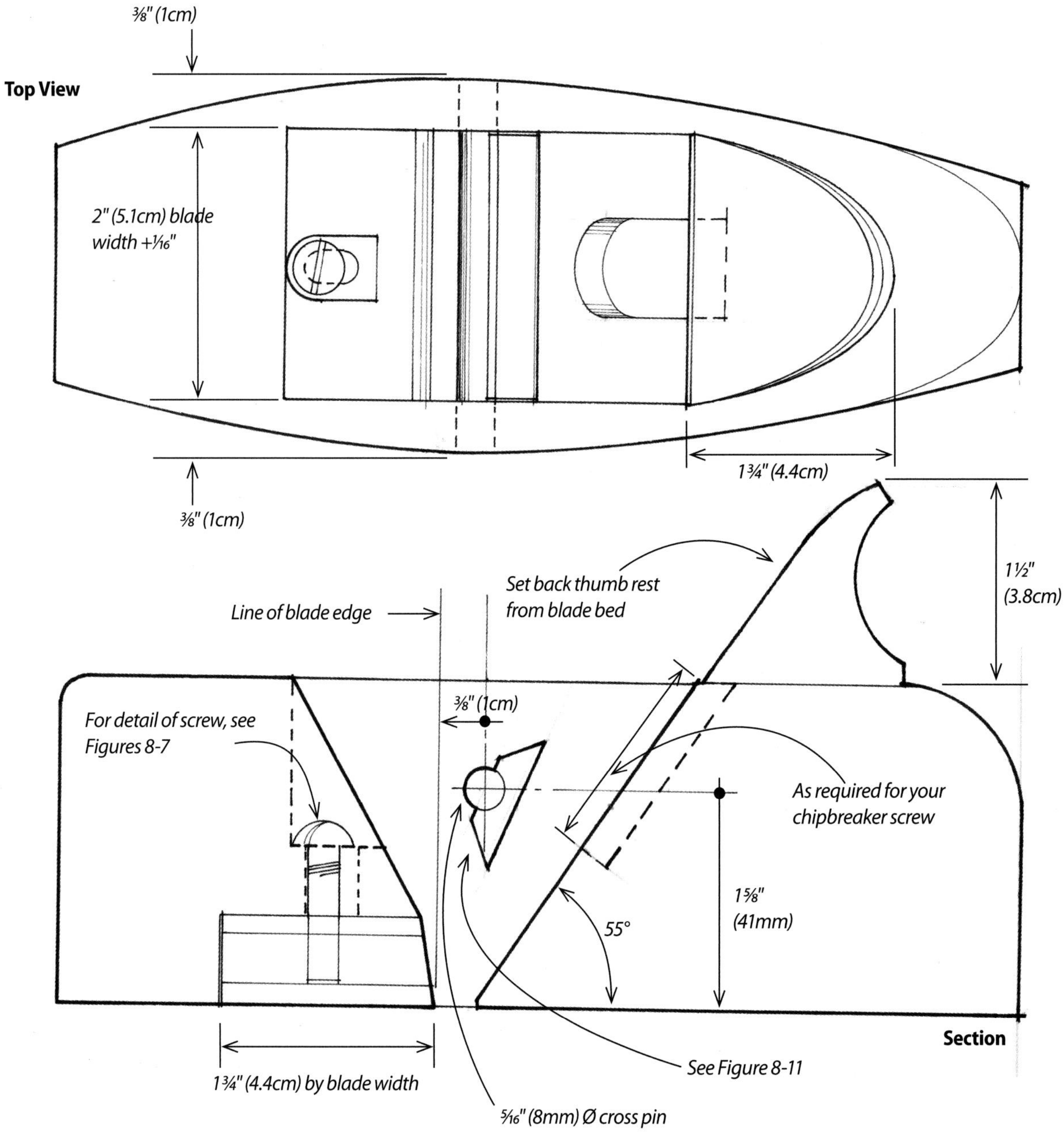

Figure 8-7. Layout of Slot for the Sole-Plate Fixing Screw

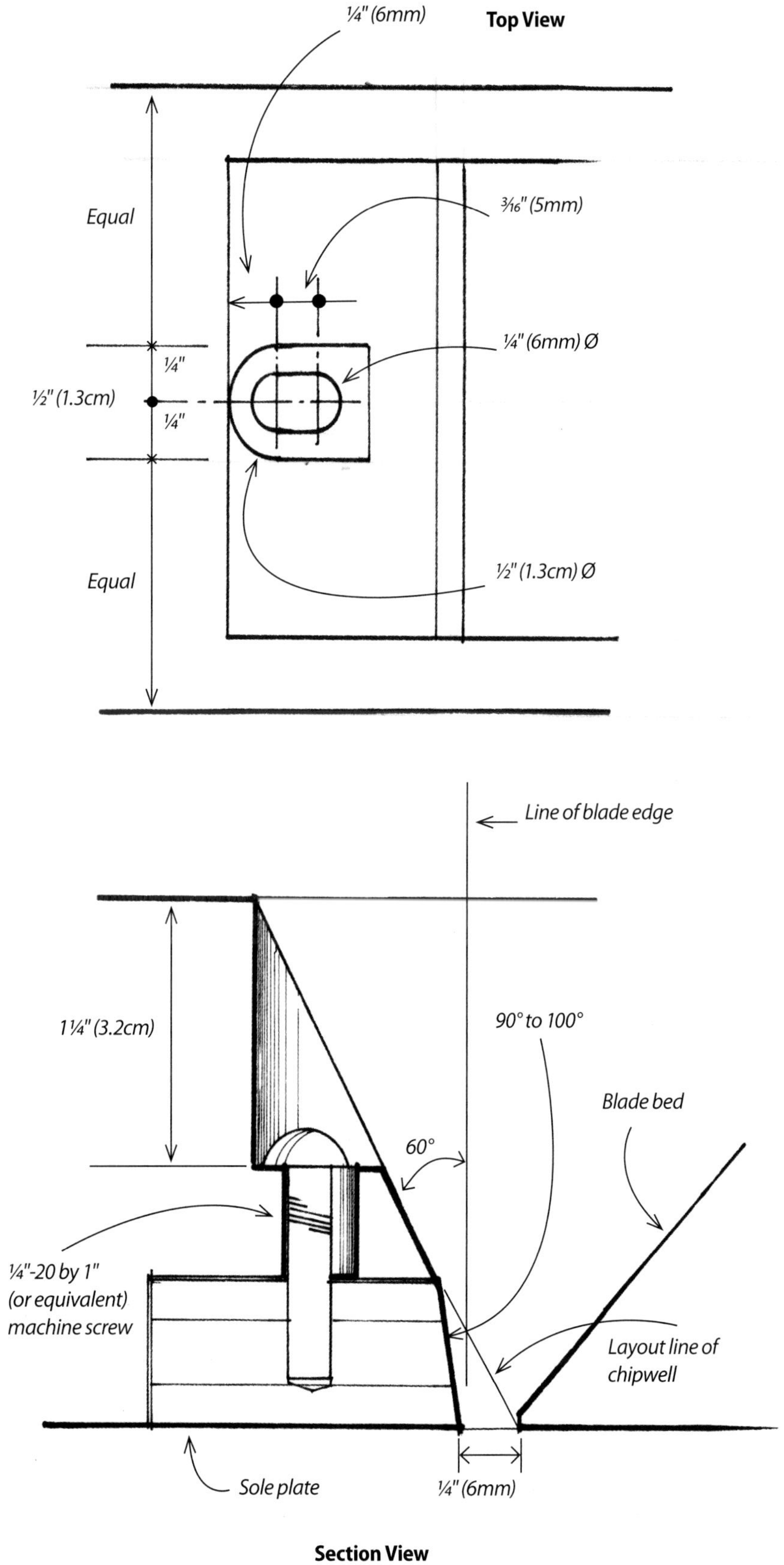

Figure 8-7. Layout of Slot for the Sole-Plate Fixing Screw (cont.)

Top View

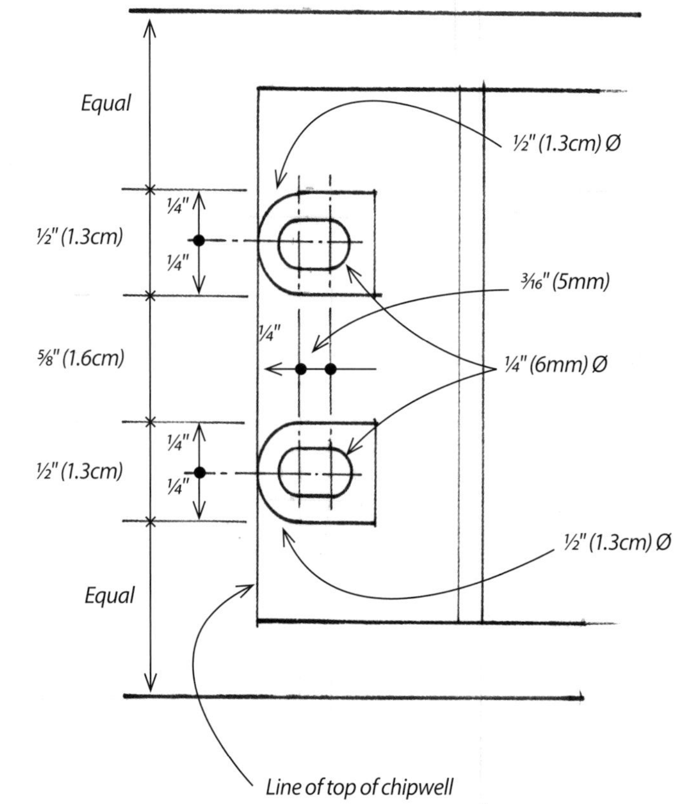

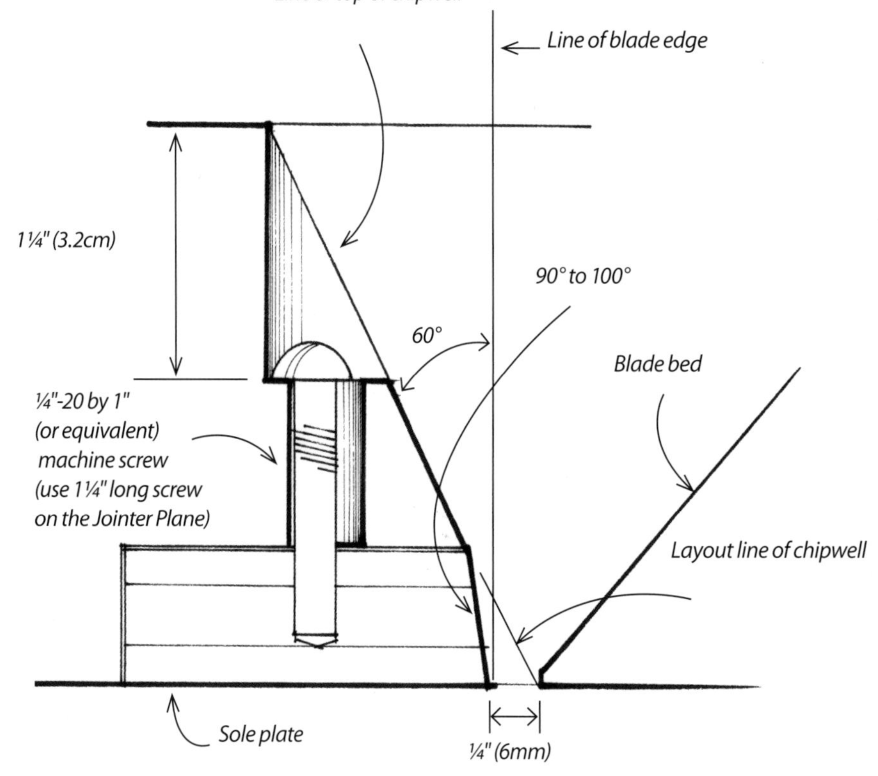

Section View

Figure 8-8. Closed Tote (full size)

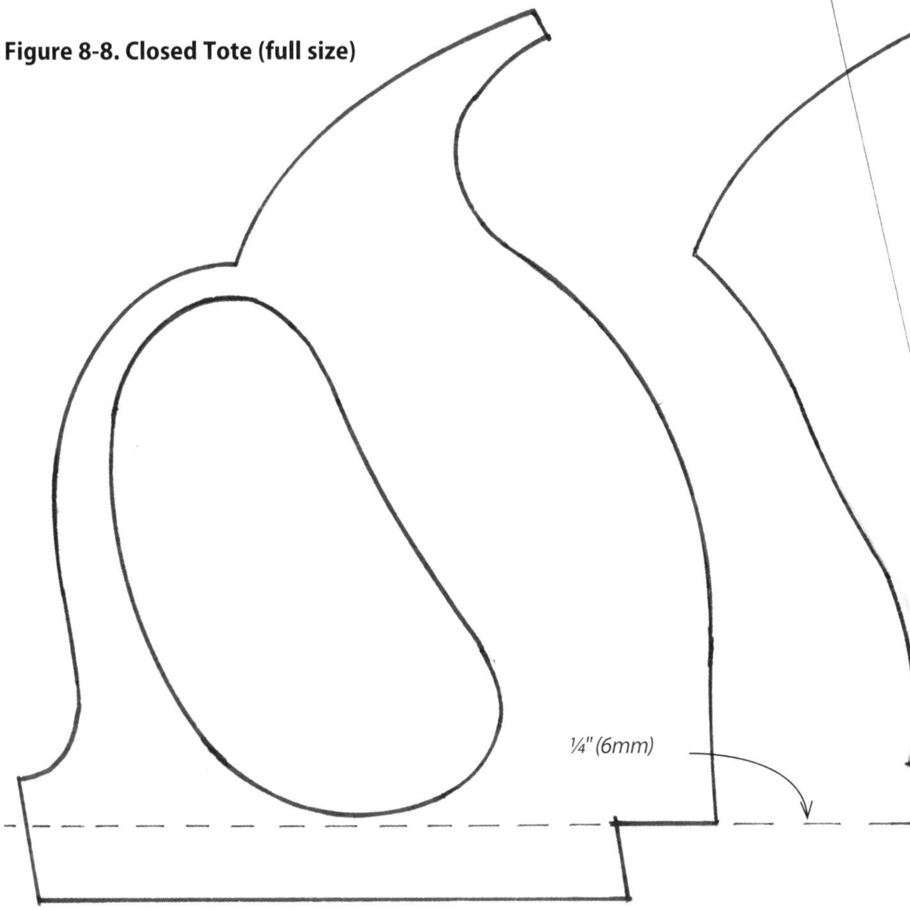

Figure 8-9. Open Tote (full size)

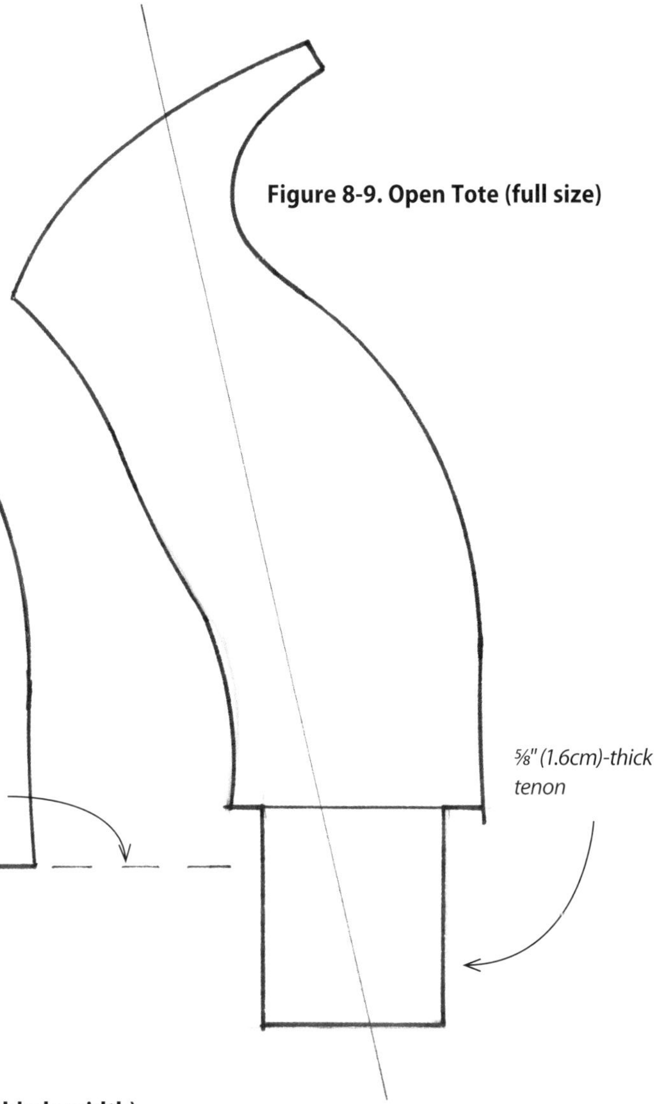

Figure 8-10. Profile of Wedge (full size) (width equals blade width)

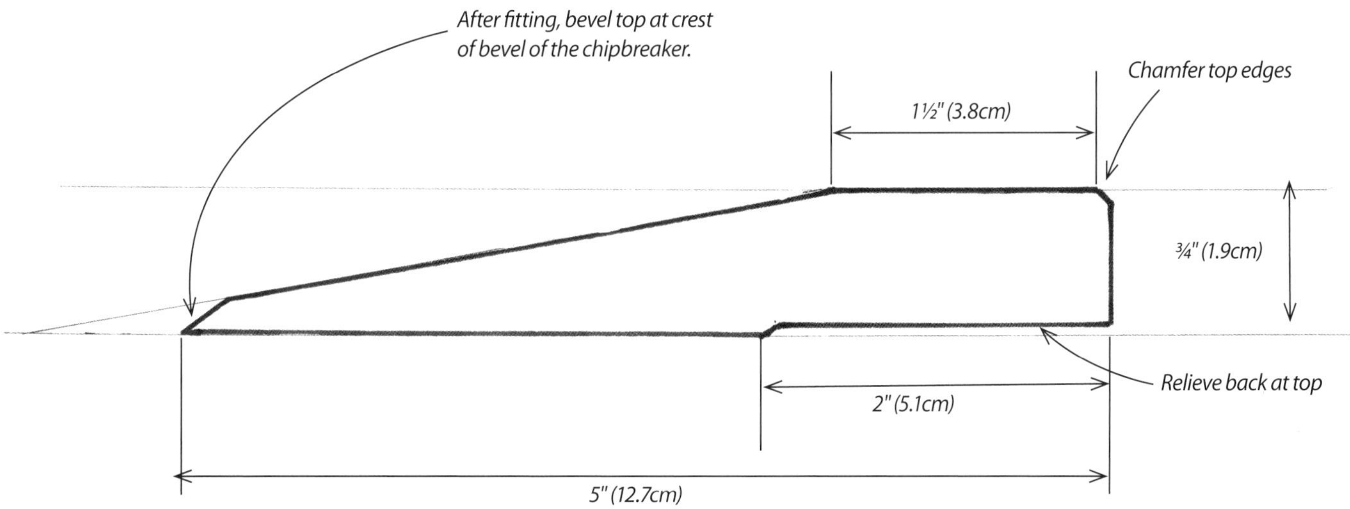

Figure 8-11 Cross Pin Bearing Plate

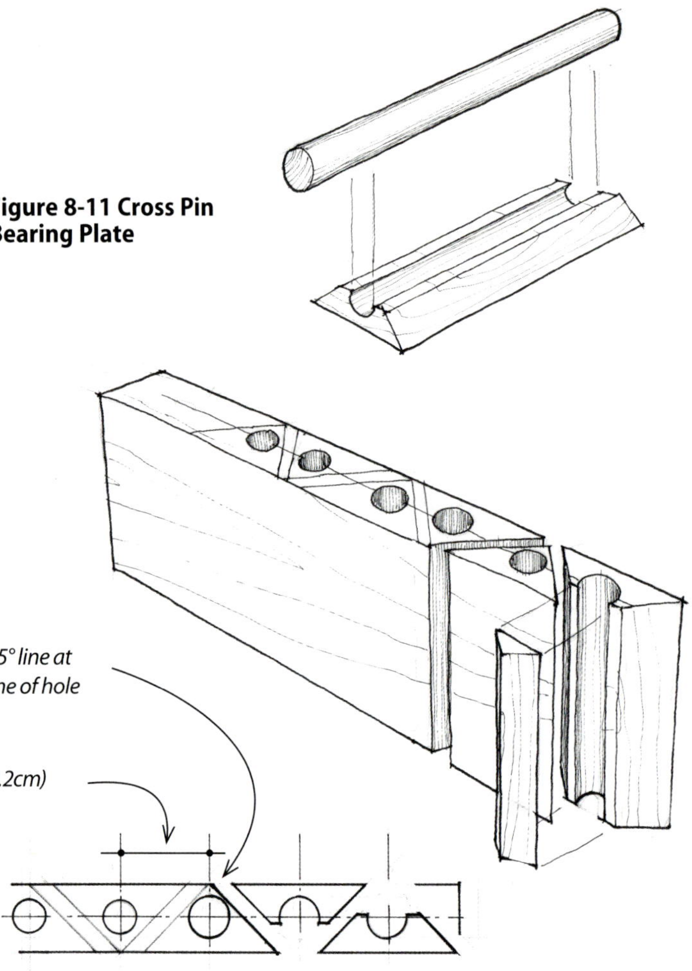

Figure 8-12. Rough-milled blanks should be stickered and allowed to settle for at least a week; six months is better.

by 4' (1.22m) long. (I glued up some 1¼" (3.2cm) thick MDF I had in stock).

You will need one mounting block for every blade angle you intend to mortise, plus one for the chipwells. Remember, the block will be the complementary angle of the angle you want to cut. For instance, a 47½° blade angle will need a block angle of 42½°; a 50° blade angle, a block angle of 40°. You will need some 1½" (3.8cm)-diameter holes drilled in the face of each mounting block for clamping (at least one for the plane block itself, plus one or two others to clamp the mounting block down, depending on the machine you are using). It is also helpful to screw a stop block on the mounting block to help keep the plane block from sliding under the pressure of the mortise chisel (**Figures 8-20** on page 176 and **8-21** on page 177).

You will have to take a good look at the capacity and limitations of your mortising setup. While I recently got a substantial stationary mortiser with good capacity, the longer plane blocks had to be positioned with one end off the table to get enough clearance under the chisel (**Figure 8-21**, bottom, on page 177). I managed to get everything to clear, but just barely. With a mortising attachment on a drill press, the table can be lowered and the plane block kept entirely on the mounting block.

However, the mounting block on a drill press will have to be clamped and unclamped with each cut because it does not have a cross vise as a stationary mortiser has. If you use a stack of wood or MDF pieces the same thickness as your chisel size as shims behind the mounting block to the fence, you can add (or subtract) one on each new cut to save you the trouble of measuring and squaring up the work to the chisel after each unclamping. Or you may be able to mount the block in a cross vise on the drill press table, saving you the trouble of clamping and unclamping

4. CUT THE BLADE BED AND THROAT OPENING

Using a ⅜" or ½" (1cm or 1.3cm) hollow chisel, cut the blade bed first through the mouth opening no deeper than is necessary for you to be able to finish the cut from the top. Err a little to the inside of the blade-bed line. Do not worry if the chisel overcuts the mouth opening, because you will be fitting a sole plate later that will fill this. (Making this first cut through the mouth serves two purposes. First, it avoids splintering on the exit of the cut. Secondly, it allows you to complete the cut whether or not your mortising chisel is long enough to do so—and it probably is not.)

Turn the plane block over to finish the cut from the top. Cut the recess for the chipbreaker screw first, then finish the cuts on either sides, cutting closer to the line than you did when you made the cuts through the mouth, to compensate for blade drift when cutting at an angle to the grain. Either this should result in a flush meeting of the cuts, or a small step-cut at the bottom that can be pared away later.

Cut all the blocks you are doing, changing mounting blocks as required, then change mounting blocks, one last time, and cut the chipwell line down from the top on all the blocks. Be careful

Figure 8-13. The blocks laid out, the sole plate blank glued up, and some of the candidates for blades that will be used (the Sta-Set chipbreaker—second from left—was not used).

Figure 8-14.

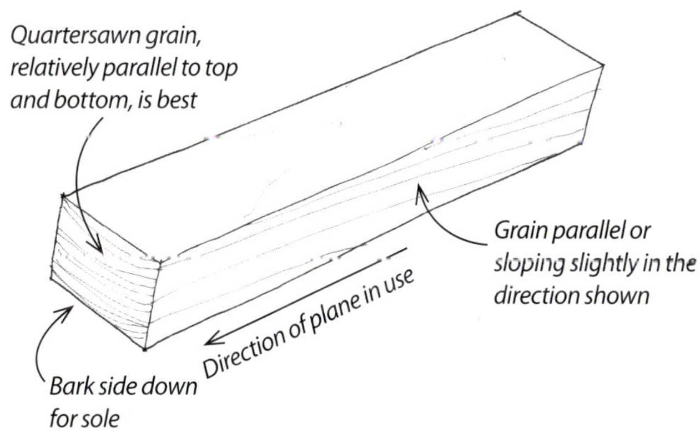

Figure 8-15.
Mark blade-edge line and transfer around block.

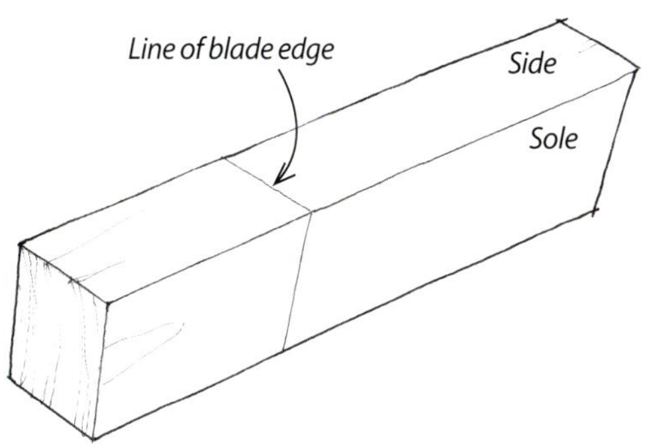

not to exceed the depth and cut into the blade bed. You can use the mortiser to cut away a lot of the waste at either side of the chipwell, being careful not to cut too deeply into the throat or blade bed and cutting away any remaining waste with a keyhole saw. Alternatively, you can cut the waste away entirely with a keyhole saw. The Fein saw, if you should happen to have one, can also make this cut (**Figure 8-22** on page 177).

Pare the waste and any irregularities on the blade bed away with a chisel. Smoothly pare the chipwell. Check the blade fit by holding the blade down with one finger in the center, then tap the four corners of the blade with another finger (**Figure 8-23** on page 178). If you hear a clicking sound on any corner, that part of the blade bed is low; pare the other corners until the clicking stops. Also, visually check the bed with a straightedge, and sight down it for twist.

Figure 8-16.
Mark the blade-bed line on the sole back ¼" (6mm) from blade-edge line. Mark blade-bed angle up both sides and connect lines across the top.

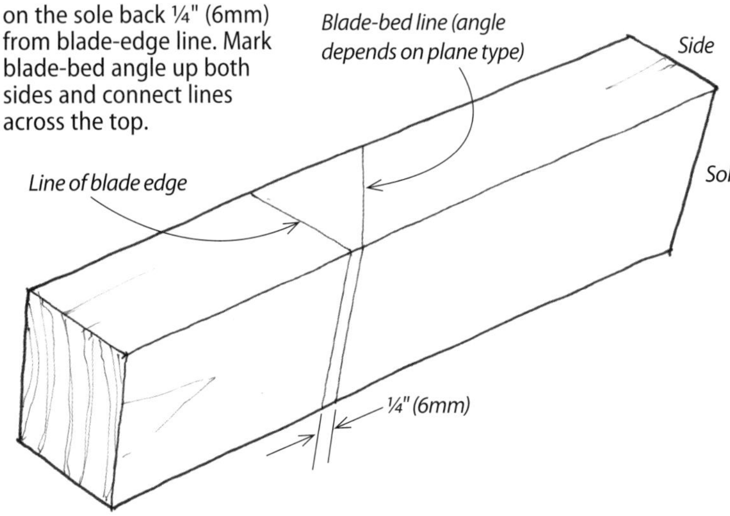

Figure 8-17.
Mark the chipwell line starting at the blade-bed line and extending up at 60°. Connect the line across the top.

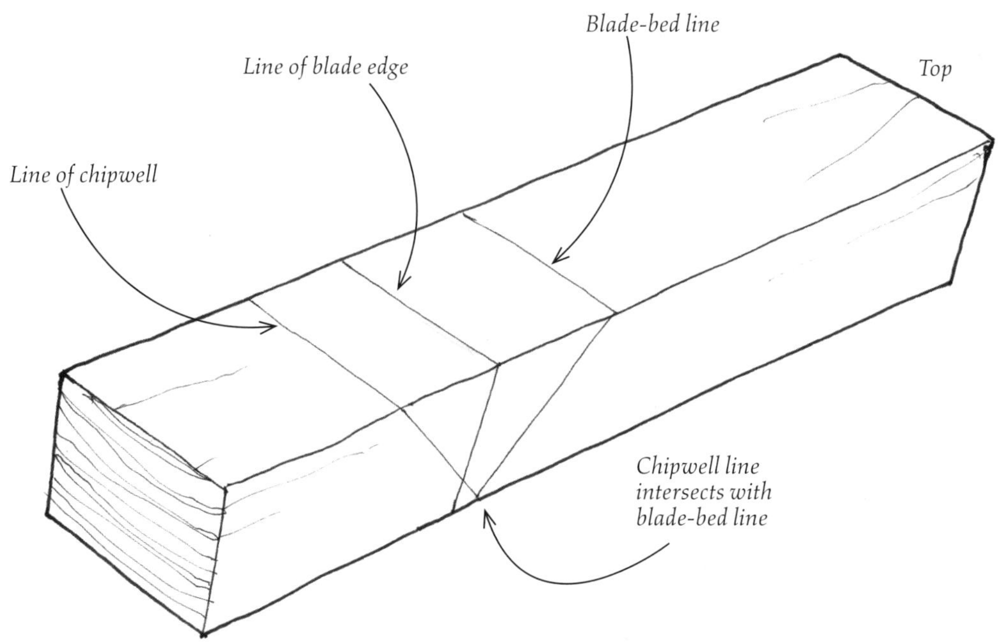

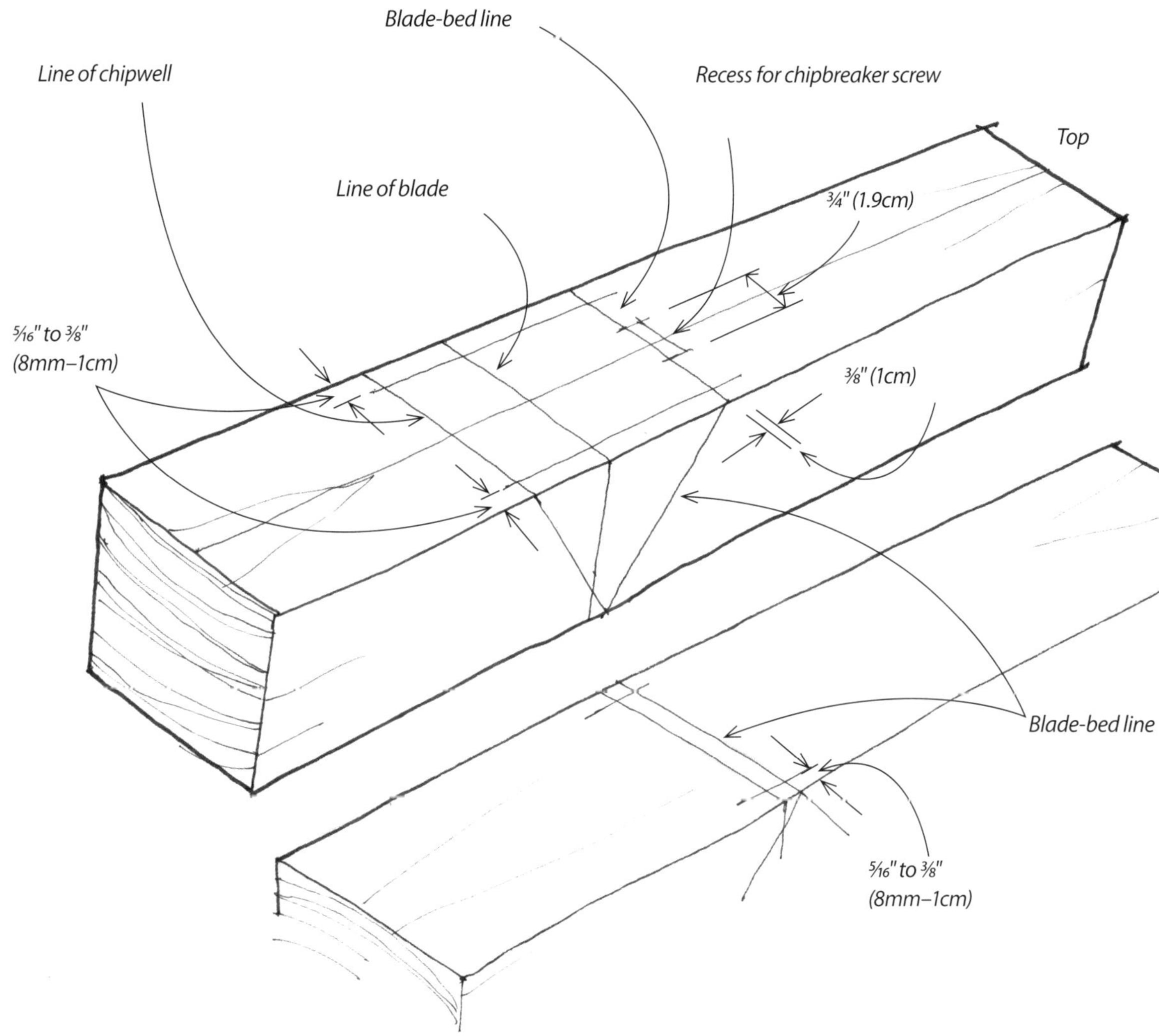

Figure 8-18. Mark the edge of the chipwell in ⁵⁄₁₆" to ⅜" (8mm to 1cm) from the sides, top, and bottom. Verify that the resulting chipwell width matches the blade width or is no more than ¹⁄₃₂" (0.8mm) wider. Mark a centerline top and bottom, and mark the recess for the chipbreaker screw.

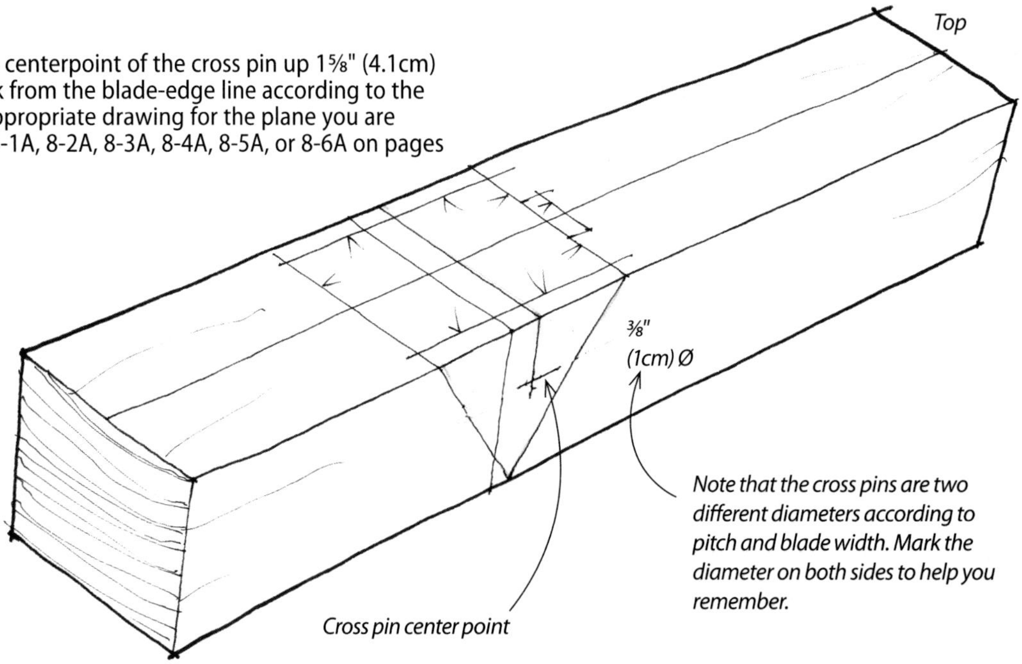

Figure 8-19. Mark the centerpoint of the cross pin up 1⅝" (4.1cm) from the sole and back from the blade-edge line according to the blade pitch. See the appropriate drawing for the plane you are making. (See Figures 8-1A, 8-2A, 8-3A, 8-4A, 8-5A, or 8-6A on pages 158–168).

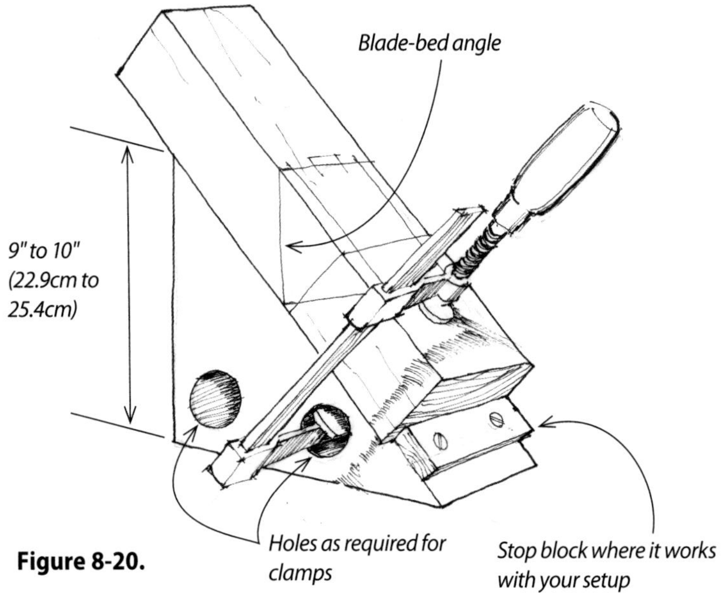

Figure 8-20.

5. SOLE PLATE

After this preliminary blade fitting and cleanup, cut the recess for the sole-plate screwheads in the chipwell using the jigs. Drill out the slot(s) in the plane body for the sole-plate fixing screw(s). Doing this before routing out for the sole plate will eliminate any split-out in the sole-plate recess from drilling for the fixing screw. Cut the recess for the sole plate with the jig. Preliminarily fit the sole plate and tap the sole-plate screws (**Figure 8-7**) (See "Fitting a Movable Sole Plate" on page 184). You can finish fitting the sole plate once the wedge is completed and can lock the blade in place.

6. CROSS PIN

Now make the cross pin. You can use standard dowel stock, though I would recommend oak rather than birch for the additional strength. Make sure the grain is straight and continuous. Or you can split (not saw) your own pin out of straight-grained stock. Either way you have to accurately size the dowel, either with a dowel sizer or by trial and error.

Make up stock for the plate that holds the cross pin out of the same material as the plane block, with the grain oriented the same way. It should be ⅝" (1.6cm) thick by the width of your widest blade by twice as long as you need to make the number of plates required **(Figure 8-11** on page 172). You will need an end to hold it when cutting the plates free. To drill the holes as accurately as possible on the drill press, scribe the centerlines and drill in from both sides. After drilling the holes, alternately cut the pieces free at a 45° angle until you have more than you need **(Figure 8-25** on page 179**)**. Cut their length to the width of their matching blades and clean up the bevels. Then cut or plane the hole away on the top (narrow) side about 1⁄16" (2mm) shy of the scribed centerline **(Figure 8-26** on page 179**)**. See if the plate can be snapped onto the cross pin. Continue planing, one or two strokes at a time, and fitting until you can snap the plate onto the pin. Carefully remove the plate, insert the cross pin into its hole and snap the plate back on **(Figures 8-27** and **8-28** on page 180**)**. Do this for all the planes.

Figure 8-21. Plane blocks and mounting blocks on the mortiser (top). Longer plane blocks may require the mounting block to be cantilevered, in order to gain enough clearance to work (bottom).

Figure 8-22. Plane blanks at various stages of production, from back to front: the first cut through the mouth, cutting the lower half of the blade bed; top cuts completed for both blade bed and chipwell; waste cleared down both sides of the chipwell; waste removed.

HANDLE SHAPE

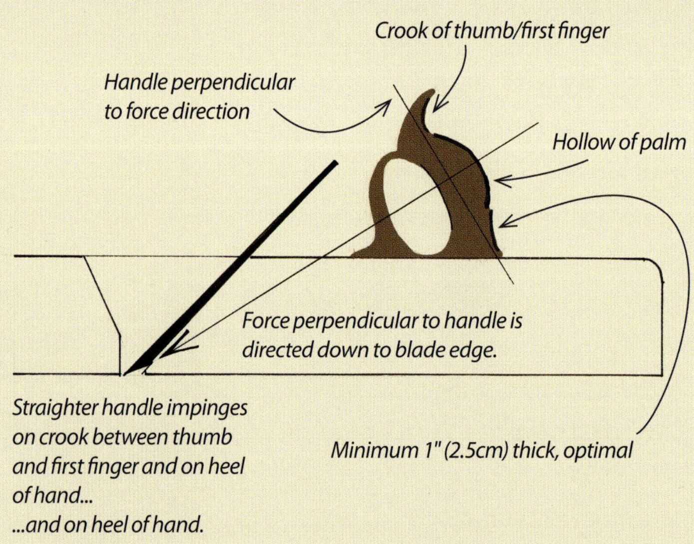

Designing a tote (or other handle) for hand-planes, begins with understanding a few fundamentals. A handle must accommodate the hand, and provide an appropriate surface area to spread the stress of planing evenly over the hand. The palm is significantly concave. The German plane's rounded end (or a coffin-sided) smoother matches the concavity pretty well; the shape of a traditional Western tote perhaps not so well. In addition, the crook of the thumb and first finger requires a properly shaped bearing area, because resistance to sliding forward up off the handle happens here. Finally, the position and angle of the handle or grip must focus the force toward the blade's edge. The implications of these considerations amount to this: The handle or tote must be *humped*, not straight or even gently curved, if it is to fit the hollow of the palm. It should be thick in order to engage as much of the hand in the area of the thumb and first finger as possible, as well as the palm. And, the centerline of the arc of the hump must pass through the blade edge. Additionally, because the plane must be returned back to the beginning of the stroke and not only just pushed, the tote must be the right circumference to be comfortably grasped and lifted. Make sure it is big enough around that the fingers of the hand do not press upon the palm before getting a good grip, and, of course, not so big that is becomes tiresome to grab.

If you look at traditional totes from wooden planes, they follow most of these mandates. Perhaps the totes could be thicker, but I am not sure what the optimal thickness would be without significant experimentation. It would also appear that a rounded-end coffin-shape in the traditional style of plane would benefit from the addition of a *neck* for the thumb and first finger similar to that on German planes.

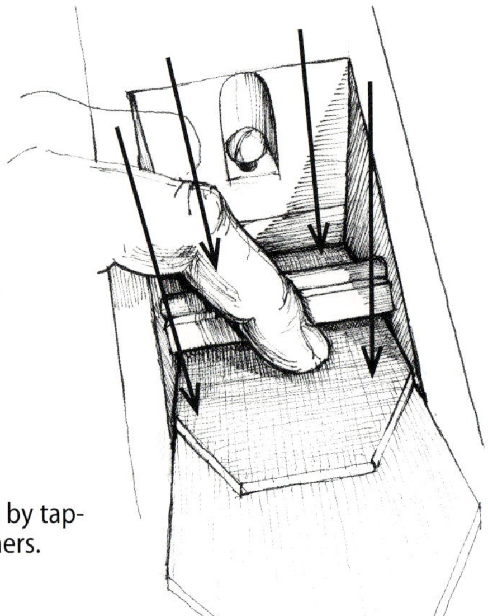

Figure 8-23.
Check the fit of the blade by tapping it on each of its corners.

7. WEDGE

Cut blanks for the wedges and then band saw a 10° taper over about two-thirds the length of the wedge (**Figure 8-10** on page 171). Clean up the cut with a plane. If necessary, cut a narrow slot in the back of the wedge for any protrusion of the chipbreaker screw. Insert the blade with its chipbreaker in the plane, and then the wedge for a trial fit. (It is easier to do this with the sole plate removed until after the wedge fitting is done.)

The wedge should descend close to the bevel of the chipbreaker before it tightens up. Remove the wedge-and-blade assembly, and fit the wedge to the shape of the chipbreaker. Carefully cross-plane the wedge until its curve matches that of the chipbreaker. Leave the underside of the wedge ever so slightly proud in the center of its length to guarantee the wedge makes solid contact at both the bottom (at the top of the chipbreaker's bevel) and the top.

Once the wedge is fit to the chipbreaker, do a trial fit of the whole wedge-and-blade assembly. Check that the blade is making solid contact with the bed and the pressure on the wedge from the cross pin is even. You can check the pressure from the cross pin on the wedge first visually—look that there is no gap at either side—and then by pushing the wedge sideways. The amount of pressure to release the wedge should be equal from both sides. If needed, plane the high side on the top of the wedge with light strokes of a block plane until the fit is correct. Do not crown the wedge—keep it flat. Once the wedge is fitted, cut it off at the chipbreaker bevel, and bevel the end to deflect shavings. Finish shaping the rest of the wedge.

8. FINISH FITTING THE SOLE PLATE

Once you can lock the blade in place, finish fitting the sole plates by planing the mouth-edge end on the shooting board until you have the mouth opening you want. You can always adjust it further later. Screw it in place when you are

Figure 8-24. Sole plates fitted, tapped, and installed on five plane bodies. At left are three sole-plate blanks.

Figure 8-25. The blank for the cross pin bearing plates (bottom), one cut from the blank (top left), and a finished one (top right).

Figure 8-26. At left, the bevel-edge shooting board is used to clean up the top faces of the cross pin bearing plate. Next to it, the regular shooting board is used to clean up edges and ends. Cut stock for the cross pin bearing plates can be seen between the two shooting boards, with the wedge blanks behind.

Figure 8-27. To assemble the cross pin and its bearing plate, push the pin home from the side and snap on the plate.

Figure 8-28. Then, install the blade assembly with the wedge to begin checking the fit of the wedge.

Figure 8-30. After installing the cross pin assembly and fitting the wedge on the smoothing planes, the thumb piece is added.

Figure 8-31. The angle cut of the thumbpiece waste at the bed line is deeply scored with a hand saw, but not cut free until after the block is glued on so as to allow it to be clamped up.

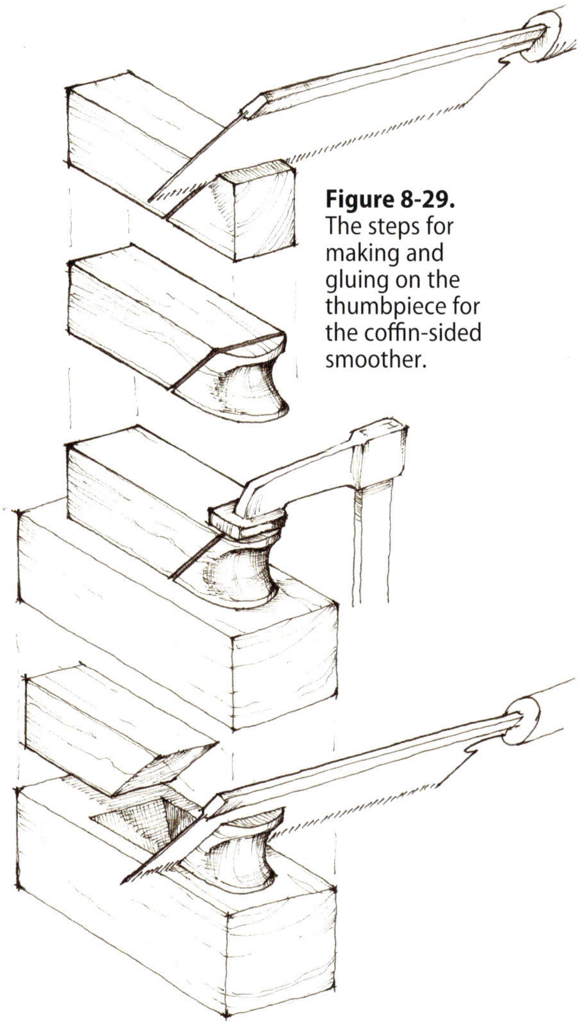

Figure 8-29. The steps for making and gluing on the thumbpiece for the coffin-sided smoother.

satisfied. You can, for the time being, leave ⅛" (3mm) or so of the mouth edge at a 90° relief angle, relieving the throat above to, or close to, the chipwell of the plane block. If you find in use that chips jam in this area, you can remove the sole plate and rework the mouth to a greater relief angle.

9. SHAPING THE SMOOTHING PLANES

On each of the smoothing planes, first mark the curve of its coffin shape on the top—it is easier now—but do not cut it. Then band saw and smooth the curve of the thumbpiece, and shape its thumb recess on a long piece of stock (**Figure 8-29**). Mark the blade angle and make a partial cut, on the line all around the piece, ⅛" to ¼" (3mm to 6mm) deep. This will help keep you from marring the plane when you cut the angle after the thumbpiece has been glued on.

Cut the thumbpiece off the stock square beyond the blade line, and glue it to the block with the cut you made on the blade line back about 1⁄16" (2mm) from the blade bed. After the glue has dried, finish cutting off the waste at this partial sawcut line (**Figures 8-30** and **8-31**). The thumbpiece should be cut and pared back from the blade line so it does not interfere with the blade if it has shifted during glue-up. Band saw and smooth the plane's coffin shape (if you leave the back curves of the plane uncut until after you shape the front, the plane is easier to hold in a vise) and then cut, shape, and smooth the thumbpiece and the back of the plane to your grip (**Figure 8-32**).

Figure 8-32. Then cut the thumbpiece waste free and give the plane its final shape.

10. MAKE AND FIT THE TOTES

On the other planes, prepare stock for the handles, or totes (**Figures 8-8 and 8-9** on page 171). Sometimes it is nice to do the totes in a contrasting wood; an argument could be made that a tote from a dark wood will look better over time, as a tote from a light color wood will show grime. It all depends on your taste and the stock you have at hand.

Figure 8-33. The totes in various stages of completion.

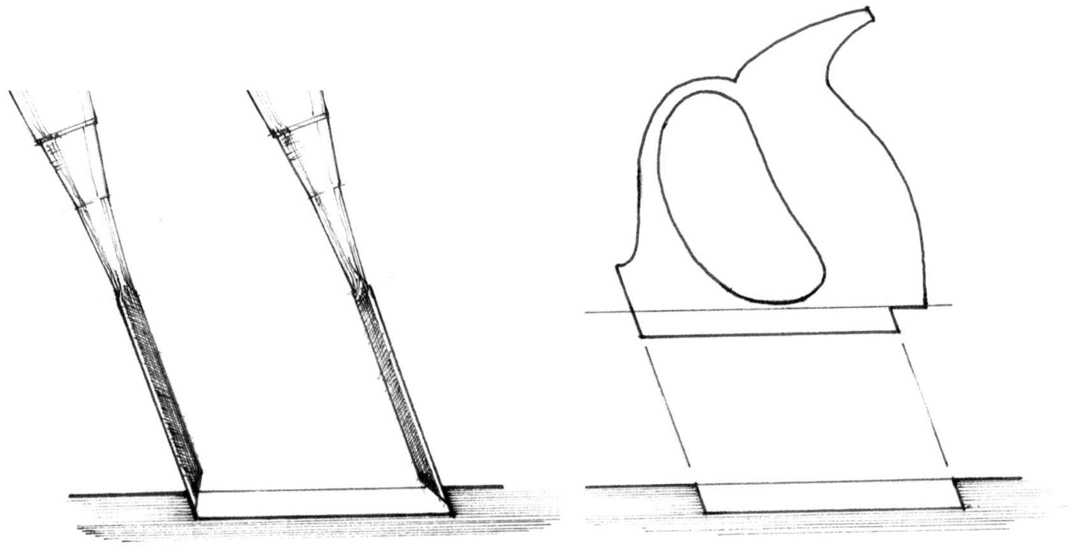

Figure 8-34. The closed totes of traditional planes are set into a shallow mortise that is undercut at the back, with a matching cut at the front, to help keep the handle from rotating out of its housing from use.

I suggest you do not cut the totes free from their stock until you have shaped the grip (**Figure 8-33**). This will make it easier to maneuver on the router table, should you want to form the round part initially with a router bit, or to hold the blank in a vise in order to smooth.

After shaping the totes, mark the location and size of the recess required on the plane. On Razee planes, make the back cutout of the block and smooth it before doing this. Probably the easiest way to cut the recess for the closed totes, since on the Razee-style planes the curve behind the blade interferes with a router jig, is to use the hollow-chisel mortiser. This leaves a rough bottom, reducing the gluing area, which can be smoothed, or adjusted if necessary, with a router plane. Cut the recess for the closed totes to its shortest length and finish undercutting the back dovetail (**Figure 8-34** on page 181). Then cut the angle of the front with a chisel. Make a template of the handle and its dovetail out of ⅛" or ¼" (3mm or 6mm) hardboard or plywood, and use it to check the fit as you work. Then finish fitting the totes. Do not glue them in until the planes are shaped and smoothed.

11. FINISHING TOUCHES

Insert the blade and wedge it securely, about 1⁄16" (2mm) shy of the bottom. Follow procedures outlined for setting up wood planes, "Configure the Sole" on page 127, to true the bottom.

Smooth the top surfaces of the plane, rounding the edges to taste. Check again that the faces of the plane are square. Glue in the tote. Form the eyes at the chipwell if you wish. They can make it a little easier on the hand should it have to work in that vicinity.

Figure 8-35. The completed fore plane.

Figure 8-36. The completed jack and jointer planes.

Find or make some length of hard hardwood dowel ⅝" to ¾" (1.6cm to 1.9cm) in diameter for the striking knob on the long planes. Drill a hole about 1" (2.5cm) deep, round the top end of the dowel (before gluing it in), cut it off so it will stand proud about $\frac{3}{16}$" (5mm), and glue it in its hole, making sure it bottoms out.

Apply a light coat of oil, if you wish, on the top surface of the plane and tote, to give a little more protection and improve grip (**Figures 8-35** and **8-36**).

FITTING A MOVABLE SOLE PLATE

A movable sole plate has a number of advantages. It increases the versatility of the plane since the mouth opening can be set for fine or coarse cuts or to accommodate unruly grain. Additionally, as the sole wears and is trued, the plate can be re-adjusted to close the mouth, rather than having to be replaced.

The process for fitting a movable sole plate is the same as fitting a glue-in repair. There are some additional steps, however. It is not necessary, but probably better, to laminate the sole plate for wear and stability. Also, slots must be cut for the fixing screw and screwhead.

Glue up the blank and let it sit overnight, preferably longer, before jointing one edge and then ripping it to width when the jig is made.

Fit the sole plate as you would a fixed plate: if it is too long, cut it so it gives the maximum mouth opening you may want for this plane when it is in its far forward position. Check that the edge of the mouth is parallel with the blade edge when the blade edge is parallel to the sole of the plane. Adjust the clearance angle of the throat to your requirements as described above for fitting a fixed plate. Then, with the sole plate in position, drill a hole the diameter of the screw shank at the front end of the screw slot to a depth just shy of the bottom of the core veneer of the sole plate (**Figure 5** on page 187).

Remove the sole plate, clean the hole of all debris, replace the sole plate, and screw the machine screw (with a washer attached) into the hole in the sole plate. This will tap threads into the wood as it goes. If you have to remove the screw and reinsert it, be careful to properly start the screw in the already-cut threads.

When the mouth needs to be closed down, after the screw is loosened, sometimes the sole plate sticks and cannot be moved with the fingers. You can cut a notch about 1/16" (2mm) deep by approximately 3/8" (1cm) wide at the front of the plate—first remove the plate, of course (**Figure 6** on page 187). Then, when the plate sticks, a small screwdriver can be gently inserted to carefully coax the plate into position. Do not forget to lock it in place with the machine screw.

Now, if the edge of your mouth is parallel with the blade and its edge is clean and sharp, you are good to go.

1

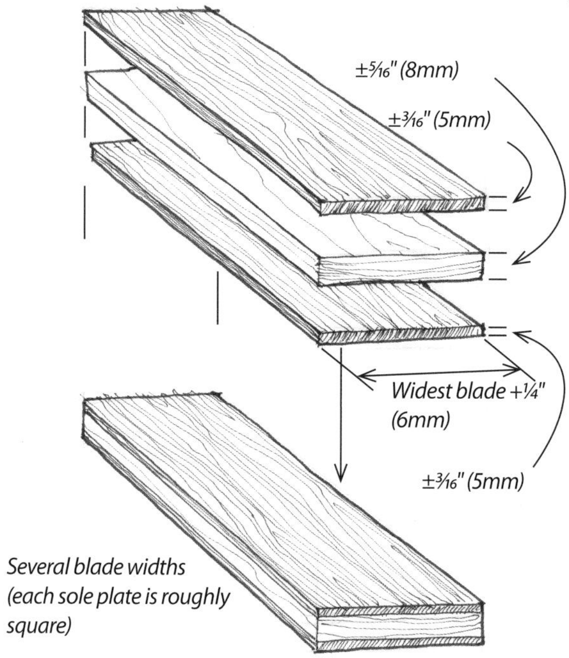

1. Begin by laminating up the sole-plate blank. Make it at least 1/4" (6mm) wider than your widest mouth opening, and long enough for several repairs. The face material should be about 3/16" (5mm) thick, each side, with a core (one ply) of the same wood as the plane body, about 5/16" (8mm) thick, and the same grain orientation as the main body of the plane. For the wood, lignum vitae, ironbark, ipé, or pau ferro are good choices; some dark tropical woods, such as ebony, can chip and sometimes leave dark streaks on light wood.

2

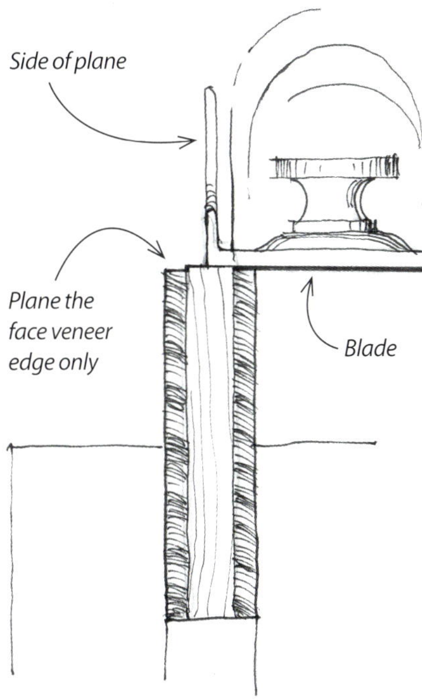

3

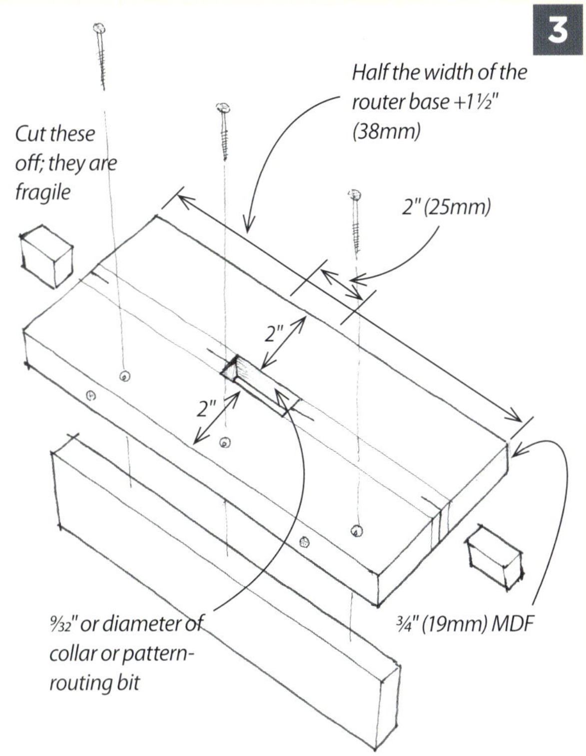

2. The procedures for making the router jig for cutting and fitting the sole plate is as shown in "Fitting a Sole Plate at the Mouth of a Plane" on page 136. Do not glue the sole plate in. Fitting the movable sole plate involves an additional step: leave the core wood a snug fit in its recess; however, plane back the width of both face veneers, one light shaving on each side.

3. Make a jig for routing the slot for the screwhead similar to the jig made to route the sole-plate recess (see page 136), using the same techniques. You can make the jig to accommodate a ½" (1.3cm)-diameter pattern-routing bit with a top-mounted bearing, or you can use a ½" (1.3cm)-diameter straight bit with a collar. Each has its advantages and disadvantages. With the pattern-routing bit, it is easy to size the jig, but also easy to damage it. With a straight bit and collar you'll have to size the jig cutout to accommodate any offset between the diameter of the collar and the diameter of the bit, but the jig is less likely to get damaged by the bit. You may have to use a straight bit anyway to get the length required. Check before you make the jig.

FITTING A MOVABLE SOLE PLATE (CONTINUED)

4

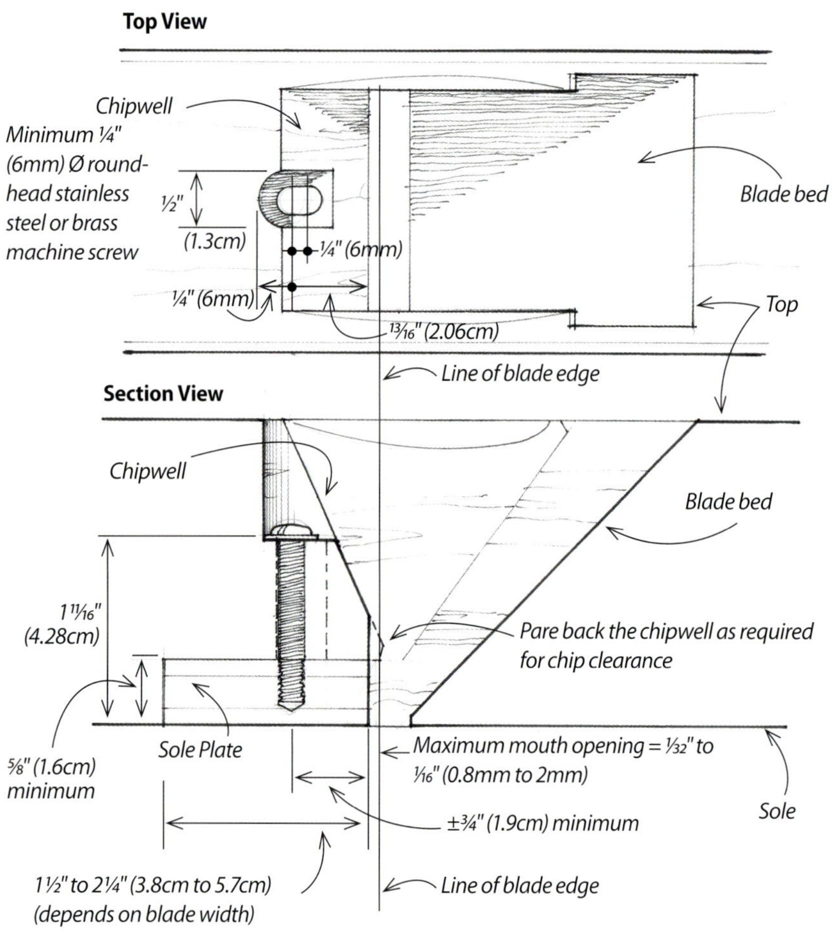

Slot for screw head must be deep enough to allow ±¼" adjustability and bearing for the screw head's washer, and be able to use a standard length screw that does not penetrate the surface ply of the sole plate.

Cut a ½" (1.3cm) slot for the screw head and its washer, and a through slot for the shank of the screw. Make both long enough to give the screw about ¼" (6mm) travel.

4. Again, if the plane is too short to clamp on top, mount a side fence below to clamp to. Mark the centerlines on the top of the plane and the front location of where the slot will be (see **Figure 4**) for calculating the position of screw. Set the jig on the centerline with the front of the jig opening at the mark for the front of the screw. Route the slot for the screwhead with a ½" (1.3cm)-diameter router bit. If you are using a pattern-routing bit, make sure the bit is long enough to reach while still keeping the bearing within the thickness of the jig. Set the depth of the bit so the bearing is within the jig before starting the router. Otherwise, you will be making another jig. Locate the centers of the screw-shank slot and drill each end and then the center on the drill press. Clean out the slot with the drill bit to get an unencumbered slot. A Forstner bit is best for this, or a good brad-point.

5

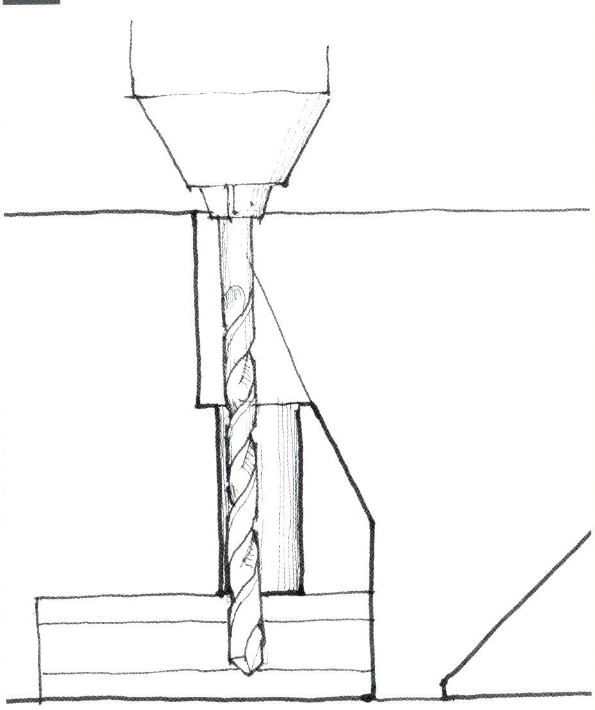

6

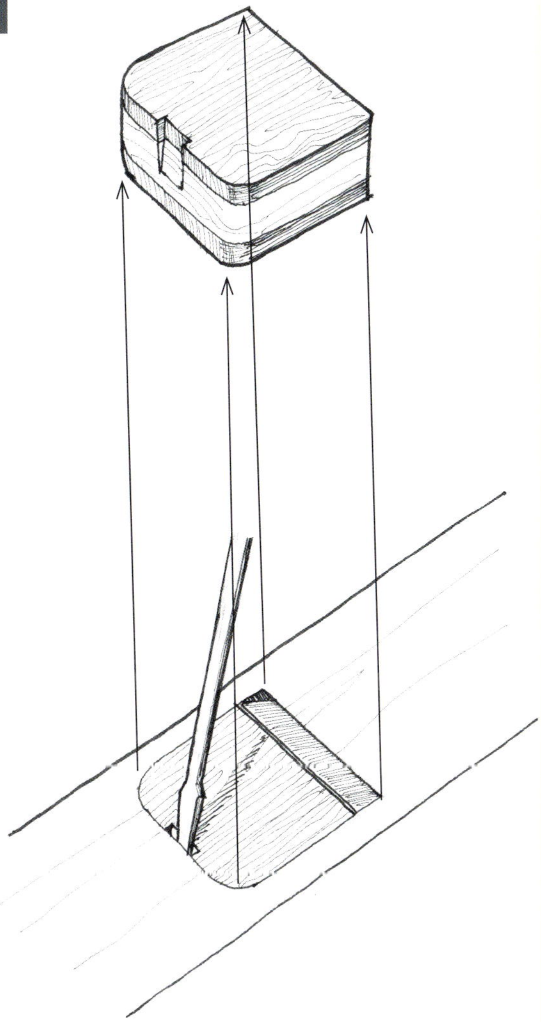

5. Drill a hole the diameter of the screw shank (not the thread diameter!) at the front end of the screw slot, to a depth just shy of the bottom of the core veneer of the sole plate.

6. Cut a notch about 1⁄16" (2mm) deep by approximately 3⁄8" (1cm) wide at the front of the plate so that when the sole plate sticks, a small screwdriver can be gently inserted to carefully coax it into position

FITTING A MOVABLE SOLE PLATE WHEN MAKING A KRENOV-STYLE PLANE

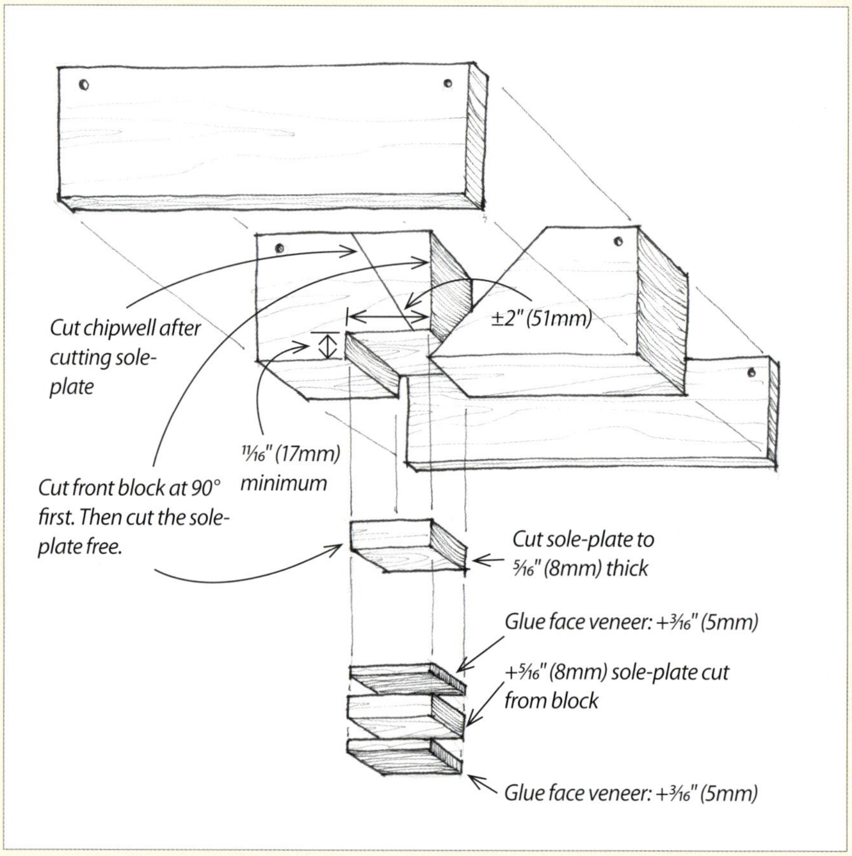

Fitting a movable sole plate when making a Krenov-style plane is relatively easy if done before the plane is glued up. It simplifies getting a very tight mouth, and allows increased versatility of the plane should that be required. Refer to *Making and Mastering Wood Planes* by David Finck (Sterling, 2000), for a full treatment of the Krenov-style planes and how to make them.

When making the plane, after the blade bed block is cut free, cut the front part of the center block at 90° at the throat line. Then cut from the front block a piece that will become the sole plate, leaving a notch 11⁄16" (1.7cm) deep by ±2" (5.1cm) long overall. Cut this notch on the table saw with a tenoning jig or clamped to a miter gauge. You can then cut the line of the chipwell on the front block.

Rip the thickness of the piece that will become the sole plate to 5⁄16" (8mm) (it should be about ½", or 13mm, before) and glue 3⁄16" (5mm)-thick face veneer on each side (see "Fitting a Movable Sole Plate" on page 184). It will be safer to rip this core piece by hand: with a marking gauge, scribe a line all around the piece at 5⁄16" (8mm), saw to one side of the line and plane it down to split the line. After it is glued up and installed, any discrepancies in thickness can be planed out when the plane's sole is conditioned. After a few days drying, trim the face veneer flush, and then a light plane stroke narrower on each side (see Figure 2 in "Fitting a Movable Sole Plate" on page 185). Proceed with completing the plane, making sure when gluing up that glue is cleaned from the recess for the sole plate.

Before shaping the plane, make the jig for routing the slot for the screwhead. Route the slot and drill the elongated holes (see Figure 4 in "Fitting a Movable Sole Plate" on page 186 for a suggested layout). Try to keep the slot within the chipwell. Finish fitting the sole plate as with any movable sole plate.

INDEX